A LIFE OF PRIVILEGE, MOSTLY

A LIFE OF PRIVILEGE, MOSTLY

Gardner Botsford

Granta Books
London

Granta Publications, 2/3 Hanover Yard, Noel Road, London N1 8BE

First published in Great Britain by Granta Books 2006
First published in the US by St Martin's Press 2003

A CIP catalogue record for this book is available from the British Library.

1 3 5 7 9 10 8 6 4 2

ISBN-13: 978-1-86207-817-8
ISBN-10: 1-86207-817-3

Printed and bound in Great Britain by
William Clowes Ltd, Beccles, Suffolk

For Janet

CONTENTS

MOSTLY

For anyone old enough to have been born during the First World War, like me, and damn near killed in the Second, also like me, war was a regular presence in the course of growing up. Our generation moved from a backward look at one war to a nervous forward look at a new one, waiting in the wings. The First World War took shape for us in the enthralling and terrifying stories told by our parents' friends who had been Over There. (One of these gave me nightmares for a week: an infantry replacement, riding in the first truck of a long convoy, fell off the tailgate and was squashed by the next truck in line, and then squashed again by every succeeding truck.) These cautionary tales were reinforced by a steady barrage of war-inspired books aimed right at our generation—books like The Boy Allies series, and books with less flat-footed titles, like *Arnold Adair and the English Aces*. The Boy Allies books, though ubiquitous, were not very believable: even our galloping imaginations could not be persuaded that the boy allies—twelve years old, like us—would have been allowed to traipse around the front-line trenches in France. But books like *Arnold Adair* were all too convincing, and scarier. ("The Boche pilot, his twin Spandaus chattering a hymn of death, came screaming back to the attack. . . .")

In the thirties, we moved from reminiscence and fiction to reality. The Japanese in Manchuria, the Italians in Ethiopia, Franco in Spain, Hitler wherever he was—all made the twin Spandaus seem trifling. In the last year of the decade, with the start of the Second World War, the transition was complete, and in the forties—well, we all know about the forties. Pearl Harbor, when it came, put our generation—put me, at any rate—in a moral pickle. The war had to be won, of course, but war, as I had come to know, was a dangerous business. I was an outspoken hawk—had been one since Hitler's early days—but when it came to replacing words with action, I was out of town. "Every new generation will respond anew to war's great seduction," Samuel Hynes writes in his excellent book *The Soldiers' Tale,* a consideration of many writings about war by men who did the fighting. Mr. Hynes not only was a Marine combat pilot in the Second World War but is a professor emeritus of literature at Princeton, so it is hard to argue with him, but I must say that I felt no tug of seduction—nothing beyond the tug of a lousy conscience. The only thing that saved me from lasting ignominy, in fact, was the draft.

My rescue from ignominy started on September 16, 1942, at four o'clock in the morning, when I switched off the alarm clock before it could ring and tried to get out of bed without waking Tass. I had a date at 6:00 A.M. with the U.S. Army Induction Center. Tass was my wife of barely two years; the bed was in my mother's house in Manhattan's East Seventies, where Tass and I were more or less camping out in anticipation of this date I couldn't break.

My efforts to go off to war unnoticed were in vain, of course;

Tass hadn't slept any better than I had. This was the first of some hard times for her—six months pregnant, convinced that she would have to raise a fatherless child, with no place of her own to live. I, at least, knew where I was going next.

The Induction Center, in Grand Central Palace—New York's old and only exhibition hall, on Lexington Avenue at Forty-fourth Street—was in a state of delirium. To increase space for the Army, workmen were tearing down walls all over the place, while I and scores of other recruits, each hugging a cardboard carton both practical and symbolic—for mailing home one's civilian clothes and cutting the final bonds to civilized life—were sent from one line to another and yelled at. Most of my future comrades in arms seemed very young, and they were—eighteen or nineteen, to my venerable twenty-five. Eventually, in groups of ten or so, we were marched into the men's room—the construction workers had left no other space available—and were sworn into service, to the music of flushing urinals. Then we were bused to Pennsylvania Station and dispatched to Camp Upton, on Long Island.

Camp Upton was the camp where one was turned from a confident, competent civilian into an insecure and incompetent Army private. The place was just as mad and seething as Grand Central Palace. Night was indistinguishable from day. Over a period of seventy-two hours, we were issued uniforms, given shots and tested for our IQs, fitted for boots and examined medically, and lectured on venereal disease and vetted for homosexuality by psychiatrists. Finally, we were sent through the shed where we would be classified as to branch of service: Artillery, Engineers, Special Services, Infantry, Signal Corps, or whatever. This was the recruit's big moment; it would determine the whole course of his Army life—even, in fact, whether he was likely to survive. What I wanted was a nice, interesting, safe job, and I figured that I was a strong candidate for Special Services, a very safe unit that published the Army magazine *Yank* and escorted important foreign dignitaries around military installations and such. My hopes were plausible: I was a college graduate, I spoke French, and I had a reasonable IQ. Because of my experience as a reporter on various newspapers, and most recently on *The New Yorker,* I figured that I would end up on *Yank.* Or maybe in Army public relations, although that lacked cachet.

In any case, I was of a calm and confident disposition when I reached the head of the line and sat down at a table to be interviewed. My interviewer, a corporal, examined my chart, made little cabalistic computations, and finally put a decisive *X* in one of the boxes.

"What's it to be?" I asked.

"Infantry," he said. He might just as well have hit me with a baseball bat.

"Infantry?" I yelped. "Not the infantry! What about the four years at Yale? What about the French? What about—"

At this moment, a corpulent sergeant came up and laid a hand on my interviewer's shoulder. "How's it going, Bernie?" he said, and looked over the pile of completed dossiers on the corporal's desk. "Not bad for your first day on the job. So what did you do with this guy here?"

"This guy was a little tough," the corporal said. I felt like a side of beef being inspected by two restaurant chefs. "He's got no qualifications on the MO list that I could see, so I put him in the infantry."

I moaned.

"Let me see his chart," the sergeant said, and took a look for himself. "Oh, no—you goofed on this one, Bernie," he said. "Look here. See those four years of college? And 'Foreign Language, Spoken'? No, he should have gone into Special Services, or maybe that new diplomatic branch."

I perked up. What a smart, perceptive fellow!

"But what the hell, let it go," the sergeant said, dropping my chart onto the completed pile, and me, irretrievably, into the infantry.

* * *

On January 1, 1943, the day my daughter Susan was born, I was in Camp Croft, South Carolina, halfway through my basic infantry training. My request to go to New York to see the new arrival was turned down. Two weeks earlier, another request had been turned down. This one asked for a transfer out of the infantry—to the Signal Corps, to the Coast Artillery, to the Norman Luboff Choir, to anywhere at all that was not the infantry. Its denial caused me to reassess my position. If I had to stay in the infantry, I reasoned, I would at least stay as an officer and be relieved of KP. This resolve came to me on Christmas Day, 1942. I was on KP—specifically, up to my elbows in one of the giant garbage cans behind the mess hall. The Army had two kinds of garbage—wet garbage and dry garbage—and the greatest sin against the Holy Ghost and the War Department was to put wet garbage in the dry-garbage can. Some numbskull had done just that on Christmas Eve, and the mess sergeant had ordered me to rectify the error—to get every teaspoonful of wet oatmeal and brown gravy and canned fruit cocktail and discarded bacon fat out of the dry-garbage can and into the wet-garbage can. The day was perishing cold, and the brown gravy had glued itself onto the wastepaper that was legitimately in the dry-garbage can, and the freezing oatmeal was giving me chilblains, and nobody in the whole U.S. Army felt as sorry for himself as I did on that Christmas Day. Officers, as I have said, did not have to do KP.

In March, I transferred to Fort Benning, Georgia, to go to infantry-officer training school, and on June 17, 1943, after thirteen weeks of the most prolonged, punishing physical work I had ever done, I was commissioned a second lieutenant of infantry. My graduation orders were so spectacularly fine that I could have written them myself: I was to report to the Army Intelligence School, at Camp Ritchie, Maryland, for an eight-week course dealing with the French Army and the Resistance. The downside was that after the ball was over I was to report back for assignment as an infantry officer, but I would worry about that later.

Camp Ritchie, where I reported on June 30, was known to be

more a country club than an Army camp. In peacetime, it had been the summer training ground of wealthy reserve officers from Baltimore—young dandies who did most of their training on the camp's golf course and tennis courts. Moreover, there were houses for rent off the base, where I could be joined by Tass and new Susan.

There was, however, one hurdle to leap: I had to be tested for fluency in French. My examiner was an infantry captain—a tough and burly Frenchman now in the U.S. Army. Somehow, he looked familiar to me, but I couldn't place him. We talked for a bit, and suddenly I got it: he was the former maître d'hôtel at Spivy's Roof, a nightclub on East Fifty-seventh Street, where Spivy, a French chanteuse of some note, used to sing, and where I used to go to hear her. He was a reserve officer in the French Army who had transferred to the U.S. Army when he couldn't get back to France. Once we had connected, my test became a cheerful social occasion. He even steered me to the off-camp living quarters I rented the next day.

Within a week, Tass and Susan had come down from New York and settled in. Life in the Army suddenly became idyllic. The weather was perfect, and the food at the camp was astonishing, cooked and served by Italian chefs and waiters, now prisoners of war. There was good company at table, too—friends I still have, like Henry Huguenin and Lucien Wulsin. The work was fascinating. It was primarily a course in the methods, operations, and makeup of the French Resistance, plus instruction in how to extract useful military information from civilians. It was taught by Frenchmen who had actually worked in France—in from England by parachute, out by submarine. The high point of the course was an all-night exercise that had a strong streak of theater about it. The stage was the command post of a make-believe infantry battalion, somewhere in France, that was trying to cross a river by capturing a well-defended bridge. The battalion commander (a staff officer at the camp) sat at a map in a blacked-out tent, directing his troops' forward progress. Periodically, reports would be telephoned in from the front: G Company has reached the river; E Company is running into heavy machine-gun fire. The map would be adjusted and new orders issued. Then a French civilian (one of the Resistance instructors, in peasant clothes) would be escorted into the tent, and turned over to us for interrogation. Underneath a quantity of ordinary peasant chaff, he would have a few nuggets of useful information—e.g., that the machine-gun position in front of E Company was manned by disabled veterans of the Russian front—which he would give up only if properly questioned. There were eight or ten of these encounters during the night, each one producing a change in the map, and at dawn the river would have been crossed—or not, depending—and we would be graded on our effectiveness.

But, of course, this idyllic life couldn't go on forever, and in September I got my orders: Prepare for overseas embarkation (destination secret) and reassignment as an infantry officer.

The day of my departure was another of those fearful drubbings for Tass. My orders were to present myself, along with twelve or fifteen others, at 5:00 A.M. in front of camp headquarters, ready for transport to a port of embarkation. Now all my training is over; this is the real thing. Tass drives me from our rented house to the camp. Pitch dark. Raining furiously. Tass in tears. We are late. No time to say good-bye properly—the other men are already lined up in formation, and I race to join them. The officer in charge of us yells at Tass—her car is blocking our route. She tries to turn it around and, in the wet and dark, backs it into a ditch, where its wheels spin helplessly in the mud. The last I see of her as we are marched off to a train—the last I see of her for more than two years—she is crumpled over the steering wheel and helplessly sobbing as the car digs itself deeper and deeper into the mud.

The train from Camp Ritchie left us at Camp Kilmer, on the Jersey side of the Hudson, opposite New York City. That night, we were ferried across the river to a landing stage huddled under the stern of a huge black ship that towered above our barge. I barely made out its name overhead: *Queen Mary*. We clambered up a gangplank to a low-level hatchway, and as each man came aboard his last name was called out, to which he was supposed to reply with his first name. When my turn came, I inadvertently almost called out "Gardner!" but I had my wits about me and shouted "Robert!" instead, and I was checked off. "Robert" was indeed my first name, though nobody but the United States Army had ever used it in all my twenty-six years. However, this was no time for a discussion of nomenclature, so I gave them the name they wanted. Then I was handed two plastic disks: one indicated the times I was to eat during the crossing, and the other the place where I was to sleep. My food disk said "3 o'clock." That meant I would eat at three o'clock in the morning and three o'clock in the afternoon—two meals a day. My sleep disk put me in a cabin on one of the lower decks—tourist class in the old days. It was a two-person cabin, now fitted with two vertical racks, each holding five canvas hammocks. In addition, the gear of all ten men had to be stowed somewhere in the cabin—helmets, bedrolls, barracks bags. The vertical space between the hammocks was so tight that you couldn't turn over unless the man above you turned over at the same instant. The air was foul; there was a porthole, but it was sealed shut and blacked out.

Since there were not nearly enough cabins on the ship to hold all the troops on board—thirteen thousand soldiers, plus one thousand in crew and staff—less conventional dormitories had been created from the barbershop, the hairdressing salon, the dress shop, the newsstand, the dog kenel, the wine cellar (empty), the gym, and the squash courts; even the enormous ornamental-fish tank on the reception deck had a resident soldier. And still there was not enough room. Consequently, a great many men had to sleep on the open deck, in shifts. Outlines of a human form had been painted and numbered on every deck of the ship, leaving only a narrow walkway along the rail. Each outline had two men assigned to it, and they alternated as tenants every four hours—four hours on the chilly deck, four hours inside in the warm. The ship's public rooms were given over to the inside men; the smell was indescribable. Every officer aboard had a shipboard duty ranging from supervising the mess lines to fire prevention. Mine was to enforce the blackout. I would patrol the body-laden decks looking for chinks of light, and when I found one—there were surprisingly many—I would go inside to smother it. A single torpedo could have produced the greatest, cheapest victory ever imagined by the German High Command. Speed was the *Queen*'s best defense against submarines; she could outrun any U-boat, so unless one was lying in wait directly in our path our chances were good. As a further defense, we zigzagged the whole way across, slowly, creakingly listing from one side to the other every two or three minutes as we shifted direction. Even so, not an hour went by without a submarine's having been sighted—or, rather, *said* to have been sighted—and at least a dozen torpedoes missed us by no more than six inches, according to wildfire report.

Four days out of New York—twenty-four hours quicker than the peacetime run—the *Queen Mary* landed in Gourock, on the Firth of Clyde, in Scotland, and a few days later I was at a holding camp outside the little hamlet of Broadway, in the Cotswolds. I was one of a small menagerie of second lieutenants waiting for assignment to an infantry division. Living quarters were bare Quonset huts, with a coke stove at one end as the sole source of heat and hot water in the autumn chill. It was a miserable life, with no end in sight—the Army had apparently forgotten us. Every chance I got, I signed out and spent the night at the Lygon Arms, a picturesque, Hallmark-card inn in Broadway. It was as old as the Domesday Book—all dark wood paneling and narrow passages, with every room on a different level—and it was generally empty and always freezing. Sometimes, I was the only overnight resident. Broadway itself, like the other marvelous Cotswold villages—Chipping Campden, Stow-on-the-Wold, Moreton-in-Marsh—was almost deserted; even the young women had been drafted into the Land Army of farmers.

On one of my visits, sitting in the bar, I was approached by a parody of a British upper-class county matron—tweeds and woolen stockings and sturdy mirror-polished walking shoes. She perfunctorily went through the usual catechism—where in America was I from, and what did I think of England—and then, after a lot of throat clearing and barking, asked if I would care to join her and her family in a little gathering in the hotel ballroom after dinner that night. Her distaste for what she was doing was very evident, and I couldn't figure her out—she certainly wasn't one of those hands-across-the-sea do-gooders, spreading cheer among the poor GIs so far from home. Then she explained: Her daughter Fiona, now conscripted by the Land Army, had turned eighteen recently, so it was time—"I don't know how you do these things in America"—for her to be presented to society. In happier days, Fiona's mother gave me to understand, the debut would have been celebrated properly, in London, with a proper dance and a proper orchestra—"but of course things are so different now." So she and her husband were giving Fiona a little dance here at the Lygon Arms, and they would be most pleased if I would come.

The county lady was right in one respect: things were different now. The ballroom of the Lygon Arms was far gone in mustiness, dimness, and neglect, and the blackout made it even gloomier. For the party, an inadequate number of twenty-five-watt bulbs had been installed, and six or seven little tables had been placed around the dance floor. The dance band was a violinist and an accordionist, neither of them a day under eighty. We were a party of about twenty—Mr. and Mrs. County; Fiona, a sullen, heavy-browed girl, bronzed by the weather; a few perfectly acceptable female cousins; a number of what I took to be aunts and uncles; and a collection of males that added up to a mother's nightmare. Dragooning them into service must have cost Mrs. County endless surrenders of pride and social position; for one thing, they were all damaged goods, because otherwise they would have been in uniform. They were of various ages and of various costumes—tight pants, baggy pants, patent-leather shoes, ankle-high boots. Mr. and Mrs. County were properly dressed in well-cut evening clothes, but Fiona was wearing an ancient dress that must have come from an attic trunk—wearing it mutinously, as though she were in drag. I had a feeling that the evening had been preceded by a tremendous family battle, which her mother had won in the last round. Fiona retaliated by pretending that she was not there at all: she would dance if asked, but not a word could be got out of her. Mr. and Mrs. County, on the other hand, were tireless in trying to create gaiety where there was none, but despite their efforts dead silence often descended on the whole company. Not surprisingly, the evening petered out very early, but British tradition had held firm. We had dressed for dinner in the jungle, and Fiona was now formally Out.

In October 1943, my orders finally came through: report for duty with the First Infantry Division, then in Dorset. This was an assignment that carried much cachet. The First Division was, as its number indicated, a Regular Army division, of great renown and a long history; one of its units—the 5th Field Artillery—went back to the Revolution. But while its history may have been exemplary, its statistics were dismayingly bloody. It had taken a terrible beating in 1942 as it fought its way across northern Africa and then through Sicily, replacing its losses as it went. Hardly a man in the present rifle companies had made the initial landing in North Africa. (By the end of the war, the division had suffered 20,761 killed and wounded, plus thousands more lost to accidents and war-related diseases.) It was not a safe place to be.

The division had recently arrived in England from Sicily, with orders to train for the invasion of France, and its various units were now spread around Dorset, from Lyme Regis almost to Bournemouth. A division, as then constituted, consisted of three infantry regiments; each regiment had three battalions, and each battalion four companies—three rifle and one heavy-weapons (machine guns and big mortars). At the very bottom of the pile was the platoon, four to a company, each made up of about forty men, commanded by a second lieutenant. I was a second lieutenant. I reported in at Division Headquarters, in Blandford, just above Dorchester, and was assigned to F Company, Second Battalion, 18th Infantry Regiment, for immediate duty; an F Company jeep would take me to F Company headquarters, in a field somewhere southeast of Blandford.

The F Company jeep dumped me in front of one of a half dozen Quonset huts on either side of a muddy, hilly Dorset road. My new boss, the company commander, was Capt. Fred Kramer, and my new job, he told me, was to take over the First Platoon as soon as the present platoon leader, Lt. Jack Summers, left for his new post as executive officer of another company. Kramer was very matter-of-fact and apparently unaware of the effect on me of what he was saying. True, all my training ever since that brainless sergeant had dropped me into the infantry had aimed me at precisely this job, but training is one thing and reality another. I was suddenly aware that I didn't know the first thing about running a rifle platoon, and the F Company jeep driver hadn't increased my self-assurance when he told me that Captain Kramer's predecessor was buried in Sicily, and Jack Summers's in Africa.

Trudging around the muddy Dorset pastures in search of the First Platoon, I pictured Summers as some kind of fire-breathing holy terror—how could a First Division platoon leader be anything less?—but he turned out to be a mild-mannered fellow, a former roofer, from Worcester, Massachusetts, who had joined the division as a replacement second lieutenant—just like me—before the landing in Sicily. He would be leaving in a week, he said, and he knew what I was going through—he'd been there himself. "But you'll be too busy to worry about it," he said.

It turned out that Summers was right. By the time he left, I was unconcernedly leading the First Platoon all over Dorset as F

Company went through training marches, rifle practice, machine-gun and mortar practice, street-fighting practice. One night exercise pitted F Company against a band of *goumiers*—short, black, wiry, evil-looking North Africans, commanded by French officers and part of the French Army. Their weapon of choice was the knife, and each man carried one. They were also famed as trackers. The point of the exercise was this: F Company, presumed to be deep in enemy territory, was to set up a tightly secured, overnight defensive position, and the *goumiers*, presumed to be the enemy, were to try to infiltrate it. If they succeeded, they would mark their passage with a piece of chalk, instead of a knife to the heart. Or so it was promised.

F Company's part of the exercise went off without a hitch: we established outposts, set up intersecting fields of fire, and sent out patrols. Then we waited. Nothing happened. By three o'clock in the morning, still nothing had happened, and I was wondering how soon headquarters was going to call off the aborted exercise and let us all go home. Finally, dawn came. There were chalked crosses everywhere—even on the backs of some of the men—and nobody had seen a flicker of movement or heard a whisper of sound. I almost felt sorry for the Germans who found the *goumiers* facing them in the front line.

So the weeks and months went by—running around in the Dorset mud all week, recuperative weekends in London. By any rational standard, London during the blackout was a grimy, underprivileged, dangerous place to be, but to me it was delicious. The grime was undeniable—gaping holes left by the Blitz, leaking sandbags everywhere, and nothing painted or refurbished in four years. Hyde Park was dotted with clusters of antiaircraft guns, which would open up deafeningly whenever enemy bombers—now infrequent visitors—appeared overhead. The deepest Tube stations had been turned into dormitories, filled with stacks of metal cots, neatly curtained to protect British sensibilities. These cubicles would begin to fill up every evening after work and late tea. Travelers waiting for a Tube train would stand at the very edge of the platform, tactfully pretending to be unaware of the busy nightlife going on behind them. In the restaurants, the endless diet of brussels sprouts and lank brown bread made Army fare seem Lucullan, and the pitch-dark blackout made a mantrap of every open areaway and iron railing. But London was a wonderful place to be. I would catch a train from Dorchester on Saturday evening, after we had been dismissed for the day, and be in town in time to pick up a girl from the English-speaking Officers' Club, on the back side of Park Lane, and take her to the Mirabelle for a splendid dinner of brussels sprouts and something indescribable and lank brown bread. Then on to a nightclub—the expatriate French *boîtes* tucked away in Soho cellars were the best. Two American officers I had met on the *Queen Mary*—Fulton Cutting and Philip Burnham—who worked at some sort of high-level operations unit in Berkeley Square, had rooms in a house on Queen Street, where there was a bed for me. Some weekends, I would leave my gear in Queen Street and head down the block to Shepherd Market, where there was a superlative pub, always full of attractive people, David Niven, then a commando, among them. My almost cousin, the publisher Harold Batsford, was another, and so was a French major named Hector Issy, who was as broad as he was tall and as gnarled as an oak. Every now and then, he would be away for a week, and if you asked him how come, he would change the subject. He later told me he was one of those in-by-parachute-out-by-submarine demolition experts, but more than that he would not say.

One night at the pub, I met an English couple—a civilian accountant, middle-aged and very pleasant, and his middle-aged very pleasant wife—who invited me to drop in at their flat in Chelsea that evening after dinner. A little party, they said—ten or twelve people they were sure I would like. I got there late, and found a gathering no different from a university-press book party in New York. I was given a drink and introduced around—five or six civilian couples of the same cut and stamp as the accountant and his wife, plus a young lieutenant from one of the kilted Scottish regiments. When I had made the rounds, my host said to the gathering, "Well, we're all here now, so we can begin." With that, a door at the end of the room opened, and out came a woman in a tiger-skin outfit that unnecessarily covered the center of her stomach and the middle of her back and nothing else. This was mesmerizing enough, but even more so was the six-foot whip she was carrying—and using. No circus ringmaster could have outcracked her; she made it snap an inch from your skin, and you knew she could leave you with a welt to remember if she wanted to. With her first snap, the room erupted in tumult. All around me, men and women were leaping out of her way as they tried to shed their clothes. The tiger lady had them circling the room like cats in a cage, laying a jolting snap right behind the laggards at every circuit. In no time at all, the only people in the room still dressed were the kilted lieutenant and I, and Miss Tiger was coming after us. Fortunately, the other guests, now buck naked, were holding her back, grabbing at her and imploring her to transfer her ministrations to them. The kilted lieutenant, skipping over chairs and dodging behind tables, was trying to get out the front door before she could put a stinger in his kilts, and I was right behind him. Just in time, he wrenched the door open, and out we shot. He was very spry, and he beat me down the stairs by a wide margin. I never saw him again. Or the middle-aged British couple, or the tiger lady.

Many of my daytime hours in London were spent in the headquarters of various Army service commands, trying to get myself reassigned out of the infantry, but without success. Then I got a homegrown stroke of luck of such majestic beneficence that I could hardly take it in: by order of the division's adjutant general, I was transferred out of F Company to Division Headquarters, assigned to the G-2, or Intelligence, section, Col. Emmett F. Carson commanding. Once again, I owed my reprieve to my ability to speak French. (In fact, I am convinced that without my French I would not be alive today; one has only to consider the mortality statistics for second-lieutenant platoon leaders, or read Robert Kotlowitz's chilling *Before Their Time*. Somebody in the division's higher echelons had combed through the personnel files to find French-speakers—after all, we were going to France—and there I was, with a dividend: my eight weeks at the Camp Ritchie Intelligence school. To be sure, the way the First Division operated, transfer to Division Headquarters was no guarantee of a long and genial life, but anything at all was better than the foxholes of a rifle company.

Colonel Carson was a rarity among the West Pointers who made up the division's command staff: he was a civilian, a former Wall Street executive. But, like a Catholic convert, he had gone all the way in his conversion, and was now more Regular Army than the Star-Spangled Banner. (In fact, he stayed in the Army after the war, and was a battalion commander with the division in Korea.)

My first assignment under Colonel Carson was to attend an Intelligence school run by the British in Cheltenham, to get the very latest line on operations in France. The school was staffed by French Army officers, and they brought us up to date on the identity and functions of the various French Resistance movements, and gave us a booklet that would help us distinguish the good guys from the bad guys. In France at that time there were scores of militant organizations with resounding names; only by consulting the booklet would you know that the Alliance for the Defense of French Soil was an okay outfit and that one called France Forever was really run by the Nazis. The booklet made for pretty dry reading, but I put it into my map case anyway. The next time I thought about it was in Normandy, where it achieved a remarkable coup.

In mid-April, a sense of urgency began to fill the air. Regimental and battalion commanders started making unannounced inspections and raising hell if things weren't exactly right. Weapons were required to be as clean as the day they were made. Short haircuts were an absolute, as I learned all too well one day when I was still with F Company. I had my platoon nicely lined up in the company roadway one afternoon when a jeep came by and Col. George Smith, the regimental commander, got out to make a surprise inspection. I was not alarmed, but I should have been. A new replacement had been added to my platoon that very morning, and I hadn't had time to learn anything about him beyond his name—Stanislaus something. The colonel went up and down our lines without comment, and then stopped in front of Stanislaus like a bird dog coming to the point. "Take off your helmet, son," he said. Stanislaus did so, and a cascade of golden curls burst forth, masses of hair, torrents of hair, down to his shoulders, down to his waist—in my consternation, my imagination ran wild. "This will cost you fifty bucks, Lieutenant," the colonel said to me, and it did, on my next payday.

Training exercises grew tougher and longer. We were divided into boatload segments and practiced boarding mock-up landing craft. Long lines of trucks and tanks snaked through the Dorset villages en route to vast holding lots in open fields near the ports. Artillery shells were stacked like cord wood alongside every road. Southern England was sinking into the sea under the weight of munitions—none of them worth a dime if the First Division failed to get ashore. Everybody knew we were going, but nobody knew where or when.

Rehearsals began. The whole division was loaded onto transports for a practice landing at Slapton Sands, in Devon, where the beaches and bluffs were said to be like the ones we would land on in France. Tension rose. In the Blandford manor house where the First Division had its headquarters, there was a tantalizing secret room guarded day and night by military police. Nobody could enter except officers of the very highest oil. Then one day in early May I was told to report to Colonel Carson inside the room. The summons was so momentous that I was prepared to genuflect as I entered the holy of holies. To my surprise, most of the room was taken up by a big playground sandbox, at table height. A closer look showed that it was not for kiddies. The sand was an artful simulation of a beach somewhere, leading up to a line of bluffs. Little metal objects that looked like bent paperclips were scattered on the toy beach, and a sergeant, scanning an aerial photograph, was moving them about. This, I realized, was the invasion beach, and the paperclips were antitank obstacles. Colonel Carson pointed to a spot on the bluffs where a toy farmhouse had been planted and told me to mark it well: it was where I was to meet Robert Mercadès, head of the Resistance network in the Bayeux area. The whole thing, he said, had been worked out by high-level British Intelligence: on D day, now set for June 5, Mercadès would make his way from Bayeux, just to the east of this beach, and work himself through the German lines to this farmhouse, where he would hand me essential information about German supply dumps and artillery emplacements inland.

There it was: I now knew the when and the where of the invasion: June 5, on a stretch of the Normandy shoreline west of Bayeux. Code name: Omaha Beach. I instantly wished I had not been told. It was probably the biggest secret of all time. There was no calculating the stakes riding on this bit of knowledge.

A week later, the stress level went up another notch: all leaves were canceled. On the first of June, the big move came: we were herded into "sausages"—giant barbed-wire enclosures shaped like sausages—in open fields nearer the coast. This was the last we would see of civilian life; once you were in your sausage, you abandoned all connection with the outside world. No one was allowed in or out. No one was allowed to call, or even wave, across the barbed wire, and a constant file of military police circled the sausages to see that no one did. Each sausage held the troops that were to board a particular group of landing craft, and it was here that the men were told where they were going and when.

Then we waited—hot, smelly, and cramped. On the fourth of June we were loaded onto our craft. Mine was an LCI—Landing

Craft, Infantry—which carried a couple of hundred men and had projecting ladders at each side of the bow, down which the men would trot off onto the beach. It was one of several LCIs tied up side by side in Weymouth harbor.

Late in the afternoon of June 4, we started out for France, scores of ships in line, each tugging a silvery barrage balloon to ward off dive-bombers, everything very tranquil and well regulated. Two hours later, we turned around and went home again: bad weather forecast. The next evening, we again paraded out of Weymouth harbor, the ships still clutching the strings of their silvery barrage balloons, like children on the way home from the zoo. Again, all was purposeful and orderly; emotions were certainly churning on every ship, but they churned silently. Nobody talked much. Even though huddled together and cramped, one felt very *private*.

The night was long, the Channel was rough, and seasickness and its prevention took charge of all one's thoughts. Then, gradually, we began to hear, above the thrumming of the LCI's engines, a heavy thudding. It got stronger and stronger, and with each thud the ship seemed to lurch. I wriggled my way up to a spot on deck to see what was going on. The thuds we had heard were coming from the guns of battleships arrayed in a line behind us. They were throwing shells as big as freight cars over our heads, deep into the interior. Every time a gun was fired, our little ship would jump in the water from the concussion, and we could hear the shell go hissing and warbling through the air above us on its way to France. There was a tentative flush of dawn in the east, and as the light grew stronger the vague presence of other ships around us hardened into shapes—scores of ships. Among them were big transports and other LCIs as well as smaller vessels, packed tight with unidentifiable cargoes, endlessly and, it seemed, aimlessly crisscrossing the gray and choppy water.

It was now about eight o'clock in the morning, and we were still a long way from the beach. Six-thirty had been H-hour, but we had no way of knowing how the assault had gone. We pushed on. Now we could near the noise from the shore—the *rat-tat-tat* of machine-gun fire, the *whomp* of artillery. I could hardly take in the immensity of the scene, which was setting the heavens roaring from one edge of the horizon to the other. Could anybody have planned all this? Could anybody control it? Our troop commander was peering at the beach through binoculars. "Something must have gone wrong," he said. "They should be off the beach and on the bluffs by now." What had gone wrong, we later learned, was the unanticipated presence of a fresh, fully equipped Wehrmacht infantry division, the 352nd, which had moved into the German defense positions for anti-invasion maneuvers too recently to be picked up by Intelligence.

We were slowly continuing our move toward shore when a dud shell hit us amidships, right over my head, leaving a neat circular hole where it had come through. It was a dud, but it scared me half to death. (A live shell would have completed the job.) It gave me my first gut awareness that there actually were people out there who wanted to *kill* me. Up to now, the day had been pure spectacle; now it was all too personal.

However, there was too much going on for imagination to take over and panic to set in. We were still pushing in. Now there were bodies in the water, facedown, and random geysers shooting up from exploding artillery shells. Survivors of stricken ships were clinging to floating debris. Far behind us in the Channel, the battleships were still hurling their sibilant freight cars over our heads. Closer toward shore, a Navy destroyer was wheeling back and forth like a dog in a kennel pen, firing spasmodically at targets onshore; the mist and drizzle and the smoke from grass fires ignited by the shelling made it impossible to see what they were shooting at. The beach itself was fully visible—we were still a good half mile offshore—and so were the steep bluffs behind it. The segment of the beach our LCI was aimed at was called Easy Red; to the right was Easy Green; to the left, Fox Green. At Easy Red, a small stream, now dried up, had carved a cleft—a little valley, called a "draw" in Army parlance—into the bluffs behind the beach, and it was in a stone farmhouse at the top of this draw that I was supposed to meet Mercadès. Getting there, however, looked to be a planner's fantasy. The only way off the beach was by means of a sort of rough track—marked "Exit E-1" on our maps—that ran up the west wall of the draw—the track used by the local farmers to bring their cattle down to browse on the salt hay at water level. It was obviously well defended. Even at our distance from the beach, I could see little figures in American helmets trying to work their way toward the cow track, and it was clear that they were taking many casualties from machine guns dug into the cliffs.

An LCI off to our starboard was also making for Easy Red beach, and when we were about a quarter of a mile from shore it took a direct hit, throwing dozens of soldiers into the water. At this, the commander of our LCI spun his ship about and headed back to sea—losing a second LCI was no way to win the war. I applauded his good sense, but not for long. Word came down that we were to load into little LCVPs, which would ferry us to shore. (An LCVP—Landing Craft, Vehicle/Personnel—was a sort of tiny scow, hardly more than an outboard, that could carry perhaps twenty-five standing men; there was a ramp at its front that could be lowered for their exit.) Cargo nets were draped over the side of our LCI for the troops to climb down and into the LCVPs. But so far there was only one LCVP bobbing alongside our ship—one LCVP for over a hundred men. Things began to come unstuck on the LCI. First, a contingent of beach engineers was ordered aboard our single taxi. Then they were pulled back, and a part of Headquarters Company was told to go. In the end, a disparate group of men, some of them beach engineers and some of them random bits of Headquarters Company—including me—was ordered over the side onto the cargo nets. But the nets were too short, leaving a drop of six or eight feet from the last handhold to the bottom of the landing craft. The driver of the LCVP, a Coast Guard petty officer who, for some mad reason, never stopped singing, was doing his best to hold his craft tight against the LCI, but the sea was rough, and he kept yawing away and then slamming into its side. His passengers, loaded down with equipment and constricted in movement by the stiff, chemically impregnated coveralls we were all wearing against the possibility of poison gas, had to judge the exact moment to let go and land in the LCVP, rather than in the water between, to sink out of sight forever. Miraculously, some twenty or twenty-five men made the jump, and the singing driver would take no more. We set off for the shore again.

Ellsworth Clark, the executive officer of Headquarters Company, had also boarded the LCVP, and he and I stood behind the raised ramp; we couldn't see much, but we thought the ramp might be bulletproof. A stray Signal Corps photographer named Herman Wall sat on the LCVP's rear gunwale, snapping pictures. He took one of me and Clark standing behind the ramp, and one of me splashing ashore at the head of a file of men after the ramp was down. A third showed Clark, still in the boat, urging the last of the men into the water. The first picture was republished in *Paris-Match* on the fiftieth anniversary of D day, and I have a copy; the second, enormously enlarged, covers a wall of the invasion museum at Arromanches.

By coincidence, our LCVP landed at about the same time as advance elements of the 18th Infantry Regiment—my old outfit—which had been in reserve. In *Omaha Beachhead,* published by the Historical Division of the U.S. War Department, the official Army historian has this to say:

> As they neared the shore, troops of the 18th had the impression that no progress had been made in getting off the beach. The beach shingle was still full of tractors, tanks, vehicles, bulldozers, and troops. The high ground was still held by the Germans, who had all the troops on the beach pinned down under heavy fire from small arms, mortars, and artillery. On the right of Exit E-1, an enemy pillbox

> was still in action. Fire from a tank supported our infantry in a first attempt to take it, but the attack was stalled until naval fire was laid on, and a destroyer about 1,000 yards offshore coordinated its actions with the infantry assault. The affair was very nicely timed: the destroyer's guns, firing only a few yards above the crowded beach, got on target at about the fourth round, and the pillbox surrendered. Twenty German prisoners were taken. . . . Within half an hour, engineers were clearing mines from the E-1 Exit.

This is a good, tight report, written by somebody who wasn't there. Nobody who *was* there could have set down anything so wide-ranging, so circumstantial. Nobody on that beach was aware of anything that wasn't right in front of his nose—and, Lord knows, that was enough. The human mind, when under great tension, closes its doors, shutters its windows, and focuses on the insignificant. When I waded ashore onto that Normandy beach, I was entering the stage set of a truly stupendous world event, yet what my mind stubbornly chose to busy itself with was a memory of my *first* landing in France, twenty years earlier, when I had debated which foot would have the honor of being the first to step on French soil as I came off the ship's gangplank. The War Department historian, writing from his civilized perch in his civilized office, could coolly record that when a tank-infantry attack on a pillbox failed a Navy destroyer was laid on to finish the job, but such breadth of vision was beyond me. All I recorded were snapshots of tiny fragments of the world's stupendous event, snapshots with no anchor in time or meaning. Sample snapshot: the hundreds of cumbersome life-preserver belts littering the water's edge, jettisoned by the troops as they reached shore. Snapshot: a makeshift aid station sheltered behind some rocks, where a medic was injecting morphine into the arm of a wounded soldier who wasn't going to make it anyway. Snapshot: five or six German prisoners—

all of them in their teens—sitting in a declivity on the beach with their hands on their heads and looking just as terrified as the nervous private who was guarding them. Snapshot: a beach-engineer sergeant with one arm in a bloody sling shouting at two of his men, who were dripping water from head to foot. Snapshot: a bulldozer filling in an anti-tank ditch dug across the mouth of the draw, its driver working as methodically as if he were building a road in Ohio.

When the ramp of our landing craft went down, I had no idea how I was going to get to my rendezvous with Mercadès or what I was going to do with the file of men who were following me ashore. As it happened, the beach engineers among them were easily disposed of: I had noticed a makeshift beach-engineer command post, marked by a yellow flag, off to the right, so I sent them along to join their fellows. That left five or six ragtag members of Headquarters Company. The first thing for them to do—for any of us to do—was to get off this murderous beach. Headquarters Company had a prearranged assembly area on the bluffs above the E-1 Exit, but the exit was still closed, and I couldn't take them with me as I tried to find the stone farmhouse—I was still determined to try for Mercadès. So I made sure every one of them knew where the assembly area was, and sent them off on their own, every man for himself, since it was suicidal to stay on that beach bunched up in a group.

Now my problem was how to get to the farmhouse. Our engineers were still clearing mines from Exit E-1, and I could see no other way out. German small-arms fire had let up for the moment, allowing freer movement, so I started for the exit myself. I had hardly taken a step when a machine gun, firing from God knows where, went back to work, kicking up divots of sod from the top of a low embankment a couple of yards in front of me. This was certified panic time. The embankment—the side of an old streambed?—offered about two feet of protection, and I flung myself into its lee, flat on my stomach, nose in the dirt. As I lay there, trying to will myself into invisibility, I slowly became aware that I was sharing my sanctuary with a soldier who no longer needed it; in my panic, I had not noticed him before. He had been running behind the embankment in a crouch, squeezing every last bit of cover from the two-foot rise, but the machine gunner had got him anyway. He had fallen exactly as he was, as though he were a cardboard figure blown over by the wind: lying on his side, still bent over in a crouch, one hand still grabbing his rifle around its middle. His helmet had rolled off, and his short black hair looked very neat and tidy. No wound was visible, and he might have been asleep, except that his eyes were open. He was younger than me, with a bright, inquisitive face, rather foxy-looking, and a long, pointy nose. I could imagine him only a few days ago vainly trying to pick up girls in a Dorchester or Bournemouth pub, crowing and boasting, in no way on track for all this.

He and I waited behind our embankment until it became clear that the machine gunner, after his first terrifying burst, had turned his attention elsewhere. I peeped over the ledge and saw that the engineers had now opened all of Exit E-1, allowing a parade of troops to move up it: a real breakthrough. I crept out and joined them.

The stone farmhouse was off to the left, at the head of the draw, and I had a hard time finding it, chiefly because it was no longer there. It must have taken a direct hit from one of those naval freight cars. If Mercadès had been waiting for me there . . . I moved on to the Headquarters Company's assembly area. Ten minutes later, Ellsworth Clark rolled in, leading a dozen Headquarters Company men he had collected in his roaming. A bullet had delicately grazed his cheek, leaving a scratch no bigger than a shaving nick; it had bled nicely, but he was afraid it wouldn't qualify him for a Purple Heart. I was mighty glad to see him.

There was no sleep that night, and by dawn the next day enough elements of Division Headquarters had come together from all over the compass to man a sketchy command post in a run-down cow shed on the bluffs above the beach. Even before dawn, I was sent off to find Mercadès—the Mercadès connection was entirely an Intelligence operation, and Colonel Carson, in his Regular Army mode, wanted to shine. I could not believe Mercadès would be hanging around the demolished farmhouse—he was either under the rubble, dead, or in a safe place, waiting out his chance to get to us—and indeed he was not. Looking for him elsewhere was hopeless—an *aiguille* in a *meule de foin*—and by noon I was back at headquarters, sitting in a ditch, trying to get two minutes' sleep. A British captain, the liaison officer from the 50th British Infantry Division—the celebrated Desert Rats of North Africa—which had landed in the invasion sector just to the east of us, was also in the ditch, trying to do the same thing. We were leaning against a couple of young trees, our backs to the fighting, when suddenly there was a ripping sound and a metallic bang, and the English officer's head jerked forward. He took off his helmet, and there, flattened against its back, was a squashed bullet. That accounted for the metallic bang. The ripping sound had come from the tree he was leaning against, which the bullet had gone through first: no tree, no Englishman. The officer inspected the bullet briefly and then got out a knife and pried it off his helmet. "Can't someone put a stop to this sort of thing?" he said.

This sort of thing. What an irritating bastard! Was he showing off? Putting me down? Couldn't he admit he'd been scared out of his socks? My huffiness was a mark of my greenness. Among old pros, fear was not something one talked about or admitted to. Nobody, I'm sure, was immune to it, but it was an unmentionable subject. The sniper's bullet had undoubtedly scared the Englishman as much as it scared me, but he was a very old pro (as well as an Englishman), and he observed the code.

The sniper had to be found. Our troops were pressing forward well beyond us, but there was no solid front line. A lot of individual German soldiers had been left behind when the fighting moved inland, and this sniper was undoubtedly one of them. The ditch the British officer and I were sitting in ran along the edge of a field, and on the inland side of the field was a farmhouse, still inhabited. Off to the left was a clump of woods. Was our sniper firing from a tree in the woods? From the farmhouse? It was a typical low-lying Norman building, stone, with a thatched roof and a storage attic. An American major, unknown to me, who had just come out of the command-post cow shed, took up the case. Had anybody talked to the people in the farmhouse? Actually, no, somebody said; the farmer only spoke French. Well, the major said, didn't headquarters have some smart-ass lieutenant who spoke French? Where was he? Get him the hell up here!

There was no way I could deny I was the smart-ass lieutenant, and in short order I was on my way to the farmhouse. It was a poor spot to be in: a sniper can see you, and you can't see him. Still, nobody took a potshot at me before I banged on the farmhouse door. After a long wait, it was unbolted and opened on a chain; through the slit I could see a classic French peasant, with a beret and a stubble of beard. "*Il y a des francs-tireurs qui nous emmerdent,*" I said, trying to show as much sangfroid as the English officer. "Open up. I want to search the house."

"*Vous êtes américain?*" the farmer asked. I said yes, I was, and so were all the other soldiers now scattered through his fields. He unchained the door. "There's nobody here but family, but you can come in," he said. The door opened onto a standard French farmhouse kitchen—stone-floored, with a great tall clock in one corner, a huge black stove (now cold) in front of what used to be an open fireplace, and an armoire of the sort French farm wives keep their bedding in. Strings of shallots and garlic bulbs hung from the ceiling, and an inimitable, slightly sour smell of furniture wax, soap, sweat, and cooking hung over everything. Two women were sitting at a big round table in the center of the room—the farmer's wife and his or her sister, I guessed. Both were in a state of almost palpable trepidation.

"So you're here," the farmer said. "You certainly took your time coming. We've been waiting for this for four years."

It was hardly an effusive welcome. Norman peasants have long been known for their grouchiness, but this one was carrying things too far. Still, despite his uncongeniality, he was a significant figure for me—an honest-to-God Frenchman on his own native, unoccupied heath, in his own unrequisitioned house. Ever since the fall of France, no one on our side had seen such a thing. For four blank years, France had simply, teasingly disappeared. Unappeased curiosity feeds on itself, and we on the outside had nothing to go on but rumors and secondhand reports. "Businessmen from neutral countries say that the Nazis in Occupied France are experiencing serious shortages of. . . ." "Swedish observers report having seen . . ." And there were little flyspecks of what may have been news or may have been the creations of the British Ministry of Information—letters from behind the wall, from somebody's old French nurse, now retired, or from the Dutch brother-in-law of somebody's cousin. There was always much homely detail—how the butcher had told off a German officer, or how the German supply trucks had developed a rash of flat tires. I still have one of these letters, which was passed from hand to hand in the *New Yorker* offices. It was not from Occupied Europe, but from England right after Dunkirk, and the fingerprints of the Ministry of Information are all over it. Datelined "July 8, 1940, Glebe House, West Grinstead," it reads, in part:

> My dear Mary:
>
> It was a great joy receiving your letter and hearing your expressions of love and loyalty to this country. We are now standing alone with the other English-speaking races. We in England will still have to face terrible fighting on the sea, in the air, and on the land. Thank God, I pray and believe that our morale is rising every day. . . . I sent my little grandson to a wonderful fishing village in Herefordshire, which we think is safer than here. My younger daughter is at the local hospital ready for anything that may happen. Libby, my married one, has gone back to her

> little house about a mile from here and occasionally gets a glimpse of her husband, who is defending the coast. . . . Our shops are full of food, and the organisation is absolutely perfect. The troops billeted all around us are in marvellous heart. One of the soldiers said to me yesterday that if the Germans did not wipe them out on that beach at Dunkirk they are not going to do it on this island. . . .

Today, no one would believe such a letter for a moment, but in the *New Yorker* offices it was considered gospel. Everyone was so hungry for news from inside the dungeon that even Glebe House, West Grinstead, served as Delphi. Our diet of information—sightings by peripatetic Swedish businessmen, reports from somebody's old nurse—had been so hopelessly thin, so consistently lacking in reality, that my real, if surly, peasant was a gold strike. If he had been waiting four years to see us, I had been waiting four years to see him. Now here he was, in the flesh, the real McCoy, and all he could do was complain. He was a big disappointment, but I refused to give up on him.

Meanwhile, there was the sniper. Where was he? "Not in here," the farmer said. "You can search all you want, but nobody has been in or out of this house for two days. Try the woods. Plenty of cover there."

I went back and reported this to the officious major, but before he could organize a search of the woods (I knew who was going to be put in charge of it), I was summoned away by my boss. For the next few days, I was so busy, I forgot all about the sniper, but a week later I happened to pass by the farm while taking a bunch of prisoners to the big prisoner-of-war cage now established near the beach. To my surprise, the farmhouse was in ruins. I asked around and found out what had happened. The troops that had moved in behind us had also been harassed by a sniper, and again a soldier was sent to the farmhouse to investigate. But this soldier hadn't turned sentimental over the world's first liberated Frenchman. When the farmer protested that there were no Germans in his house, this soldier brushed him aside and did his own searching. He found nothing on the ground floor, and then started up the ladder to the attic. At the top of the ladder there was a trapdoor; he had to push it up to get in. As he did so, the sniper turned from the attic window and shot him dead. With that, of course, all hell broke loose. The solder's colleagues outside heard the shot and tore into the house to find him. They flushed out the sniper with concussion grenades, and arrested the farmer and the two women. The three were handed over to the French tribunals that had by then been installed near Bayeux. It turned out that the farmer was a full-blown collaborator. The two women were released, but he was executed. For a long time, I had a nightmare in which I was the one about to push up that trapdoor.

The primary objective of the First Division after it got off Omaha Beach was to seize the village of Caumont, about eight miles inland, on the crest of a Norman hill. Caumont was a key objective, because from its church steeple you could see the Channel in one direction and practically to Berlin in the other. By June 15, the First Division had taken the town and a long, narrow corridor leading to it—a thin finger pointing east into the German lines.

After ten days in France, the division had pulled itself together and was operating with its old efficiency. I could not say the same for myself. There is no day or night for an infantry outfit in action, and after ten days of combat, I was a case of no sleep and bad nerves—the price of greenness. One afternoon, I was trying to catch a nap when Colonel Carson yanked me awake and sent me down to one of our rifle companies to check on a young Frenchman who had entered our lines on what he said was a mission of mercy. This was about the ninth nap Colonel Carson had interrupted, and I was feeling more than a little irascible when I finally found the Frenchman, sitting on the edge of a horse trough in the yard of an abandoned farmhouse. He was in the custody of a private, who was half-asleep in an armchair he had dragged from the house. I envied him the armchair.

The Frenchman was about eighteen and tall, with dark hair, black eyes, and big ears. He was wearing hiking boots, an old pair of corduroy pants, and an incongruous city-suit jacket, nipped in at the waist. He was hardly worth interrupting a nap for. With very bad grace and low expectations, I started questioning him. His story was this: He was working as an orderly in a civilian hospital near Caen (to the east of our salient, and still in German hands). The day before, the civilian hospital in Saint-Lô (to the west of our salient, and also in German hands) had run out of a vital serum of some sort, and since the Caen hospital still had a good supply, he had volunteered to hop on his bicycle and take a bottle of the stuff to Saint-Lô. The only direct road between Caen and Saint-Lô, he pointed out, was Route 31, which cut across our salient, and he hoped we would give him a safe-conduct pass to cross through our lines—it would save him cycling many extra kilometers.

I inspected his bottle, and it looked all right to me—thick and yellow and sealed with medical-looking hieroglyphics. But *he* didn't look right—that city jacket. Did he come from around here? I asked. No, he said with some disdain, he was from Paris; he had been sent to Normandy a couple of days earlier. Sent by whom? Sent by his youth club, he said; he was part of its medical-assistance corps. Because of the high number of civilian casualties in Normandy, the director of the club had sent him here to help out.

"What was the name of the club?" I asked.

"Groupement Français des Jeunes," he said. That meant nothing to me, but I suddenly remembered my Cheltenham booklet, still in my map case. In no time, I found the Groupement in it, even including the name of its director, Fernand Volet.

"What's your director's name?" I asked.

"Fernand Volet," he said, and the balloon went up: the Groupement Français was bang in the middle of the list of Nazi-controlled organizations.

"How did you get here from Paris?"

"By train and bus to Caen."

"Who met you at the bus station?"

"Nobody. They told me in Paris to go straight to the hospital."

"Did Volet give you any other instructions?"

"No. He just told me to go to the hospital and help out."

These answers were beginning to get my back up. How could this unrepentant junior Nazi have the nerve to tell me so many lies? I took out my pistol and put it in his ear. "I don't believe a word of any of this," I said. "Before I blow out your brains, I want to know every single thing you did after getting off the bus. Who you talked to, where you went, what you saw. Everything. I'm going to count to three. One . . . Two . . ." But before I could say "Three" he talked.

He had known his club was controlled by the Nazis, but that was all right with him: the Germans were fighting for their lives in an unjust war. He had wanted to do his bit. When he got to Caen, he had gone, as instructed, not to the hospital but directly to the German headquarters, in a château just outside the town, and there had been fitted out with his bottle of yellow stuff and his bicycle. Then he was told to cut across our salient and take note of our artillery positions.

There was one thing more, the most important of all: where was the German headquarters? He pointed out the château—a black oblong—on my map.

Leaving him in the charge of the armchair private, now very awake—the business of the pistol in the ear had wonderfully brought him to life—I returned to Division Headquarters. There I told the air-liaison officer that I had a possible target for him. He said there were a couple of RAF Typhoons just overhead, so we worked out the coordinates. He radioed the data upstairs, and the Typhoons took off. The château was too far away for us to see the action, but when the pilots radioed back in they said they'd hit the building dead on, and black and gray Wehrmacht uniforms had come bursting out of the doors and windows like ants out of an anthill. A glorious victory. (A glorious stroke of luck.) We didn't learn just how glorious until a good bit later, when word came down that the château the Typhoons had hit was the headquarters of the German army corps commanding our entire section of the front. As for my French bicycle spy, I never heard of him again, once we turned him over to the French authorities.

B*efore I blow out your brains*"—what a way to talk! What melodrama! But not entirely so. Behind the gangster-movie bravado one fact remains: I really might have pulled that trigger. It is perfectly possible, perhaps even probable, that I, who had always waited for the light to turn green, who kept off the grass when told to, who never, never spit in the subway, would have snuffed out a young man just because I didn't like the way he talked. What had happened to me?

The answer is not hard to find. What had happened was the inevitable wearing down of civilized standards by the three abrasives inherent in war: fear, exhaustion, and the pervasive brutishness of the world one lived in. Of the three, fear was the most complex. It came in three strengths: immediate (the sibilant whisper of an incoming mortar shell), potential ("What's around that corner?"), and general (an enduring unfocused anxiety, sometimes almost subliminal). In one strength or another, it was ever present. As for the other afflictions, I remember trudging across an open field one pitch-dark night in Normandy and being so worn out after two sleepless days on the go that I literally couldn't take another step. I pulled my field jacket over my head and fell to the ground, asleep before I landed. That was exhaustion. When daylight came, I saw that my feet were paddling about in the entrails of a German soldier, disemboweled by an artillery shell. I felt no revulsion; I felt nothing. I simply pulled up some grass and wiped off my boots. Then I searched the poor bugger's remaining pockets for useful information, as I had been taught. That was brutishness.

If, today, I can no longer see myself in the role of the hotshot with the pistol, it is because, happily, I can't re-create the atmosphere in which he lived. You can remember that a kidney stone hurt like hell, or that a skid on the ice scared you skinny, but you can't bring back the *feel* of the thing, and it's the feel of the thing that's gone now—especially the feel of fear.

Dealing with fear was the one subject left out of Army training. By the time the drill instructors were finished with me, I was a very model of a modern second lieutenant, but I knew nothing about the distorting effects of fear. Military training proceeds without ever acknowledging its existence, yet training without fear is like playing poker for paperclips and matches. From my first day as a recruit, I had known perfectly well that our training was play-acting: a god-awful day spent lugging a mortar around in the mud on a tactical exercise would end in a hot shower in the barracks. There was no place for fear in the process—quite the contrary: satisfaction was more like it. By the standards of the day, lugging that mortar around was a Good Thing. Mortar-luggers were much admired on the home front, and basking in that admiration was almost as satisfying as the hot shower. The war was unmistakably a popular one, and you were a hero simply by being in uniform. Everybody said so—the screenwriters said so, the advertising copywriters said so, the songwriters said so. The natural consequence of this repeated refrain was to think of the war as a sort of B-movie morality pageant, where the forces of righteousness would overcome the forces of darkness by spiritual superiority alone. It was a comforting notion, which led inescapably to tutti-frutti sentimentality. Here is an ad for War Savings Stamps that appeared in the summer of 1942 in *The New Yorker*, a magazine of sophistication, quiet reason, and good writing. Scene: a bomber factory. A woman in coveralls is working on a plane fuselage, with her little son at her feet. (What is a kid doing on the floor of a bomber factory? Don't ask.) The kid speaks:

KEEP 'EM FLYING, MOMMY!

Yes, Mommy, YOU! I look to you, Mommy, 'cause you're the little woman who finds the money, somehow, even when there isn't an awful lot, to give me the best of food, and things.

So keep those protective wings over me, Mommy. . . . And buy War Savings Stamps till we have enough—to buy a bomber. Babies and their mommies in conquered lands say I ought to tell you, Mommy—Keep 'Em Flying!

It was ever so. In Paris awhile back, a museum show dealing with the history of journalism featured an engraving from a 1915 issue of *L'Illustration* that showed three invalided French *poilus* of the First World War making their way through a Paris park. One has been blinded (at least, his eyes are bandaged), and he is being led along by his two pals, one of whom has a leg missing and the other an empty right sleeve. Their progress is being observed from a park bench by a civilian whose face is contorted by an emotion that is hard to interpret until one reads the caption: "*L'Envie.*" The picture, according to the museum's descriptive legend, was immensely popular in Paris in 1915, and it probably would have been equally popular in New York in 1942, when adulation, and thus envy, of the gloriously maimed was not uncommon. I remember being at a party on Long Island when a Royal Canadian Air Force flight lieutenant wearing a chilling black glove on an artificial hand came in; the reception he was accorded was almost pure adulation, and I, the feckless civilian, hated him for it.

Mercadès, I should report, had not been buried under the rubble of the farmhouse. He showed up, on his bicycle, a couple of days after my encounter with the churlish peasant. This was quite a different sort of liberated Frenchman. He was a captain in the regular French Army, and after the defeat at Dunkirk he had gone underground and eventually opened a bicycle shop in Bayeux, from which he directed the operations of six or eight agents. The region around Bayeux had been divided into sectors, and each agent was responsible for one sector and for one sector only; if he saw something, no matter how spectacular, going on next door, he was to ignore it and leave it to his adjacent colleague—whose identity he did not know, and thus could not reveal, even under torture.

For his meeting with us, Mercadès had put on what remained of his Army uniform of four years earlier; he had lost a lot of weight, and it flopped about him like a toga. He was a slight man to begin with—dark hair, olive complexion, sharp brown eyes, about thirty years old. In his baggy, low-comedy uniform and his outdated French Army helmet, he cut an odd figure in our midst, but he paid no attention to that; he was all business. He had brought with him a roll of French Army maps, and on them he pointed out the Forêt de Cérisy, a heavily wooded area, impervious to aerial reconnaissance, about a mile and a half beyond our lines. In the forest, he said, the Germans had stockpiled large quantities of fuel at this point here, and ammunition at that point there—both points within range of our artillery. Nobody really believed him—they couldn't get past his vaudeville uniform—but the coordinates were passed along to the artillery anyway. A couple of minutes later, a tremendous cloud of smoke suddenly appeared in the direction of the forest as the ammunition dump blew, followed by a second cloud, darker, as the gasoline went up. From that moment on, Mercadès was a respected figure among us, and he was fitted out with an American uniform and helmet. I saw a good deal of him over the next weeks, escorting his agents to various points where they could slip through our lines and into German territory, yet we never became real friends. He was too much all business for that. When the French Army got back on its feet, Mercadès was recalled and put in command of an infantry company near Metz, but our connection was broken off before that, when I got wounded and sent to England.

I had just left a barn after a futile search for a downed RAF pilot and was walking across a field when I heard the *r-i-i-i-i-p!* of an incoming shell. It was close, and a second shell, an instant later, was even closer—too close. A shell splinter plowed through my butt, cutting a ligament or something, so I couldn't walk or crawl to get out of the way of a third shell. This one felt as though somebody had driven a white-hot wire into my side. But once the smoke and surprise and panic had cleared, I realized that I had got what was called a million-dollar wound—not really dangerous, but serious enough to get me out of the line, away from the front.

The first stop on my way out was the battalion aid station, the medical facility closest to the front lines, where surgeons under tents worked on a never-ending assembly line of the wounded—slam-bang, rough-hewn surgery intended to get the casualty patched up well enough for transport to a bigger, more sophisticated medical unit to the rear. That same night, Division Headquarters had been bombed, killing the air-liaison officer and wounding many others, so the surgeons were extra busy. At the aid station, one of them removed the shell fragments from me (he left the two pieces of shrapnel in a gauze bag tied to my stretcher, and I still have them), following which I was flown (after an agonizing delay) to an Army general hospital near Manchester. There were thirty or forty of us wounded in the plane, and a fleet of ambulances picked us up at the airport. Being admitted to an Army hospital is exactly like being admitted to a civilian hospital: a delay of X hours is required in the admissions office—longer if the case is urgent. All of us on the plane were stretcher cases, and because there was not room enough for so many stretchers in the admissions office, we were parked outside in the July sun. We were not only hot but foul—unshaven, dirty, often caked with blood. No mark of rank distinguished the officers from the enlisted men—such a mark would have been a bonanza for snipers—and we were all wearing identical filthy undifferentiated uniforms. We all smelled alike, too, since not one of us had been out of that uniform for days. All I could think of was the clean, dry, white hospital bed that awaited me.

The moment came, and with it a Buster Keaton comedy routine: Two orderlies picked up my stretcher and trotted me to a distant ward. There, they rolled me into the dreamed-of bed, where a beautiful nurse named Molly started cutting off what was left of my uniform. (The surgeons in the battalion aid station had razored away only enough cloth to do their business.) Her touch felt wonderful. I closed my eyes. This was bliss. Suddenly, a male voice broke in. "Hold it, Molly—this guy doesn't belong here. He's an officer. Admissions thought he was a private because he didn't have any insignia." Molly dropped her scissors in horror, and the two orderlies were called back. They put me on the stretcher again, trotted me to a ward that was in every way identical to the first one, rolled me onto a bed exactly like the other, and left me in the charge of a beautiful nurse named Polly, who finished cutting off my uniform. The Army is no place for Rational Man.

I stayed in the hospital for a month. In the last week of that month, I was on my feet again, and the doctor told me that as soon as my biggest bandages were off, I could have a three-day pass to London. A million-dollar wound indeed. Two days later, still wearing a picturesque assortment of smaller bandages, I got my orders. I could forget about London; I was to report back to the First Infantry Division without delay, bandages and all. I howled in protest, but fortunately it did no good—fortunately, because otherwise I would have missed the liberation of Paris, a day of such happiness, release, celebration, and joy, reaching into every crevice of the city, that no day like it will ever occur again.

Within a week of leaving the hospital, I was in a transient holding camp near Melun, twenty-five miles south of Paris. Another First Division officer—Bobby Brown, a company commander in the 18th Infantry Regiment, returning from his *third* wound in action—was with me. We were part of a shipment of hospital returnees and infantrymen just off the boat from the States—replacements for the casualties suffered by rifle companies in the line. Bobby, a Regular Army veteran, was about ten years older than me. He had been promoted from sergeant to lieutenant in Africa, when almost all the officers in his company had been killed in a single action. He was a Georgia Cracker and the only man I ever met who really loved warfare; for him, it was like hunting, which was his favorite pastime in his Georgia backwoods, and in pursuit of his German prey he did some truly frightful things, all as a matter of course. Before the war was over (we kept in touch), he had been wounded eight times, the last time in an action that won him the Congressional Medal of Honor. It also left him so heavily concussed that he never fully recovered. But the Regular Army takes care of its own, and after the war he was assigned to West Point, where he was put in charge of the basketballs used by the West Point team.

It was while we were in Melun, awaiting a further move toward the front, that news came of the imminent fall of Paris. For me, this was what the war was all about, and the idea of vegetating in a replacement camp at such a moment was unthinkable. Consequently, I proposed to Bobby that we go absent without leave and join the merriment in Paris. Bobby was all for it. He had heard wonderful things about all those mademoiselles they had in Paris. So we arranged for another guy to answer our names at roll call, hitched a ride on a farm truck carrying produce to the city, and finally set foot in La Ville Lumière at the Porte de Charenton, in the southeast corner of the city.

From that moment on, the parade of events was nothing short of astounding. We had arrived early on a brilliant Sunday morning, the first free Sunday in Paris in four years, and Bobby and I were very likely the only Allied soldiers in town. The French armored division that had taken the city had moved on, and the rear guard of service units—the quartermasters, the paymasters, the military police—had not yet arrived. Every Parisian who could walk was out on the streets in the sun, in the suddenly free air—hugging, kissing, weeping, simply shouting—and here in their midst were two American soldiers to be hugged and kissed and wept over. The moment we jumped off the truck, we were almost drowned in adulation. No one could do enough for us: we were offered four thousand drinks and kissed four thousand times. My hand was numb from being shaken. It was a day without equal, for them and for us. The city was still in its German dress; every lamppost was hung with German Army directional signs—ZUM P.G. d.B. HAUPTQUARTIER and such—and every blank wall was pasted over with broadsheets issued by the German High Command, instructing the Parisian populace to do this or that. New orders were pasted on top of old orders; if one scraped deep enough, one could probably get back to May 1940. The big outdoor-advertising signboards that once sold Dubonnet and Suze and Michelin tires were now selling the virtues of hard work and civic duty. Nothing was new: nothing was being built or remodeled; no paint was fresh. Everything looked gray and used—hardly the stage setting for the circus of exhilaration that was going on. And this was only Charenton, a workaday part of the city.

Bobby and I made a date to meet at five o'clock at the gate of the deserted American embassy, on the Place de la Concorde—a spot that even a man who was already dipping into the ocean of free drinks could find—and we parted. I had a sort of courtesy aunt—my stepfather's sister Josephine, now in New York—who had spent most of her life in Paris, living in a charming little house near the Bois de Boulogne. She had fled back to the United States when the German threat became a reality, and I thought I might take a look at her place for a report home. The cognac and the girls could wait; they weren't going to disappear.

So I started out on foot, but hardly alone. Apparently, half of Charenton wanted to see Aunt Jo's house, too. It was slow going, but the sun shone down, the air was dry and crisp, and more and more people, all dressed in their best, were streaming through the streets: it was not only liberation; it was Sunday. There was even dancing to an accordionist in some of the squares. My rivals in the hero line were the Paris cops, some of whom had flowers stuck in their képis; they had started fighting the Germans even before the French armored division arrived, and around each of the many barricades they had thrown up (some even composed of the classic cobblestones), a crowd would be gathered to hear a cop participant or a local know-it-all tell how the great victory had been won. There were many detours and stops so that I could be shown where this dreadful thing had happened last winter, or this heroic thing had happened last week. At the Place de la Nation, I was taken to see the clandestine short-wave radio by which the local Resistance unit kept in touch with London. As a moment of revelation, of poignancy, it was a letdown. The heroic transmitter was in the dingy back room of a perfectly ordinary, anonymous third-floor apartment, now empty. The scene was totally banal: no secret panels or trapdoors under the rug, no effort to camouflage the transmitter as a bread box or a tennis press—just a plain, feeble-looking radio, sitting on a plain, wobbly table scarred with a hundred cigarette burns. It was hard to imagine a nervous operator tapping out his information to London—maybe even unwittingly tapping out his own death sentence—but, I was assured, this was the real stuff.

I could see that I was not going to get to Aunt Jo's house at this pace; I might not even make my date with Bobby Brown. The Place de la Nation is a long way from the Place de la Concorde, so I hitched a ride with a bunch of carousing youths driving around in one of those tinny, rattly little German Army jeeps. The youths—they were already spilling over the edges of the jeep, but they somehow made room for me—were drinking out of bottles and singing and waving an enormous French flag on a long pole, a flag so big on a pole so long that it almost capsized the jeep every time they swung it. The youths were all wearing white armbands with FFI printed on them—Forces Françaises de l'Intérieur. The FFI were the benchwarmers and spear-carriers of the Resistance, and we had noticed all across France that their ranks grew prodigiously as soon as the Germans were out of sight. It is possible that the FFI did some good, but not much. Compared to the disciplined, patient, deadly Resistance, they were a Central Park pickup team. But the youths finally got me to the Place de la Concorde, and here, for the first time, you could see that Paris had been seriously fought over. A burned-out German tank stood in a corner of the Place, in front of the Hôtel Crillon, which had been the residence of the very highest of the German High Command in Paris. At each side of the hotel entrance, barbed wire had been strung far out into the Place to force pedestrians into a long detour around the hotel's front door and prevent them from tossing a bomb into the lobby. The Germans in the neighboring Ministère de la Marine must have put up considerable resistance, because one of the enormous columns on the facade of the building had been shot out, and the whole place was pockmarked and splintered.

The Place de la Concorde was the closest I got to Aunt Jo's. By the time we reached it, the afternoon was fading, and I had to keep my date with Bobby Brown. Somehow, I escaped my retinue and made it to the gate of the American embassy. Bobby was already there, or partly there; enormous quantities of girls and booze had rendered him almost inoperative. He'd had enough, he said. Another day like today would kill him. He was going to go back to Melun and rest. I could stay on in Paris if I wanted to—he would look after my interests in the replacement camp—but he'd had enough.

So he went, and I stayed. In fact, I stayed for three days, which could have got me shot for desertion if I had been caught; in wartime, being absent without leave is automatically upgraded to desertion after a lapse of three days. For the moment, there were no MPs in town. But there would be soon, so I obviously needed to go underground.

Just around the corner from the American embassy, on the

Rue Boissy d'Anglas, there was (and is) a standard little sidewalk café-bar, the Café de l'Ambassade. I stepped in there for a beer and some thought about my next move. The bartender-manager of the place, a roly-poly, round-faced, black-haired man with an enormous smile and something of the clown about him, was standing behind the bar with his arm in a sling; in front of him on the bar was a shot glass with a spent bullet in it, and he was telling an enthralled audience just how the bullet had produced the sling. He had been on a barricade in the Rue Florentin, he said, when this German suddenly appeared with a rifle (elaborate miming of the German taking aim), and—*paf!* There was this terrible pain in his arm, but he ignored it and brought his *flingue* (pistol) to bear on the German (elaborate miming of a cowboy drawing a bead on a rustler), and—*paf! paf!*—the *salaud* was eliminated. And here—here in this glass for all to see (it was passed around)—was the bullet the doctors had retrieved from his arm after an operation of the most exquisite difficulty.

It was a wonderful performance, and I warmed to the performer instantly. His name was André Boutonnet. When it came my turn to examine the bullet—my appraisal as a professional was eagerly awaited—I said that it was a .30-30 slug from a Mauser rifle, one of the most dangerous weapons in the German arsenal (complete horse water on my part), and Boutonnet beamed on me like a father whose son has won the elocution prize. Here, I thought, was a man who could help me disappear, and I put the matter to him. Leave it to him, he said. Furthermore, I said, I needed a doctor to change my bandages. Very simple, he said—the doctor who had removed his bullet was only a block away. Nothing could be easier.

And nothing was. He took me up the street, across the Rue du Faubourg St. Honoré, to a decrepit, anonymous three-story building that must have been put up in Richelieu's time. It was a hotel (though nothing so identified it) used by the farmers who came in from the countryside to sell their produce at a little back-street market just behind. (Today, the market square is a nest of expensive wine shops and boutiques, and the hotel has acquired a sign and a name—the Hôtel d'Aguesseau.)

The d'Aguesseau was a perfect hideaway. The proprietress, who looked like a beer-truck driver in drag, refused to take any money from a liberator of Paris and set me up in a top-floor room with a feather bed. There I stayed for three nights. The proprietress would give me coffee in the morning, I would trot around to the doctor to have my bandages changed, and then I would spend all day, in continuing brilliant weather, covering every inch of the Paris I knew, inhaling the smells, recognizing the sounds, talking to and being talked to by dozens, scores, of citizens, every one of them as eager to know about me and my world—was the war really almost over?—as I was to know about them and their world during the Occupation. But none of them was as good a chronicler as Boutonnet. He was a born raconteur, a great tricolor ham actor from the Auvergne, like most of the *cafetiers* of Paris. He was married to a hometown girl, Augusta, formerly a chambermaid at the Grand Hôtel, on the Rue de Rivoli, and they had a daughter, Simone, about seven years old, who spent all day in school. Boutonnet was the manager and bartender of the café, and Augusta ran the cash register. (I don't know who owned the place.) In 1939, he had been called up by the French Army, as a mess sergeant, and in 1940 had been taken off the beach at Dunkirk by the British; his commanding officer, Capt. Julien Saussol, had stayed behind with a number of wounded men in his company and had been captured. (I later met Julien Saussol. He was by that time the equivalent of a deputy chief inspector at police headquarters on the Quai des Orfèvres. He said that Boutonnet had saved his life when he got out of prison camp. He had been so frail that he could hardly walk, and was morbidly depressed as well. His old mess sergeant had fed him up and cheered him up and pulled him back into the world.)

Though Boutonnet owed his life, or at least his freedom, to the British, he had nothing but scorn for them, for the things they ate (the only two words of English he knew were "bins," for "beans," and "cawley-floe-ver,") and for their little idiosyncrasies (vigorous imitations of the nasal noises in British speech and of the way the British walk). I forget how or when Boutonnet was repatriated, but when he got back to Paris, the war was over for the French, and he took on his job at the Café de l'Ambassade. In no time, he became the head sachem of the *quartier,* a sort of Tammany Hall district boss and unordained pastor of the local flock. His second in command was the coiffeur whose salon was next door, a tough, enterprising fellow who looked like a proper mate for the proprietress of the d'Aguesseau. Despite the fact that the café was directly across the street from German headquarters in the Crillon, it became a safe-house, mail drop, and message center for the local citizens in their plans to defeat German rationing or steal German gas. It was exactly the right milieu for me, another defier of military authority.

I might well have stayed in my secret hotel for a month without being discovered, but something told me that I was storing up big trouble for myself with every passing day: Bobby Brown could not be expected to answer my name at roll call forever. So I reluctantly hitched a ride back to Melun—in the nick of time, it turned out, because the next day the First Infantry Division sent a jeep all the way back from Belgium to pick up Bobby and me—pure First Division elitism. The Regular Army always takes care of its own.

By the time I rejoined the First Division, it was stuck on the bluffs overlooking the city of Aachen, just across the German-Belgian border. Not only the First Division but the whole Allied offensive had stalled, because it had outrun its supplies—no fuel, no ammunition, and, for a while, no food. We were reduced to eating emergency D rations—rock-hard chocolate bars full of artificial nutrients. Three chocolate bars a day can make you very tired of chocolate bars. The Germans still occupied the city below us, and all we could do was watch as they brought in reinforcements. To fill their time, the First Division's engineers devised an Army-type entertainment. Up on our level, above the city, was the home barn of Aachen's trolley cars, with tracks leading down the hill to the center of town. What could be more entertaining than to wheel one of the trolley cars out to the edge of the hill, fill it to the roof with high explosives and a timing device, and give it a push? Despite the ammunition shortage, there was enough stuff lying around—redundant land mines, leftover artillery guncotton, beehive antitank charges, concussion grenades—to produce an edifying bang. The trolley was stuffed with this diet until not another rifle cartridge could be squeezed in. An artillery wizard was brought in to compute the time it would take the trolley to reach the center of town, and then affix the timing device.

All this took time. Three-quarters of the way down the hill was a dug-in German outpost, visible through binoculars but untouchable during our current deprivations. Its crew observed our preparations, and you could almost hear their minds clicking as they worked on the problem. In the middle of the second night, they made their countermove: they laid a log across the tracks. This was a master stroke, requiring strategy meetings up on the hill. It was finally decided to go ahead anyway—maybe the trolley's bumper would push the log out of the way.

At last, the big moment came. Scores of spectators gathered around as the blocks holding the trolley in position were removed, the timing device was set ticking, and a forward push was administered. Would the trolley make it past the log? The Germans in their outpost were no doubt wondering the same thing when it suddenly dawned on them that if it *didn't* make it the damn thing would explode right in their laps. At the last minute, they darted out of their bunker, pulled the log aside, and darted back. Cheers rose from the hilltop spectators as the trolley, gathering speed, rolled past the outpost and on down the hill. It passed through a built-up area and providentially negotiated a switch that might have sent it down the wrong track. Up on the hill, the spectators were jumping up and down like horseplayers rooting home the favorite. Then a groan went up: the tracks beyond the switch made a curve, and the trolley, now going too fast, rocketed off the rails into an open field. A couple of instants later, there was an explosion that anywhere else would have won the war. We went back to our chocolate bars.

The stalemate continued. I spent a lot of the empty time with a new arrival at Division Headquarters, a Belgian civilian named Freddie de Berck. He was the managing director of a big family-owned shoe factory several miles to our rear, and he had attached himself to the First Division as it rolled through his town. This was not unusual; the division often picked up civilian advisers along the way, generally local personages who could provide the latest information on German doings in the area and afford insights into local politics—who was good and who was bad. Freddie was one of these. He was no local personage however. He was an international personage of the finest flower. About forty years old, he had a broad education and a flawless command of English. He was at home all over the world. His binoculars were from Huet, in Paris; his working uniform consisted of jodhpurs from Savile Row and riding boots from Peel; and he considered Voisin a better restaurant than the Colony in New York. He was a little sleek for my taste, but in our undeniably grubby midst he was a vivid, exotic anomaly. He showed up every morning clean and well pressed, having spent the night back home attending to factory business. In the days before the war, the factory had very profitably manufactured luxury shoes that it sold all over the world, from Nome to Montevideo, but nowadays, I gathered, its operations were on a more humdrum level. His wife used to do the paperwork, Freddie said, but she had been away for more than a month now, and he was stuck with it.

One afternoon, he asked Ben Honecker, another Headquarters lieutenant, and me if we would like to come to his house for dinner and the night. Indeed we would, and we did so. Freddie met us at his front door, and we allowed a butler to take away our helmets and pistol belts. Then to the library for drinks, which were served by a footman from a rolling trolley. I took champagne; Honecker, more down-to-earth, had bourbon. Freddie apologized for his wife's absence—"We'll just have to be bachelors together"—and soon led us to the dining room, where three places had been set at the end of a long dining table—linen napkins, candelabras, paper-thin wineglasses. In the candlelight, the place settings shone like gold, and I surreptitiously lifted the edge of my service plate to see why. It weighed a ton—it not only shone like gold; it was gold. Dinner was served by the butler and a uniformed maid; its main ingredients were steak and an accompanying Pomerol. I hadn't seen a steak in I don't know how long; and neither had Honecker or anybody else I knew. Yet here was a perfect one, beautifully cooked. After dinner, we returned to the library for coffee and cognac or Calvados, and were offered cigars from an enormous humidor—Ben took one—as we lay back in deep, comfortable chairs listening to some wonderful Yvonne Printemps records on the phonograph. Then to bed, on linen sheets.

On the way back to Division Headquarters at dawn the next day, Ben Honecker asked me if I didn't think there was something funny about the way Freddie was living in times like these. I told him to forget it—if Freddie asked him back for another night, would he say no? I knew, of course, that Ben was right. There was something extremely funny about the de Berck setup, but I was so corrupted by the civilized ease and *comfort* of it all that I had no room for bad thoughts.

Freddie never did ask us back, but he worked his way through most of the other junior officers at Headquarters (he no doubt knew he couldn't swing the general or the colonels), and those who didn't make the list were pretty sniffy about it. One of the sniffers was Charley Gershon, a captain who was in charge of security at Headquarters. He thought Freddie was, at best, a fraud and a con artist (he hadn't seen the gold plates) or, at worst, a dangerous fellow.

Around this time, I was sent down to one of the battalions for a couple of days on some chore for Colonel Carson, and when I got back Freddie was gone. "A Belgian colonel and a woman were here yesterday and took Freddie away with them," Ben told me. "They had a long palaver with Colonel Carson and then beat it. That's all I know." Charley Gershon was more informative; he had talked to the woman in his official capacity. "I *knew* that guy was bad news," he said. "That famous shoe factory of his! It was making boots for the German Army, and using slave laborers to do it. Dozens of them. A lot of them died. He was a real slave driver. He was so mean and brutal that his wife—that was his wife who was here—left him. And it was a year and a half ago that she left, not just last month. The Germans were still here. She couldn't go far, and de Berck was after her, so she took refuge with the Communist underground. She's a red-hot Communist today. When liberation came, she went to Belgian Army headquarters and turned de Berck in. I hope they shoot the bastard."

I clucked in sympathetic agreement, but it was a feeble cluck. I was wondering what I would do if Freddie should suddenly reappear and invite me back. Would I have the moral character to say no? I would like to think I would, but I wonder. That steak and Pomerol! Those linen sheets! Yvonne Printemps!

With the division's front feet firmly planted in Germany, my role in the Intelligence section had become precarious, since French-speaking was no longer much in demand. I was sorely afraid I was going to be sent back to F Company, but somehow I was overlooked. Eventually, I became a sort of odd-jobs man and courier: Colonel Carson would send me all over the place when there was something he wanted to know, and especially when the field-telephone wires were down. I also had to help Phil Dunlay with the daily Intelligence report, and keep tabs on the prisoner-of-war cage to see if anybody interesting was going through.

All too soon, there was plenty for me to do. Supplies began flowing in again, and the big operation to capture Aachen started rolling. Street fighting is a bloody, nasty business. You never know who is in the next street or the next block—your guys or the other guys. Or who is behind that window curtain—a terrified grandmother or a machine gunner. Or both. And all those upstairs windows make perfect shelters for snipers.

After a lot of this sort of fighting, Aachen was finally taken. One of the casualties of the assault was my friend David Lardner. A son of Ring Lardner, he was about my age and had worked on *The New Yorker* as its nightclub critic. I have known four Lardners—Dave, Susan, Rex, and James—and they have all shared one characteristic: a predisposition to silence. They listen and nod and smile and refill your glass, but they hardly *say* a word. Dave Lardner would come to my office around quitting time and murmur, "How about a drink at the Cortile?" and if I got more than twenty more words out of him during the drink, it was a big evening. Nevertheless, we were good friends. He had bad eyes and was exempt from the draft, but he could not bear to be out of the war. His brother John was writing very good stuff from the Pacific for *Newsweek,* and that may have been the reason. In the end, Dave got his wish: he somehow wangled a job as a war correspondent for *The New Yorker*, and he showed up, fresh off the boat, at First Division Headquarters during the fighting for Aachen. He was with a jeepload of other correspondents intent on covering the fall of the first big German city to be taken by the Allies.

I had a warm, semispeechless reunion with Dave, but then Colonel Carson, ever on my back, sent me into the city to find out if a certain big block of buildings had been taken over by the Wehrmacht or was still full of civilians. (The trip was a memorable one for me: it was the first and only time I unmistakably shot someone. I was sneaking down a street toward my objective when I saw a German soldier leaning out a second-floor window and firing at a target I couldn't see. I hit his outstretched arm with a shot from my .45 automatic, and the weight of the slug spun him around like a puppet on a string before he fell back into the room. I did not wait to investigate further.) Having ascertained that the Wehrmacht had not yet occupied the building block, I was on the road back to Headquarters, taking the long way around that had been marked by engineers' tape as being free of mines. Halfway along, I saw a puff of smoke off to the right—the kind of smoke made by an exploding mine. The first thing I heard when I got back was that the mine had been under Dave Lardner's jeep. His driver had foolishly ignored the engineers' tapes and had tried to take a shortcut. Dave was the only one killed. He was buried in the American cemetery at Henri-la-Chapelle, in Belgium. I went there to see if his grave was properly marked (it was), and I believe he is still there.

If the fighting in Aachen was bloody, the fighting in the Hürtgen Forest, where we moved in November, after the city fell, was even bloodier—in fact, it was the worst fighting of the whole war, though largely unreported. Mud a foot deep, freezing rain, incessant artillery fire, tree bursts—an incoming shell would hit the treetops and explode *downward*, so that an ordinary foxhole provided no cover. The casualties were endless. It sometimes happened that the truck bringing fresh replacements to the rifle companies would return to the rear with several of their bodies. To be an infantry replacement was hard enough at any time, but in the Hürtgen Forest it was totally demoralizing. The new man was hustled to the front line directly from the ship that had brought him to France, and shoved into a rifle platoon before he could catch his breath or write his mother. He didn't know where he was, or who all these people were who were yelling at him to do this or that. Everything was new to him—the machine guns, the artillery, the muddy foxhole he had inherited from a dead man. He knew nobody, and nobody knew him—not even his name. His fellow-riflemen didn't trust him, because of his greenness, and resented his being alive when their good friend, the man he was replacing, was dead. Yet he was supposed to fit in like an old-timer, and his life depended on his not making a mistake. It's a wonder more replacements didn't go back in the trucks that had brought them up.

Conditions like these wore the First Division down, no matter how many replacements were trucked in. The rifle companies were at half strength. The artillery had fired all the rifling out of its gun barrels and couldn't hit any target smaller than a rural county. The supply trucks had been so badly mauled that not many were left, and these barely functional. And the mud got deeper.

Finally, in December, what was left of the division was pulled out of the line and sent to the little Belgian town of Eupen for rest and repairs. Max Zera and I, as part of our personal rest and repairs, put in a request for a three-day pass to Paris, and it was granted, to start December 17. Max, a captain, was my best friend at Headquarters. He was from the Bronx, built like a tree stump, fluent in Yiddish, and a man of volatile temperament and instant emotions, which he expressed in a voice that was part trombone and part chain saw.

On December 16, the day before we were to leave for Paris, the Germans opened their big counteroffensive—the Battle of the Bulge. That night, the Sixth Panzer Army came pouring through the American lines south of Eupen. The main body of the German armor headed west, while a subsidiary force turned north, toward the vast U.S. Army supply depots around Liège. The First Division—unrested and unrepaired—was ordered to head south and stop the Germans from coming up the main road leading to Liège.

Only a patchwork force could be scratched together from the bankrupt division, and Sgt. Eddie Rojas and Max and I were among those tapped. Late that night, we started south in a jeep, along with a stray major from one of the infantry battalions. The weather was frightful—bitterly cold and snowing, with a high wind howling through the dark. I was wearing every stitch of clothing I could lay my hands on—including a much admired rabbit-fur vest I had bought from a Belgian farmer's wife—and I was still frozen stiff. Nothing is colder than an open jeep in winter. We were the last vehicle to leave the rest-and-repair area at Eupen. Just ahead of us on the road were perhaps a dozen trucks of riflemen, plus the remnants of a field-artillery battalion. And somewhere ahead of them—though nobody knew where—was the German armored column, coming up the road right at us. To make matters worse, the panzer troops were using a number of captured Sherman tanks still bearing their American markings. You could be shot dead by your own tanks. And there was more. To create even greater chaos, hundreds of German parachutists—*English-speaking parachutists, wearing American uniforms*—were being dropped in the area of the German attack. Although the snow made it impossible to see anything in the sky, I was delegated to ride backward, with my legs dangling over the jeep's tailgate, to fend off any parachutists with an M1 rifle. Fat chance, but nobody could think of anything better.

The night was as black as pitch. We could not use headlights, of course, so Eddie Rojas blindly followed the dim and shielded tail light of the truck in front of us. We rode in silence, sealed in by the snow, deafened by the vicious wind. Every now and then, the blackness would be rent by a great flash in the east as the Germans fired another V-1 at London; the deadly little robot machines putt-putted over our heads so low that I instinctively ducked as they went by. Above the V-1's I could hear real planes in the air—planes carrying disguised parachutists, as we all knew but refrained from saying. In fact, nobody had much to say about anything, never mentioning the really big question: just how far up this lonesome road had the Germans penetrated? Sooner or later, the question was bound to be resolved in confrontation, and nobody in our jeep was very optimistic about the outcome.

A nervous hour went by as we crawled along. We passed four or five abandoned gun emplacements—*American* gun emplacements—with brand-new 90-mm antitank guns dug in alongside the road, and nobody to shoot them. Then, ahead of us, we dimly made out two figures at the side of the road; one of them was waving at us to stop. The waver turned out to be a woman so bundled up that she was almost spherical. She was supporting an American soldier whose right foot was encased in a bulkily wrapped bandage—and at that moment I realized we had fallen into a trap; a German parachutist's boot was undoubtedly beneath that bandage. As for the woman . . .

The stray major with us put his pistol in the man's stomach. "What's up, Bud?" he said. But Bud, whatever his nationality, was beyond speech. He looked wildly at the major, at all of us, and choked, unable to say a word; if he was a parachutist, he was also a great actor. The woman, however, had a lot to say. She had found him lying in the snow outside the front door of her farmhouse, where he had come for help. He couldn't walk, and she thought he had broken his foot. She had taken him in and bandaged his foot, but what he needed now was a real doctor. Eddie Rojas, who had been examining the guy's dog-tags and gone through his pockets, announced that he was legitimate. "Probably broke his foot running away from those antitank guns back there," he said. "Panicked."

We had already wasted too much time on the soldier. We told the woman that somebody better equipped to take care of him would be coming along—not adding that it might well be a German tank column—and drove on.

Now we no longer had the Cheshire-cat taillight of the truck ahead to guide us; we were alone on the silent road. Eddie Rojas was bent over the steering wheel, with his eyes almost out on sticks as he tried to find his way through the snow, and for another four or five miles, we crawled along in a frozen silence.

All at once, we heard an ominous clanking sound, coming from somewhere up ahead. Eddie stopped and cut the motor. Now the clanking was louder, and it was headed our way—the tank we had been so long expecting, the lead tank of the German panzer force. Time to retreat. Eddie started the jeep and made a first pass at turning around, but it was no go; the snow was too deep and we were in a cut in the road, between two low embankments. "Everybody out!" the major whispered. We jumped down and spread out. Rather than climb the embankment, which would have taken time, I threw myself into the ditch alongside the road and put my face in the snow, never stopping to think that I would show up dark against the white.

The clanking grew louder and louder, and so did the hum of a powerful engine. I slowly turned my head to take a peek, and I saw a monumental tank, with a gun the size of a telephone pole, weaving up the road toward me. About fifty feet away, it stopped. Dead silence, except for the hum of the engine. A long wait. Still flat in the snow, I watched that big gun swivel around until it was aimed directly at me—right down my throat. I stopped breathing. I could not even think. Another wait. A slit opened above the driver's seat and a voice called out, "Hey, you!" Not "*Achtung!*" or "*Sieg Heil!*" or whatever—"Hey, you!" But what about those English-speaking parachutists? Those false Sherman tanks? Could one of them . . . ? "Hey, you, I see you! Stand up!"

I stood up. I don't know whether I was more relieved to hear English or terrified to be so visible and so vulnerable. The tank's turret opened, and a head poked out, telling me to keep my hands up and approach slowly. I did so. The tank man climbed out of his turret and jumped down into the road. He took a look at me and then leaned forward for a closer look. Suddenly, he threw his arms around me and almost squeezed my breath away. It was Nelson Works, who had sat right behind me in Sociology 102 all sophomore year at Yale.

Nelson, a tank-destroyer officer, had got separated from his people during the chaos of the German breakthrough and had been running around loose behind the German lines ever since. To escape detection, he had been using back roads, and had thus missed our infantry column on the road ahead.

As it happened, the Germans never did come up that road; they had probably heard about those 90-mm antitank guns. So they decided to try a road to the west, where the 30th Infantry Division was dug in, and they failed.

Four or five days later, I was sent over to the headquarters of the 30th Division on some sort of liaison mission—our G-2 picking the brains of their G-2. It was an absolutely brilliant day. The snow had finally stopped, and now the sun was out in full array. The countryside glistened, and the trees of the forest looked like Christmas cards. Nobody had yet traveled the road that Eddie Rojas and I had to take, but we moved down it easily enough through the trees. At a point about halfway along, we emerged from the forest into an open field, and here the snow was deeper. Nevertheless, we managed quite well until we hit an unexpected snowbank that was just a bit too deep for us. Here we stalled, wedged on top of the snow, with our wheels spinning uselessly in the air. Eddie and I had got out and were surveying our problem when we heard a sudden rumble from the east, and a low-flying German fighter plane—a Messerschmitt, I think, although I never could tell the German planes apart—streaked overhead. It was going so fast that I barely glimpsed its Luftwaffe markings, and I don't think the pilot even noticed us down below. But where there was one Messerschmitt there could be more, with more observant pilots, and Eddie and I redoubled our efforts to rock the jeep off its pedestal of snow. As we were heaving and pulling, another jeep, following our tracks, emerged from the forest and stopped a few yards behind us. A figure in an American helmet got out and clomped over to us through the snow. "Need a hand, buster?" said a voice I knew well. It was my brother Peter. I could not have been more surprised if it had been Mahatma Gandhi. I knew that Peter, a lieutenant in the artillery, was in Europe, but, what with poor mail and the censorship, I hadn't yet heard anything more precise than that. I was mighty glad to see him, but explanations would have to wait. Peter, too, had heard the Messerschmitt, and he knew we had to move fast. Fortunately, his jeep was equipped with a winch, so we cabled the vehicles together and pulled my jeep off its pillar of snow. Eddie backed off from the snowbank and then charged at it full tilt. This time, he made it. Once he was on firm ground, Peter and I climbed into the backseat and rode together to the 30th Division HQ trailed by Peter's driver and jeep. Now I got my explanations. Peter, it turned out, was with the 106th Division, the unhappy unit that found itself directly in the path of the main assault of the Sixth Panzer Army when it broke through our lines. By pure chance, his artillery battalion had been bypassed by the German thrust, and it was now regrouping in an assembly area not far from the First Division's lines. Peter, who knew I was with the First Division, had given himself the day off to look me up. At division headquarters, my colleagues had told him where he might find me, and now here he was. When he told me what his role was with his battalion, I wondered at his being here at all. He had just about the worst job in the Army: artillery forward observer. Forward observers are the eyes of the gun battalions, which, of course, can't see what they're shooting at, a mile or more away. The forward observer sets up for business in an advanced position with a big view—a church steeple, a rooftop, the crest of a hill—and if there is one person in the world the enemy, with good reason, wants to put out of action, it is the forward observer. (Peter was twice wounded before he was through.)

And so we talked and talked all the way to the 30th Division—family news (I hadn't seen Peter or anybody else in my family for almost two years), news of friends, gossip, shoptalk about our entirely different daily lives. But too soon it all had to end: he had to go back to his battalion, and I had to carry my maps and messages back to G-2. I didn't see Peter again until New York.

A month later, toward the end of January, Max and I got our deferred three-day pass to Paris. He and I and two sergeants also on leave drove a jeep from wherever we were in Germany down to Paris—three hundred miles on a blowy, gray, frozen day that made it clear, once again, that nothing is colder than an open jeep in winter. The drive was even worse than the one down the Eupen road, because it was longer, and it introduced me to new levels of low-temperature misery. Driving through Liège, where life was supposed to be calm and civilized, we had a serious scare. We were going down a residential street lined with tall and gloomy apartment houses when there was a titanic explosion behind one of the houses. The concussion lifted our jeep right off the street and loosed a cascade of flying bricks and rubble upon us. A piece of masonry the size of a shoe box came hurtling down and glanced off my helmet; my ears rang for days. The whole thing was inexplicable. We had heard no anticipatory whine of an incoming shell, and there were no planes in the sky above. We thought we were well beyond the range of ordinary German artillery, but if the Germans had a gun that could throw a shell as big as this one as far as this one, we were in big trouble. It was only on our way back from Paris that we learned what had caused the big bang: one of the very earliest of Wernher von Braun's V-2 rockets, which came out of the stratosphere so fast that it outpaced its own sound. In any case, I now had an interesting historical dent in my helmet.

When we finally got to Paris, the four of us were literally almost frozen into shape. We had pulled up in front of the main Red Cross office, on the Boulevard des Capucines, to be assigned hotel rooms, and we could barely get out of the jeep. I was struggling to straighten up, and Max was on the sidewalk circling around in a stoop, as though trying to find a lost penny. A splendidly dressed lieutenant who was walking by stopped and tapped Max on his back as he circled. "You can't leave that jeep here, soldier," he said. "And stand up straight when I'm talking to you." (As usual, none of us were wearing any badges of rank or grade.) When the lieutenant tapped him again, for more attention, Max hit him a tremendous wallop, and the sight of the lieutenant sprawled on the sidewalk so magically restored our circulation that we were able to jump back in the jeep and get out of there before the MPs could arrive.

Near the Gare St. Lazare, we found another Red Cross office, and there we were assigned rooms—each of us in a different hotel, for some reason. I drew the Hôtel St. Anne, in the Rue St. Anne, just behind the Avenue de l'Opéra. We left the jeep in a U.S. Army car park and agreed to meet at 6:00 A.M. three days later for the trip back to Germany.

Paris was no warmer than the jeep. The city had no heat at all, and very little electricity. No matter where you went, the indoor temperature was the same as the outdoor temperature; the only difference was the absence of wind. Moreover, it was quickly apparent that the whole city had gone straight downhill after the heady days of my last visit. The exuberance and undiluted joy (and glorious warmth) of August were gone, and now there wasn't enough to eat. The people looked gray and tired, and why not?—they were half-frozen as well as half-starved. Furthermore, I was no longer a unique and honored hero; I was just another goddam American, indistinguishable from the officious lieutenant Max had slugged.

But at the Café de l'Ambassade, everything was the same. Boutonnet, with his street smarts, had a sufficiency of food (I refrained from asking how), and I, with my Army smarts, had thought to bring along some canned rations begged from our mess sergeant, in particular a canned pound of bacon that almost reduced Boutonnet to tears of happiness. We feasted, and we certainly drank—Boutonnet and I and the coiffeur from next door and various other friends, including, at last, Julien Saussol, still thin as a string but lively—huddled together in candlelight at one of the café tables behind drawn blinds. During the day, I walked about the city, checking up on this and that, and finally got to Aunt Jo's house on the Villa Saîd. It was empty and looked dingy and dispirited, in serious need of attention; a neighbor told me that it had been occupied the whole time by two very quiet, very correct German Army doctors.

All in all, there wasn't much gaiety in Paris. I did go to a party near Les Invalides (I had looked up the sister of a French Army officer I met in Normandy), and got warm for a while, but it was a long, cold walk home. Then, on the night before the four of us had to go back to Germany, it snowed. (It never is supposed to snow in Paris.) Walking back to the Hôtel St. Anne from Boutonnet's around midnight, full of booze and bacon, I was awash in self-pity. Frozen to the bone, slush underfoot, icy bed in prospect, up at five to get to my rendezvous with the others, an endless, frigid jeep ride back to the place I least wanted to be. Good-bye Paris, hello German artillery. Then, on the deserted Avenue de l'Opéra, I ran across someone who was no better off than I was—a whore, slowly turning into an icicle in her mangy rabbit-fur jacket and her little whore's dress. With the snow falling, and not another human being in sight, I was her last chance. To me, she looked like my electric blanket, my bed warmer. Fifty francs, payable in advance. The concierge at the St. Anne never even looked up when we entered.

Up in the room, where at least it wasn't snowing, we were in bed in an instant, still with most of our clothes on, clutched together like Siamese twins, trying to generate body heat. A stocky young country girl, she was deliciously warm, and under the spell of that warmth she got loquacious, and so did I. She was nineteen, from somewhere in the middle of France, she told me, and had come to Paris because life was so boring in her village. Her old man was a religious fanatic who wanted her to become a nun, and her mother was hopeless. She couldn't find any work in Paris, but she hadn't tried very hard, because a friend of hers had told her of the easy money to be made on the street, with all the American soldiers in town, and her friend was right. She'd been on the street for six months now, but lately, with the cold, she had just about decided to go back home, father or no father. And what about me? she asked. I must want to go home, too, no? Oh, yes, I said, still feeling boozily sorry for myself, and then the cinematic sentimentality of the whole situation—the young lieutenant, so cold, so far from home, in bed with a tenderhearted whore in Paris during the last hours of his leave—overcame me, and I couldn't stop talking. I talked about my life at home, and the daughter I'd hardly seen, and about meeting my brother in the Ardennes, and about my other brother in the Pacific, and about a dozen other things of no possible interest to her. Quite sensibly, she went to sleep, and I guess I did, too, but not for long, because at five o'clock the night porter banged on the door, and I had to pack up for the trip back to Germany. The girl watched me from bed, and then asked me to get her handbag from the dresser. As I was going out the door, she called me over and gave me back my fifty francs. I played my role, too: I wouldn't take them. Movies have been made of less.

On and on we went. The First Division reached the Rhine just downstream from Bonn (Beethovenland). The city fell without much of a struggle, and Colonel Carson sent me and Ben Honecker into town to see if we could identify the German units that had been defending it. When we got there, there was nobody around we could ask. The place seemed to be completely deserted. Ben and I banged on doors, but nobody answered. Even the civilians seemed to have all run away. We found one door that was unlocked, and went in. It was a nice, comfortably furnished middle-class apartment—nice but empty. An open book was lying facedown in one of the upholstered chairs, and on a small chairside table there was a half-empty stein of beer. A hissing sound we heard from the kitchen turned out to be a propane stove, under a big pot of some kind of soup; the owners had left in such a hurry that they had had no time for their lunch. So Ben and I ate it for them, and it was delicious vegetable soup with a lot of noodles.

The division was on the Rhine, but not across it. Nobody on our side was across it. The river, running from Switzerland to the sea, was the one last barrier that could hold off the Allied advance from the west. At Eisenhower's headquarters, great plans were being laid for a massive parachute drop, coupled with a concerted offensive that might succeed in putting a pontoon bridge across the water, but the cost promised to be murderous. Then came news of the capture of the bridge at Remagen, several miles upstream from Bonn. It was the only bridge in the thousand miles of the river that had not been blown by the retreating Germans, and it was captured intact by an American rifle-company patrol (I forget which division) that overran the German engineers even as they were trying to detonate the charges that would knock the bridge down. It was an achievement that shortened the war by many months and saved a great many lives.

The Germans knew that they had to destroy that bridge before the trouble they were in got worse. They sent what was left of their bomber fleet to bomb it, they floated frogmen downstream with TNT to blow it up, and they brought every artillery piece within range to bear upon it, including some truly gargantuan railway guns wheeled up from the interior. I was taking a nap in an abandoned farmhouse when a shell from one of these monsters fell about a quarter of a mile away. The bang wasn't as big as the bang at Liège, but it was pretty good. A shell fragment the size of a two-battery flashlight flew through the open window above my head and halfway through the brick wall across the room. I burned my fingers when I tried to dig it out; if I had sat up at the wrong time, it would have taken my head off.

Despite their every effort, nothing worked for the Germans. Their target remained upright until a bridgehead had been established on the east side of the river. Then, its structure weakened by the battering, the bridge fell of its own accord. But by that time a pontoon bridge had been thrown across the river, so it didn't matter.

The First Division crossed the Rhine at Remagen, adding its weight to the bridgehead on the far side. On our first night there, I took up residence in an elegant villa with a splendid river view, which had obviously belonged to somebody with a lot of money.

I prudently moved into the cellar for the night, but upstairs I had seen, among other marks of affluence, a handsome library of many shelves, with a ladder to reach the top ones. The next afternoon, things were quiet enough for me to go upstairs and see what a proper modern German was reading these days. What this particular proper modern German was reading, it turned out, was pornography, and a lot of it—pornography by the yard, by the acre. Every book in the room was pornographic, some ancient and venerable, in crumbling bindings, others beautifully bound and illustrated. Most were in German, some in English, others in French and Italian, and for all I know, in Rumanian. Plus a big section of Oriental naughtiness. Anthony Comstock would have had the best day of his life romping through the collection.

After the First Division moved out of the Remagen bridgehead, its objective was to help seal off the Ruhr Valley, Germany's great industrial wellspring. Now that the Rhine had been crossed, the going was swift, and the debris of war—human debris as well as military—had not yet been tidied away. Hundreds of slave laborers and prisoners of war had suddenly and unexpectedly found themselves free, with no place to go. Often they would band together by nationality and set up housekeeping cooperatively. Eddie Rojas and I came across one such commune—a French one—living on the third floor of an enormous china and glass factory. They were doing very well for themselves. They got their provisions by bullying nearby farmers, who would now do anything to make friends and stay out of trouble, and they even requisitioned wine from the cellars of local big-time landowners. They invited Eddie and me to lunch, and it was excellent. We were twelve or fifteen at table—a long one, set up between the high stacks of finished chinaware—and the method of serving was prodigal. Everything on the menu—carrots, potatoes, rabbit—had its individual plate, plucked from the surrounding stacks of dinnerware, and each toast—there were many—was drunk from a clean glass. By the time we finished singing the Marseillaise, the table was piled high with dirty dishes and glasses, but the cleanup was as expeditious as it was labor-saving: four or five men picked up the laden table, carried it over to an open window, and tipped the whole mess into the courtyard below. The diners had been doing this twice a day (no breakfast) for about two weeks, and they still had two floors of chinaware to go.

Speeding along in the wake of our troops, Eddie and I went through villages, towns, and hamlets so rapidly that I remember none of them. Some were ruined by gunfire; others were miraculously unscathed. One day, we had just passed an abandoned warehouse that was now the living quarters of a Polish commune (we knew it was Polish because the residents had hung a bedsheet painted with the word "Polski" out a window), when we came to a village that I do remember, vividly. It was a nice place, untouched by the war, with perhaps a dozen big houses facing the main street behind tall trees and well-tended gardens. Eddie and I stopped at the village fountain (still running) to get water, and while we were there, a woman came running up to us from one of the houses—a well-dressed, handsome woman in, I would say, her late forties. "I'm so glad you've come," she said in excellent English. "We were hoping you could do something about this horrible smell. Our men would take care of it if they were here, but they are all gone now, so maybe you could. . . ."

I had not noticed any smell, possibly because neither Eddie not I had taken a shower in weeks, but now I did pick up the trace of something rotten in the air.

"Where's it coming from?" I asked.

"I'll show you," she said, and led us to an open field behind the houses. In the center of the field was a stout stockade—a sort of open corral—encircled with barbed wire eight feet high. It was easy to see where the smell was coming from: inside the corral, three emaciated corpses were sprawled on the hard ground. It was impossible to tell whether they had died of starvation or had been shot.

"Jesus Christ!" Eddie Rojas said. "Who are they?"

"Prisoners of war, I think," the woman said. "They work in the furniture factory. I believe they're Polish. Or maybe Russian. Do you think you can do something?"

"You're damn right we can," Eddie said, and I was with him all the way. We took the woman back to the jeep, parked her in the rear seat, and returned to the bedsheet of the Polish fraternity. The fraternity brothers were very happy to see us. It turned out, fortunately, that one of them could speak a little French. He said he would be more than glad to help out; in fact, he could hardly wait. We put him in the jeep with the woman and drove back to the stockade, stopping first to pick up a shovel from her garden shed. In the stockade, we gave the shovel to the woman and told her to start digging three graves. To the Pole, we gave a German rifle we had picked up somewhere along the way and a couple of boxes of K rations, and told him to see to it that she did as ordered. The woman was outraged. She had never been treated like this in her life before, and she said so, with force. She threw down the shovel and started to walk away, but the Pole grabbed her and slapped her hard. The woman could not believe it. She wept and then started cursing us, but when the Pole raised his hand to whack her again, she picked up the shovel and started digging, still cursing and wailing. At this point, Eddie and I had to leave; we would have to step on it if we were going to catch up with our column. I looked back as we pulled away: the woman was digging, and the Pole was sitting on a rock with his rifle, watching her.

On April 13, 1945, I was in the Hartz Mountains (canaryland), sitting in a disabled German tank with Max Zera. We were taking cover from an enemy artillery sweep. Max was in the driver's seat and I was in the copilot's seat, with the great breech block of the tank's 88-mm gun between us. Max was fiddling with the tank's radio, which still seemed to be in working order. Suddenly, an English voice blared out. It was the Foreign Service of the BBC: "We must bring you the melancholy news that President

Franklin D. Roosevelt died in Warm Springs, Georgia, yesterday afternoon."

Max erupted. "Melancholy news!" he said. "*Melancholy!* My God!"

I think Max and I were the only liberal Democrats in Division Headquarters. Most of the high brass were West Pointers, and West Point does not breed liberal Democrats. It would be surprising if it did. The Army is an essentially authoritarian organization—as it has to be if the thing is going to work at all. There is no time for discussion or a vote. Orders are orders, from top to bottom, and it is the insignia on the sleeve or shoulder that carries the weight; I outrank you, so my word is law. Don't argue, just do it. A liberal Democrat has a hard time surviving in a climate like this.

I must add that I don't agree with Max that that "melancholy" was such a feeble word, because it burned itself into my memory so effectively that today, half a century later, I can still hear every shading of the BBC announcer's voice as he took hold of it.

While we were in the Hartz Mountains, control of the First Division was transferred from First Army, Gen. Luther Hodges commanding, to Third Army, Gen. George S. Patton commanding, and we moved south. About a week later, Colonel Carson sent me and Eddie Rojas and another sergeant back to Third Army Headquarters, twenty miles behind the lines, for reasons I no longer remember—something to do with maps. The three of us were in our usual state of sartorial collapse, and we looked very out of place among the spiffy vehicles and drivers back at Celestial Headquarters. Even our jeep looked intolerably ratty. However, we were able to do whatever it was we were supposed to do and were tooling along unhurriedly on our way home to the First Division when two MPs on motorcycles roared up from behind us and signaled us to move over, off the road—something big was coming through. We had hardly got out of the way when two more motorcycles appeared, followed by an open command car with a single figure sitting in the very center of the rear seat, leaning forward, with his hands on his knees, peering this way and that, the master of all he surveyed—Gen. George S. Patton. He looked like an overstuffed owl seeking out mice. Sartorially, he was in full fig; even his helmet appeared to have been lacquered and then polished. So had the helmets of all the others in his retinue—his driver, his aide (a stiff-faced major, in the front seat), and even the four motorcycling MPs. As an ensemble, they would have made a fine-looking float in a Fourth of July parade.

The gaudy motorcade whizzed by us but then came to a stop about a hundred yards down the road. Pretty soon, one of the motorcyclists rode back to us. "General wants to see you," he said, and we followed him to the seat of power.

"Who's in command of that jeep?" Patton asked.

"I am, sir," I said. "Lieutenant Botsford, First Division."

"If you're an officer, where's your insignia?" he asked. "Where's the stripe on your helmet?" Then, in a singsong voice that was evidently meant to be amusing, he recited, "Uniform regulations require every officer to have a vertical white stripe, one inch in width, on the back of his helmet, and every noncommissioned officer to have a similar stripe placed horizontally." He paused to let that sink in before adding, "You're out of uniform."

"Sir, the First Division is in the line, and in the line we don't wear insignia or show stripes," I said. "Snipers."

"You're out of uniform," he said again. "So are those two men with you. You have a choice: fifty-dollar fine or a court-martial. Take your pick."

I refrained from saying that if he wanted to make some real money he could go back to the division with us and extract fifty dollars from every officer and noncom in sight. Instead, I signed the printed form he pulled from his pocket, thus making it a hundred bucks I was out for reasons of personal grooming—fifty to Colonel Smith for all that hair, and now fifty to the big owl for the virgin helmet.

* * *

On the first of May, the headquarters of the First Infantry Division was in Cheb, Czechoslovakia, twenty-five miles from Carlsbad (German nomenclature) or Karlovy Vary (Czech), the celebrated health spa so favored by the Victorians. That morning, Max Zera and I were summoned to the classroom in a schoolhouse where our intrepid leader, the commanding general, had set up his command post. The general, Clarence Huebner, was (exceptionally) not a West Pointer. He had enlisted in the Regular Army as a young man and had spent his entire military career in the First Division, rising to sergeant, then to lieutenant, and, ultimately, to his present exalted role. He had never spoken a word to me, nor I to him.

"I have here a report from the commandant of military police in Paris," he said as Max and I stood like show-window dummies before him. "Dated last January. Came to me through channels. The commandant says a jeep with First Division markings was illegally parked on a Paris street and that an occupant of the jeep struck an officer who pointed out the violation. Do either of you know anything about it?"

"No, sir," said Max. I was unable to speak.

"What was the officer wearing?" the general asked unexpectedly.

"He was all gussied up," Max said. "Looked to be on his way to a dance."

"A dance," the general said. "A dance. Well, don't do it again. Dismissed."

Outside the general's classroom, the war was in a peculiar state. The stream of German Army prisoners coming through our lines had become a torrent. The roads from the east were clogged with soldiers and civilians frantically trying to get away from the Russians, who were coming on like a freight train at their backs. The crush was so great, we had had to set up a roadblock to keep them out of our lines, but it was being circumvented, and any movement along the Cheb–Karlovy Vary road was becoming impossible. At noon, Max and I were sent down to try to get the traffic off to the side of the road so the war could continue.

When we reached the roadblock, it was clear that the problem was worse than anybody at headquarters had imagined. Wehrmacht soldiers, women auxiliaries, renegade Russian troops—to say nothing of civilians by the hundreds—were headed for our lines, using every conceivable means of transport: wheelbarrows, Army troop transports, civilian buses, pushcarts, horses and wagons, dump trucks, civilian sports cars, generals' staff cars, bicycles, buggies. Every vehicle was festooned with hopeful prisoners-to-be. The crush was out of control, the sergeant at the roadblock said—everybody wanted to surrender.

However, Max and I had our orders, and we decided to attack the problem head-on. We got the sergeant to let our jeep through the roadblock and moved into the crush. Eddie Rojas was driving, and Max, standing up in the rear of the jeep and looking more like a tree stump than ever, glared and shouted at the flotsam impartially. "Off the road!" he bellowed in his foghorn voice. "Make way! *Schnell,* goddammit!" Then he roared the same thing in Yiddish. I don't know whether it was his voice or his looks or his Yiddish that did the trick, but the sea parted before us.

We continued like this for several miles—Max roaring and Eddie Rojas nudging the dilatory with the nose of the jeep—without realizing that we were moving deeper and deeper into enemy territory. Karlovy Vary (pop. forty thousand), with its dozens of hotels serving the spa, had been turned into a big German Army hospital center, and now it was emptying itself down our road. Panic was increasingly evident. *"Russkis! Russkis!"* men would shout, pointing over their shoulders to the east. (Actually, the Russians were still a couple of days away.) By the time our jeep reached the center of town, the entire civilian population must have been out in the street. We could hardly move. Out of the babel I suddenly heard a woman's voice speaking English—clipped, cultivated English. "I am British!" she shouted. "I have been forced to stay in Germany against my will. It is not my fault. Please take me with you. I have a right to go with you. The British are your allies." She was deep in the crowd, and all I could make out was that she was about fifty and was dressed far better than anybody else in this mob.

I never found out who she was, because an important-looking man in an odd kind of courtier's uniform had pushed his way through the crowd and was talking importantly to Max, who answered him in important-sounding Yiddish. "He says he's from the burgomaster's office and we should go to City Hall with him," Max told me. "They want to surrender the whole goddam town to us."

City Hall was an ancient stone building (Karlovy Vary was founded in the fourteenth century) and the burgomaster's office was on the second floor, a big room, paneled in dark wood, with a high ceiling and tall windows. We walked in, leaving Eddie Rojas standing by the door with his rifle to fend off random surrenderers and to keep an eye out for anything untoward—after all, we were behind enemy lines. The burgomaster, an old geezer in a velvet coat, was wearing all his chains of office. He spoke pretty good English. "General Schwaben is on his way," he said, and with that, right on cue, General Schwaben, a short, pinch-faced man, who was very conscious of his importance, arrived. He was accompanied by two aides-de-camp, and all three of them were military fashion plates, personifications of the German Army dress code. Their leather riding boots, belts, and pistol holsters gleamed, their uniforms were spotless and well pressed, their various decorations were polished to a shine. They marched into the room and came to attention, clicking their heels in unison. The general looked us over with pursed lips; Max, Eddie, and I were, as usual, in no way fashion plates. Dirty, unshaven, caked with dust, we were an affront to the U.S. Army dress code. It was quite clear that if we had been under General Schwaben's command he would have had us court-martialed for criminal attire.

"Gentlemen, I present to you General Schwaben," the burgomaster said. "He does not speak English, so I will translate." General Schwaben stepped forward and clicked his heels again. "It is the general's wish—and mine—to surrender the city of Carlsbad to the American Army. Do you represent the American Army?"

"We *are* the American Army," Max said grandly in Yiddish. General Schwaben looked as though he had just stepped in something disgusting. We were not only scruffy, we were *Jewish*! He started for the door but then stopped. I was willing to bet that he had reminded himself of the Russians. "Let us proceed," he said, via the burgomaster. He undid the flap of his holster, pulled out his Luger, and, holding it by the barrel, presented it to Max. His aides also disarmed themselves, placing their pistols on the burgomaster's desk. Then all three stood back, came to attention, and clicked their heels again.

Max stuck the general's Luger into his pants belt and said in his Roman-emperor mode, "My first order as military commander of Carlsbad is that General Schwaben get all the personnel under his control off the road to Cheb and await further instructions." This was conveyed to the general, who bowed. Then Max said, "I hereby appoint Lieutenant Botsford civil administrator of Carlsbad, effective immediately." The burgomaster, with some reluctance, got up from his desk, and Max motioned me into his chair. "Now, General, I think you should start carrying out your orders," Max said. The general and his aides did an about-face and marched out of the room, the burgomaster following them.

Eddie Rojas closed the door behind them. "I'll be goddamned!" he said. Max gave Eddie and me the aides' Lugers. "I don't trust that guy," he said. "He's bound to wake up to what's happened pretty soon. I think we'd better get out of here."

And that's what we did. Two days later, the G-2 log for the First Division carried the entry:

> At 0815 hours on 7 May 1945, the First Infantry Division received an order to cease firing, an order for which the

Division had fought since 8 November 1942, from Oran, North Africa, to Cheb, Czechoslovakia.

The war was over—our part of the war at least—and the recently appointed burgomaster and military commandant of Karlovy Vary were out of a job; the Russians had started moving in. I yearned to return to my fiefdom, the city I had once held in thrall, but I had no luck for about a week, when Colonel Carson sent me there on an errand that even he realized was fruitless. (If he had thought otherwise, he would have sent a more imposing envoy.) The problem was the repatriation of the hundreds, perhaps thousands, of liberated prisoners of war and slave laborers still wandering loose in the area. Colonel Carson's idea was that the Russians might be willing to help out, since many of the wanderers came from countries now under Soviet control.

I set off for Karlovy Vary with a Polish jeep driver who could speak enough Russian to get by. The first Russian we saw was an MP directing traffic at an intersection on the outskirts of town. He waved us through, gaping at us as we passed; American soldiers and jeeps were still strange and extraordinary phenomena to him. We got the same response all the way into the center of town and had no trouble being directed to the Russian division's headquarters, in a big hotel on the main street. At headquarters, we were passed along with great friendliness to the third-floor office of the division's commanding general and told to wait. The anteroom overlooked the main street, and down below I could see the rear elements of the general's division still pouring into the city. This division was one of the elite units of the Russian Army. It had come all the way from the Crimea, fighting over every mile—and the troops looked it. A number of them were wearing recognizable Russian uniforms, but most looked like laborers coming home from a hard day in the factories or the fields. Their vehicles were equally disparate: A few were American two-and-a-half-ton trucks (lend-lease, no doubt), but most were of more exotic origin, picked up along the way—farm trucks, delivery vans, stake trucks, dump trucks. I would bet that most of them still had their Bulgarian, Hungarian, or Austrian license plates. Actually, there were more animals than trucks in the procession: horses pulling artillery pieces whose origins were as kaleidoscopic as the vehicles. (But what did they use for ammunition? No answer.) Astonishingly, there were even a couple of elephants and several camels—the division must have overrun a traveling circus. It is hard to imagine how such a horde could have not only withstood but vanquished the highly disciplined, well-coordinated Wehrmacht.

The general, when we were admitted to his presence, turned out to be a short, stocky, bouncy man of about fifty, with a gray crew cut, and a rather high voice. He was bursting with hands-across-the-steppe friendliness and he hugged the jeep driver and me half a dozen times with little yips of welcome for his fellow victors. But when I asked him, via the jeep driver, if he could help with the repatriation, I might just as well have asked him what he thought of Willa Cather's novels. His only answer was to say it was time for lunch and that he would call Colonel Vlasov, one of his regimental commanders, to join us. With considerable flourish, he addressed himself to a field telephone—an American field telephone, I noticed—on his desk and gave it a crank. I assumed that Colonel Vlasov was across town, or maybe not even in Karlovy Vary at all, but as the general cranked I could hear the bell ring down the hall, no more than fifty feet away. A man at the other end answered the ring in a voice so loud that it caromed down the hall all by itself. The general replied with a yelp of his own, and the ensuing conversation was conducted in shouts and yells that needed no phone for transmission. In a few minutes, Colonel Vlasov appeared and we went downstairs to lunch.

In the end, about twenty of us sat down to a menu of thick vegetable soup and chicken, preceded by—unimaginable!—giant mounds of caviar. (I noticed, however, that the juniors at the far end of the table were passed over when the caviar came by.) For drinks, there was vodka, as if from an open faucet. The jeep driver and I, sitting on the general's right and left, were the center of attention, questioned about everything from life in America to the D-day landings, but it was slow going. The jeep driver's Russian was not all that good, and mine was nonexistent. There were many dead stops, therefore, and whenever silence fell, somebody would get up and propose a toast—to the American Army, to Russian-American cooperation, to absent friends, to absent girlfriends, to anything that moved and breathed. Gallons of vodka were poured and drunk. Halfway through, I could see that I was going to be in big trouble at this pace, so I started faking it, taking a tiny sip instead of a swallow, and when we got to a toast to the horses we once rode and loved, I stopped altogether. Nevertheless, I was very glad to get back to our jeep finally and head for home, where I told Colonel Carson that the Russians were nuts about Willa Cather but had flunked out otherwise.

I sailed home from Le Havre in mid-October 1945 on the *Kingston Victory,* bound for Boston—nine days. For the voyage, I was in nominal command (I was now a captain) of an ad-hoc group of 150 soldiers from various units who, like me, were going home to be discharged from the Army. From Boston, we were to take a train to Fort Dix, New Jersey, and there be released into the real world. On the wharf in Boston, I had the troops line up for a head count, with each man's pair of barracks bags—containing every single thing he owned in the Army—on the ground in front of him. Then each man picked up his bags and lugged them into the train that was waiting on a siding just behind us. Once the train was sealed, we took off for Dix. At Dix, I had the troops line up on the platform, again with every man's bags in front of him. Two soldiers were left over, bagless. "We can't find our barracks bags, Captain," one of them said. Two months earlier, this would have seemed normal Army routine that had to be dealt with—there were always two boneheads who could manage to lose their barracks bags on a sealed train—but with release so near I couldn't play the game any longer. "Oh, for Chrissake, don't bother me!" I said, and marched the 148 other men off to their happy ending.

Five days later, I, too, was a free man, and I caught a train for New York. Tass was living with Susan, now almost three, in an apartment at 161 East Seventy-ninth Street, and I knocked at the door—no key to my own apartment—at around 10:30 that evening. . . .

Stop for a minute. Who is this bargain-basement Odysseus returning from the wars? When we first saw him, more than three years ago, he was a nervous civilian, hoping to slide off unnoticed for his date with the Army. Then, just a week ago, we see him striding up and down a railroad platform like a new-day John Wayne, barking orders at a bunch of perfect strangers. And now here he is, standing outside his own front door, a civilian once again, with the tra-la-la notion that, once inside, he can pick up his life exactly where he left it so many years before. Obviously, something has happened. There has been a change, several changes—a metamorphosis, in fact. If we are to make any sense of these changes, if we are to understand the platform strider and give a third dimension to the newly minted civilian, we must first know more about the nervous fellow climbing out of bed at four o'clock in the morning to go be a soldier. Who was *he?*

It's a legitimate question, and answering it properly makes for a long story—there are a lot of years to cover. But the sun is up and the sea is calm, and since it is my story, I see no reason to shorten it. Instead, we will open with a digression that takes us well into the past—to the 1920s and 1930s. Then, to give comfort to the restless and fainthearted, we will slide into a narrative that returns us to our road-company Odysseus waiting impatiently for Penelope to put down her weaving and answer the damn door.

PRIVILEGE

I

THE LEADING PLAYERS

I:	Robert Gardner Botsford, born July 7, 1917, in New York City. I was named for my great-grandfather Robert Gardner, but I can't think why: my mother detested the nickname "Bob," and saw to it that I was never called anything but "Gardner." To the U.S. Army, however, a first name is a first name, and stop making trouble, so for three years I was Robert Botsford, always a beat late in recognizing myself when called or yelled at.
My mother:	Née Ruth Gardner, born June 23, 1894, in Quincy, Illinois; died in 1950 in New York City. Married (1) Alfred Miller Botsford, on October 17, 1914; (2) Raoul Fleischmann, in 1920; (3) Peter Vischer, in 1938.

My father:	Alfred Miller Botsford, born August 9, 1884, in Quincy Illinois; died in 1967 in Hollywood.
My stepfathers:	(1) Raoul Fleischmann, born August 17, 1895, in Bad Ischl, Austria; died in 1969 in New York City. (2) Peter Vischer, born on Staten Island, birth date unknown; died sometime in the 1960s.
My first wife:	Katharine Hastings ("Tass") Chittenden, born January 11, 1915; died October 21, 1974.
My second wife:	Janet Malcolm, born July 8, 1934, in Prague.

In the twenties and thirties, Neysa McMein was the most celebrated woman in New York City. Other women had their moments, but they were not taken up by the people who create celebrity—the artists, actors, gossip columnists, musicians, and writers of the time. Neysa had everything required for celebrity. She was young, good-looking, bright, gregarious, unconventional, and an artist herself. (She was the contract artist for the covers of *McCall's* magazine and did many for *The Saturday Evening Post,* as well; they were enormously successful examples of the commercial art of the period.) She became the pet of the celebrity-makers, and her studio, on West Fifty-seventh Street, across from Carnegie Hall, was overrun by her fan club. "If you loiter in Neysa McMein's studio, the world will drift in and out," Alexander Woollcott, the drama critic of the *New York Times,* wrote. "It's the first place the Missing Persons Bureau looks—everyone is there." At one time or another, "everyone" meant Feodor Chaliapin, Robert Benchley, Janet Flanner, Jascha Heifetz, Harpo Marx, Edna Ferber, Anita Loos, Anaïs Nin (she was Neysa's paid model), Otto Kahn, Dorothy Parker, Robert Sherwood, Irving Berlin, Tallulah Bankhead, Paul Robeson, Helen Hayes, Ring Lardner, H. G. Wells, and George Gershwin. When she died, in 1949, a memorial fund was established in her name at the Whitney Museum by most of those people, plus George Abbott, Bernard Baruch,

Charles Brackett, Howard Dietz, Walt Disney, Raoul Fleischmann, Ruth Gordon, Jane Grant, Averell Harriman, Moss Hart, George Kaufman, Fredric March, Cole Porter, Richard Rodgers, Cornelia Otis Skinner, and Clifton Webb. In an obituary, Noel Coward wrote, "Never, in all the years I knew and loved her, did I see her foolish or flurried or mistaken. . . . In case I should be accused of overidealization . . . I will add that her clothes were erratic, her political views frequently unsound, her spelling appalling, and her luck at games of chance maddening."

Neysa was born in Quincy, Illinois, and so was my mother, six years later, on June 23, 1894. Except for the erratic clothes, Neysa and my mother were a lot alike. In fact, they were brought up together: Neysa's father was a drunk, and my grandmother, who liked Neysa—she was a classmate of my mother's sister, Marion—took her in. (She was Margaret McMein then, and became Neysa only after a numerologist in New York told her that she needed a *y* and an *s* in her name, and certainly fewer *m*'s.) In his biography of Neysa, *Anything Goes,* Brian Gallagher writes:

> A significant and lasting appearance of Quincyana in Neysa's New York life was the arrival of Ruth Gardner and her husband Alfred Botsford. . . . Ruth was a celebrated small-town beauty. In 1914 she had married Alfred Miller Botsford, like her a child of one of Quincy's leading families. Within a year they found themselves woefully bored with Midwestern life—Botsford had already spent four college years in the East, at Williams—so they took the first opportunity to hie themselves off to New York, he to try his luck on the stage and she to see how far her small-town beauty and social gifts would get her in a much larger, more competitive arena. Ruth immediately made contact with her sister Marion's great friend Neysa McMein, and Neysa, just then making her way into the more

> exciting reaches of New York's literary-artistic set, was able to introduce Ruth and her husband to a number of her new and important friends. The young couple was launched.

Gallagher is only partly right about my mother, and less than that about my father. She was a small-town beauty all right, but her small-town beauty had already served her well in some much bigger cities—London, New York, Paris, Munich. As for her social gifts, she became an international heartbreaker at sixteen, when she graduated from the venerable National Cathedral School, in Washington, D.C., and was sent to Europe for a year to improve her cultural education. "Went to the Salon's new 'Impressionistic' School," she wrote in her diary in Paris in October 1910, and added, showing off, "Never saw such frightful canvases. Some good—Sisley, Manet." That December, her father wrote her from Quincy: "Now Ruth, you must take care of yourself if you want to continue your European schooling. Keep warm and avoid drafts—far better to pay extra for coal fires in your room than doctor bills." He addressed this letter simply "Miss Ruth Gardner, Paris, France," adding, as an afterthought in a bottom corner, "33 Rue Francois ler." (In Quincy, such precision was unnecessary, even though Quincy was a city of some forty thousand addressees. Most of the letters my mother received there—I have a box of them—were simply addressed "Miss Ruth Gardner, Quincy.")

Miss Gardner evidently paid for coal fires, because she stayed warm enough to lay waste to any number of young men in England, France, and, especially, Germany, where she spent several months at a pension in Munich run by a Mrs. Hartman, an American woman who served as chaperone and tutor. The leading suitor in Munich was a young cavalry officer named Fritz Scheiblein ("I will send a picture of my squadron with me at the head of it"), who went completely overboard. ("I must kiss your sweet hair in thought, and hold your dear little head close," he wrote from Straubing, where he had been temporarily posted.) Here is an extract from her diary:

> *Feb. 14, 1911:*
> Herr Scheiblein sent me some roses, my only Valentine. Went skating.
>
> *Feb. 17:*
> A letter from Scheiblein from Frankfurt, and what a letter! Had my hair shampooed.
>
> *Feb. 24:*
> Mrs. Rupprecht telephoned Mrs. Hartman saying that Scheiblein wants to marry me and that she has promised him she will talk to me. I hope the interview never takes place.
>
> *Feb. 26:*
> Scheiblein has written Father. Horrors!
>
> *Mar. 1:*
> Fritz S. here. He is such a darling. Whatever possessed me to flirt with him! If he would only hate me for it! It is really Mrs. Hartman's fault. She said he was only a flirt.
>
> *Mar. 2:*
> Mrs. Rupprecht came and talked at great length with Mrs. Hartman about me and F.S. Don't know the outcome. Mildred and I went skating.
>
> *Mar. 6:*
> I saw F.S.'s beauty horses—four perfect wonders. Dad coming April 6th.

Apr. 21:
Telegram from Daddy—they have landed!

Records do not reveal what Daddy had to say about darling F.S., but whatever it was, he said it forcefully, for on June 23, her seventeenth birthday, Miss Gardner sailed home from Liverpool. Six weeks later, a letter from Fritz followed her to Quincy: "You say that you have found a nice young man who is like me," he wrote. "I hate you."

My mother had a magnetic field that picked up men like Fritz Scheiblein as though they were iron filings (also customs officers, headwaiters, train conductors, postmen, and cops). I saw it happen time and again. A fellow would start off all formality and politesse, and five minutes later he would be lighting her cigarettes too eagerly, jumping up too athletically to fetch her handbag, and laughing too loudly at everything she said. Letters show that even after my mother's marriage, stricken young men from all across the country refused to give up. "Nevertheless, I still will tell you that you are a fascinating woman," Cyril somebody wrote her from Wilkes-Barre two months after the ceremony. Tacoma was heard from: "You and Bots should afford each other excellent material for a passing fancy. I sincerely hope that if you get your fingers burnt you will once again think of your devoted friend Donald McFadon." And Overton Harris, of Louisville, sneakily wrote, "Dear North Star: I considered calling you up by telephone, but a conversation with Alfred hanging on each syllable would be worse than none. You are one of the few young ladies who retain their interest even after marriage. I hope that you are happy and contented, but I doubt it."

As for my father, Alfred Miller Botsford, he was not quite the Quincy hayseed with an eastern education that Brian Gallagher implies. His father (who had had an eastern education, too—Princeton, 1874) was editor of the *Quincy Herald-Whig,* and *his* father was a clergyman in Philadelphia. When my father graduated from Williams, in 1906, he stayed east. He was stagestruck, and he tried his luck in the New York theater long before Brian Gallagher says he did. He appeared in several Broadway productions, a couple of them quite successful, and he once worked as John Barrymore's understudy. Barrymore even then was a dedicated lush, but my father was out of luck: Barrymore, drunk or sober, managed to show up for every performance.

Struggling actors make very little money, even in New York, so in the end my father had to return to Quincy and go to work on the *Herald-Whig,* as he had done before, during lean periods. While there, in October 1914, at the age of thirty, he married my mother, twenty, and, as Gallagher says, returned with her to New York. This time, as Gallagher does not say, he stayed with journalism and got a job on the *New York Evening World.* When I was born, on July 7, 1917, he was the paper's night city editor, a position that sounded more impressive than his paycheck indicated. Because he would not spend my mother's money (it is entirely possible that she had none to contribute—that her father, a rich man but a famous penny-pincher and cheapskate, saw no reason to support a married daughter), my father, like so many newspapermen before and since, moved over into advertising, where the pay was better. The job he got was in the advertising department of Famous Players–Lasky, a movie company in Long Island City that eventually evolved into Paramount Pictures. He stayed with Paramount for the rest of his working life.

My mother and father were as solidly American as Becky Thatcher and Tom Sawyer (who, in fact, lived right across the Mississippi from Quincy), and were thus entirely different from my first stepfather, Raoul Fleischmann, whom my mother married in 1920, when my brother Stephen was only a couple of months old and I was two. Raoul was a New York boy born in Austria (his parents were taking the waters in Bad Ischl), perfectly mannered, dark-haired and romantic-looking, urbane, Jewish, rich (Fleischmann's Yeast), impeccably barbered, fluent in languages, owner of a monogrammed dressing gown. And Raoul, in turn, was entirely different from my second stepfather, Peter Vischer, whom my mother married in 1938. He was a descendant of the fifteenth-century family of German sculptors, and he can best be defined as a disarming hustler—disarming, that is, until you saw what was underneath. Outside, he was all breezy, gregarious charm and bonhomie; underneath—as we all discovered too late—he had the makings of a Nazi.

In the hands of a good playwright, a set of characters like these might have been shaped into a plausible comedy of manners, a tale of shifting alliances and subsequent estrangements, starting in the first years of the century and ending fifty years later in a denouement that would unmask insidious Peter Vischer. To begin with, my father and Raoul were classmates and best friends at Williams. It was through my father that my mother met Raoul, and it was through Raoul that Peter Vischer met his first wife (who divorced him and disappears from this narrative). The link between Peter Vischer and my father was slighter: their paths crossed only because both had worked on the *New York Evening World*. My mother met Peter Vischer through his first wife before the divorce, and never failed to invite him to her parties after it, because he played such jovial piano.

These were the sort of knotted relationships that a Noel Coward or a Terence Rattigan would have untied in the last act to everyone's satisfaction, but there was no art in the way things actually played out—no comedy, no tragedy, nothing but a great enveloping mess. After five years of marriage, my mother divorced my father—who never really recovered from the blow—and went off with Raoul, once his best friend. After fourteen years of marriage to Raoul, she divorced him, too, and he never really recovered either. (I never knew, nor could imagine, why they divorced.

There was no visible third party on either side, and they were invariably courteous and easygoing with each other. I didn't ask, because I knew as a solid fact that if I did, she would have told me, in effect, to mind my own business, and he would have said, in effect, that gentlemen did not ask such questions.) Four years later, she married Peter Vischer, but soon realized that she had made a mistake. She moved to a New York hotel, where she attempted to divorce him but failed, and died there, in her hotel room, in 1950, at the age of fifty-six, angry at having been taken in by a con man. As for Vischer himself, he, too, did nothing to provide the play with a satisfactory denouement. His exposure for what he was never came off; instead, he switched from pre–Pearl Harbor German sympathizer to post–Pearl Harbor superpatriot. He found a comfortable spot as a colonel in the Army ("This is Colonel Vischer calling. Could you reserve a table for four at eight-thirty?") and died, still calling himself "Colonel," in the sixties.

The key character here, obviously, is my mother. When she is onstage, everything goes along nicely, or seems to. When she moves off, everything falls apart, and in the end she falls apart, too. She is a hard one to figure. In many ways, she was a Victorian—Victorianism died slowly in Quincy. She was rigorous about Doing the Right Thing, and she was more than that about good manners. To her, good manners were not fixed, but open to analysis and reinterpretation, and she enjoyed working out their finer points—should children having lunch with their parents in a restaurant stand up if a parental acquaintance pauses at their table to say hello? The answer, arrived at with the ice cream and *gaufrettes* (we were having lunch in the clubhouse of a golf course in Le Touquet), was no—only if the acquaintance tarries long enough to be introduced.

Such punctiliousness represented the Quincy-Victorian streak in my mother; in other ways, she was a 1920s liberated woman, like Neysa. She was competent, intelligent, assured, and always fair, with a high sense of humor. She had a nice social laugh, but when something really funny took her by surprise, her laugh was more a bellowed exultation than a laugh. My mother was a soft touch for anybody in trouble, especially for an animal in trouble. She was naturally sympathetic and would go out of her way to help. But there was nothing saccharine about her. For balance, she was at times stubborn, judgmental, and authoritarian. She managed her children with a surprisingly steady hand—a Victorian hand—but she had too much humor to be a true Victorian dragon. When she told you off for your transgressions, she would leave the impression that while they were, of course, great transgressions, they weren't all *that* great. When my brother Steve and I concealed a Whoopee cushion (an inflated flat rubber bladder that emitted an interesting sound when sat upon) in one of the living-room chairs before a big party, and stuffy Mrs. Travis sat upon it, my mother dressed us down vigorously the next day. We would have to write Mrs. Travis a letter of apology, she said, and then broke out laughing. "Well, I don't know how you're going to explain what you're apologizing *for*," she said. "For causing that silly woman to make a rude noise?"

I think it was this ability to laugh at herself that made her such good company—that and the unexpectedness of her thinking. You never knew what she was going to say next, but, once said, it always seemed like the only sensible thing that anybody could say. In short, I really liked being with her, even though—or it may even be because—I was mostly out of her orbit. From the age of eleven on, that is, I was away at school and only vacationed at home.

I left home in the spring of 1929, after a winter of bad colds, and even pneumonia. My mother, like all mothers of the day, attributed every childhood frailty to the impure air of the city, and when I had my second bout of pneumonia, in February, she took action. Her friend Elizabeth Clark was at that time subsidizing the Beasley School, a small school for boys in Cooperstown, New York, where the Clarks had an immense country estate on both sides of the Susquehanna River. Ostensibly, Mrs. Clark was underwriting Headmaster Beasley's innovative theories of education. One of these was that concentration could be taught, like algebra. Every day before classes, the assembled students would be given a text to read, and while they were reading, he would do everything possible to distract them—blow on a bugle, take both sides of a loud argument, stand on his head. Then the students would be tested for their comprehension of the text. Beasley's theories may have been right: the fact that arachnids have eight legs may still be with me because I learned it to the sound of a bugle.

Actually, Mrs. Clark's interest in the Beasley School had nothing to do with arachnids or bugling. She kept it going because it provided a scholastic perch for her son Bobby (my contemporary and soon my best friend), who had already, even at his age, been kicked out of practically every school on the Eastern Seaboard. (He died in Paris of cirrhosis of the liver at the age of thirty, which must be close to a record.) Nor did my mother care about arachnids; all she wanted was cold, clean air, and Cooperstown certainly provided that. So off I went, in time for the spring term, and from that moment on I lived at home only three or four months a year—a perfectly rational way of life, it seemed to me.

Home for me—my home away from home, so to speak—was a converted brownstone at 151 East Seventy-fourth Street, between Lexington and Third. It was bought by my mother and Raoul in 1922; they had been living in a house on Ninety-second Street, but when my half brother, Peter, was born in that year, they moved to Seventy-fourth Street, where there was more room. The house was standard New York brownstone in layout: kitchen and dining room on the ground floor, with French doors opening from the dining room onto a sunless garden in the rear. On the second floor, two big rooms, front and back. The front room was "for best"—that is, it was the most elegantly furnished room in the house, and nobody would have thought of sitting in it except during a party. The back room, called "the library" because of four built-in bookcases filled with books that nobody read, was where we sat *en famille*. It had a huge, comfortable sofa, almost the size of a double bed, in front of which stood a low brass tray table from India, three feet across, an offshoot of my mother's decorating business. I never liked it much, but the Great Decorator Upstairs must have decreed that the tray and I should be bonded for life. After several years in the library at Seventy-fourth Street, it was exiled by my mother, who didn't like it much either, to the offices of *The New Yorker*. When I followed it there, fifteen years later, it was ornamenting the front lobby of the magazine's editorial floor, and for forty years I walked by it every day on my way to my office. Today, following vicissitudes too complex to relate, it is in the basement storage room of my apartment on Gramercy Park, and I still don't like it much.

Another feature of the library at Seventy-fourth Street was the Atwater Kent radio, on which, on December 11, 1936, we heard King Edward VIII announce his abdication because of "the woman I love." This occurred at about five o'clock in the morning; Mother had hustled us all out of bed for the occasion, which she took almost personally, since she had met the king (who was her exact twin) when he was on a trip over here as Prince of Wales, had danced with him, and had made a big hit. In her mind, Wallis Warfield Simpson was only her surrogate.

The rest of the house was bedrooms—Mother's and Raoul's on the third floor (separate bedrooms; very European), and children and servants on the two floors above. It was a tight squeeze on the top floor, because there were five live-in servants: Sabine (French; cook), Minna (Austrian; parlor maid), Hedda (Czech; Mother's personal maid), Nellie (Irish; laundress), and the butler of the day—there was a string of them, and they never lasted long. (Raoul's valet, Becket; my mother's secretary, Julia Kiely; and the family chauffeur, Dan Grady, did not live in.) The women servants had two uniforms: a gray or light blue one, with denim apron, for the day's work, and a black one, with a frilly white apron, plus a cap, for evening. (Nellie was not issued evening wear.) The butler's formal wear was a black morning coat and dark gray trousers.

The day started with the household split in three. The children would be in the kitchen, having their breakfast before being put out the door to walk to school. (I, and in their turn Stephen and Peter, attended the Allen-Stevenson School, on East Seventy-eighth Street—still there, and still pursuing me for alumni funds.) My mother would be in her bedroom, breakfasting off a bed tray brought by Hedda. Raoul would be in the dining room by himself, making do with coffee and brioches before leaving for his job as manager of the Bond Bread bakery, at Eighty-first Street and East End Avenue. (The Fleischmann Yeast connection led quite naturally to the baking business.) My mother was generally in action before any of the rest of us—in action but not out of bed. Her letters and the newspaper came in with her tray, and she went through them with her first cup of coffee; with her second, she got down to work, both on professional matters (her decorating business) and on household management. All negotiations were conducted from bed. First, Sabine would come in to discuss menus and the number of guests expected that day; although my mother couldn't boil a carrot, and never once did, to my knowledge, she knew a lot about cooking. Sabine would be followed by Miss Kiely, with secretarial matters, both social (invitations, appointments, and such) and business ("Mrs. Tefft didn't like the green damask and wonders if gray is available"). She, in turn, would be followed by Grady, to receive his driving orders for the day. Those were the regulars, but there were also moments for Minna and Hedda.

Today, it is almost impossible to imagine how many duties the servants had, and how hard they worked. We were a family of five with a staff of eight servants, five of them resident—an imbalance of numbers that was never brought into question. The relationship that then existed between master and servant—between, in effect, the upper and the lower classes—was nothing less than feudal, and it was fully accepted by both sides. To my mother and Raoul, the disparity between the two levels seemed preordained; they never doubted that the disparity was right, and had always been right—that their money, their education, and their social position made it so. This gave them complete self-assurance in dealing with salaried employees. Today, such an attitude would breed resentment, if not outright defiance, but the fact of those times was that all our servants respected Raoul and went even further in regard to my mother: they really liked her—worshiped her, in Grady's case. I speak as an authority on this, because we children spent a lot more time belowstairs with the servants than we did upstairs with the quality, and we saw and heard. But I also think the servants obeyed because my mother and Raoul, impregnable in their self-assurance, spoke with such unclouded expectations of compliance that neither side could imagine not obeying.

Some people still have the knack of unalloyed command, but it is rare. Bobby Brown, my colleague in the First Division, had it. When he and I were released from that hospital in England to return to the First Division, we were put in charge of a bunch of infantry replacements, fresh from the States, who were being sent over to bring the rifle companies up to strength. They were not happy with their lot. When our party landed in France, in the middle of the night, we were supposed to be met by a fleet of trucks that would take us to a transit camp closer to the front, but no trucks had arrived. So Bobby and I herded our crew into a cow pasture just off the main road to await transport. An hour and more went by. The replacements scattered all over the pasture in little complaining groups, invisible in the dark but audible. Finally, the trucks arrived. "Get the guys up and start to load while I sign the papers," Bobby told me, and I moved to the center of the field to do so. I couldn't see a solitary replacement in any direction, but I could hear mutterings. "All right, you guys—on your feet and into the trucks!" I called into the dark. Nothing happened. "Everybody up! Get a move on!" I shouted. Out of the blackness came a ripe Bronx cheer and a derisive "Ah, go fuck yourself!" I was trying to think of what to do next when Bobby Brown came up.

"What's the delay?" he said.

"The bastards won't move," I said.

"They won't move?" he said with utter incredulity, as though I had told him they had all grown wings and flown away. "What do you mean, 'They won't move'?" Then *he* yelled into the dark, in his old sergeant's voice. What he yelled was pretty much what I had yelled, but his voice had that freezing hint of the unspeakable reprisals that would follow disobedience. It was the voice of total self-assurance and unclouded expectation of compliance, and it worked: the replacements came shambling out of the dark and climbed into the trucks. I don't think Bobby wondered for an instant what he would have done if they hadn't moved; it simply never occurred to him that such a thing could happen.

Considering what our household servants were required to do just to keep the house running, it is surprising that my mother and Raoul never heard a sharp retort from the darkness. Nellie, for instance, had to get through truly stupendous stacks of laundry—all of it washed by hand and then ironed. She was faced with the clothes of three dirty children, the sheets and towels of ten people, and all the napkins and tablecloths—the only labor she was spared was doing my mother's things (Hedda's province) and Raoul's shirts, of which there were two a day. (He always put on a clean one for dinner: a formal evening shirt to go with his dinner jacket if there was company, which was often, or an ordinary one—ordinary but silk—for dinner *en famille*. His shirts were done by a laundry, no doubt French, and were picked up and delivered by a uniformed man who wore puttees; the clean ones were put on shoulder-shaped wooden hangers by Raoul's valet, Becket, and hung in Raoul's closet. All of them were made to order by Sulka.) Sabine, of course, had little respite from her stove. There were not only the big dinners of twelve or fourteen in the dining room, but also much subsidiary eating in the kitchen, first by us kids and then by the staff. As for the butler, he had hardly a minute off from polishing the silver—the knives and forks and spoons, of course, but also the tea service and trays, the serving dishes, the candelabras, the after-dinner coffee service, the gravy boats, the two silver pheasants used as table ornaments, the labels on the cruets and decanters, the picture frames and cigarette boxes and ashtrays all over the house. Until 1933, when Prohibition was repealed, the butler of the day would also have to keep track of supplies in the wine cellar. "We're getting a little low on dry vermouth," he would say to Raoul, and Raoul would make a note to call his bootlegger. I never knew the bootlegger's name, but he was as familiar to me as was the delivery boy from the Daniel Reeves grocery store. A burly, middle-aged Irishman with roguish ways, he would drive up in his derelict Buick sedan, park it in front of our house—you could always find a place to park on a city street then, except at night in the theater district—pull the necessary bottles, or possibly a case, of contraband out of the car trunk, and bear them into the house with a certain panache, as though he were an Irish estate owner distributing Christmas puddings to needy tenants. He pretended to have an insatiable lust for Sabine. "*Voulez-vous coucher avec moi*?" he would invariably say to her—he had been in France during the war—and she, just as invariably, would histrionically threaten him with a frying pan. As far as I know, Sabine and her frying pan were the worst hazards he had to face in his professional career. Not once did a cop or a Prohibition agent disturb him during a delivery, although there were plenty of both on the public payroll—enforcing Prohibition was a big source of jobs during the Depression. The newspapers were constantly running pictures of lawmen busting up rows of bottles with axes or pouring kegs of beer down sewers, but to our household Prohibition agents were no more troublesome than postal inspectors.

Of far more concern to our household and to every other law-defying household in the country was the authenticity, or at least the medical benignity, of the bootleggers' wares. These were the subject of constant discussion. Where today the chief topic of conversation at cocktail and dinner parties is real estate, then it was booze and its provenance. Having a bootlegger of moral integrity was more important than having a good cook. A bad cook might cause a guest to think twice about ever coming back, but a rascally bootlegger might put him in the hospital. As everyone knew, there was much skullduggery afoot, and it could crop up anywhere. When Richard Whitney, the well-known Harvard oarsman, Wall Street grandee, and ornament of the *Social Register,* went to jail for chicanery in the stock market, an auction of his effects was held at his great country estate in New Jersey, and I attended it with my mother. I wanted to buy his Harvard oar, which he had mounted on a wall of his study, but my mother had more catholic tastes. She had her eye on five unopened cases of Johnny Walker Scotch, which Whitney had laid down during Prohibition. She reasoned that anyone bearing the Whitney name would have had an honest bootlegger, possibly even a titled one, and she bought the lot. We opened a bottle when we got home, and it was full of tea. So were a third of the other bottles. Nor did I get my oar. I was prepared to go as high as ten dollars for it, but it went for many hundreds, bought in by a Harvard alumnus, presumably to save it from infidel hands.

The skullduggery was not all on the bootleggers' side of the fence, either. Even Raoul, ordinarily the most upright of men, would sometimes give way to lawlessness in the matter of gin. Whenever our bootlegger went dry ("Can't oblige just now, Mr. F. The goddam Coast Guard sank the whole shipment"), he would make his own—not in a bathtub, as was commonly done, but in one of Nellie's wash boilers. The process involved five gallons of denatured alcohol (available at most drugstores), a pound or so of grated coconut charcoal (also easily had), and a specified amount of juniper juice and other flavorings (sold in pre-measured sets at the drugstore). You sprinkled the charcoal over the alcohol in the boiler, and a great foaming ensued as the denaturing ingredient was neutralized. Then you ran the five gallons through cheesecloth, to remove the charcoal, added the flavorings, and poured the result into legitimate House of Lords gin bottles (saved up for the purpose), to deceive your friends. Not once, in my hearing, did a friend mention the deception, though Raoul considered the stuff almost undrinkable.

The Calvary for the servants, though, was not the care and maintenance of the wine cellar, nor the Himalayan masses of laundry, nor even the fourteen for dinner. It was the household's annual change of scene for the summer—to the country house or to Europe. It is hard to say which destination was more testing for the staff. In the days when Raoul was running the bakery, we had no summer house of our own. We rented one—sometimes in New London, sometimes in Oyster Bay—and that meant the transport of practically the entire contents of the New York house, since my mother did not believe that anyone who would rent his or her house to strangers could be expected to maintain a proper ménage. So everything that my mother's imagination deemed necessary for survival was packed up for transport—sheets, clothes, plates, silverware, blankets, kitchen utensils, the lot. Raoul would requisition fifteen or twenty bread crates from the bakery—big tin-and-wood containers, four feet long and three feet deep—and the female staff would spend a week or ten days packing them. On the big day, a delivery truck from the bakery would arrive, and Grady and the current butler and the bakery driver would wrestle the crates down the stairs and into the van. The truck would limp off, and we would follow more majestically in the Lincoln town car.

Then, when the family had finally departed, the house itself had to be made ready for the summer. Everybody's winter clothes, back from the cleaner's, had to be folded and moth-balled and packed in heavy fiberboard boxes. Roll-up striped awnings had to be installed over every window. The silverware that was being left behind had to be wrapped in flannel envelopes and put away in a special place in the cellar, where, presumably, no burglar could find it. Dust sheets had to be draped over the furniture. Pictures had to be lowered from their places and turned to the wall to avoid bleaching. Every lamp shade had to be removed from every lamp and wrapped. The rugs had to be sent off to the cleaner's. The mattresses had to be stood up alongside their beds and then dust-sheeted. Every year, we re-created Miss Havisham's house.

After we acquired a summer house of our own—on Long Island, in Port Washington—Mother was able to put aside her xenophobia, and moving day became much less formidable. But nothing made the trips to Europe less trying for the servants. The volume of goods to be transported was less, naturally, but the selection process was prolonged. The great steamer trunks—they stood on end and opened vertically down the middle, one side being a sort of closet with hangers and the other side a stack of drawers—would be hauled up from the cellar and distributed to the bedrooms: two for my mother, one for Raoul, one for us kids, and a spare for overflow. This was when Mother's personal maid paid her dues. Every dress—every garment—that my mother owned would be brought out and evaluated and then put back or packed. But in which trunk should it go? One trunk was the cabin trunk; the other was labeled NOT WANTED ON VOYAGE and would not be seen again until the other side. Since everyone in first class (our class, it goes without saying) dressed for dinner every night of the voyage except the first, at least four evening dresses would be required—five or six on a slow boat. Thus, many decisions had to be made, and the next day Mother would change her mind, and everything would have to be done all over again. When, finally, the contents of the trunks were 80 percent agreed upon, it was time to start on the hatboxes and shoe boxes and cosmetic cases and writing cases and lingerie cases, and ordinary suitcases. For weeks before sailing day, it was impossible to move around my mother's bedroom: "The carpet was now almost entirely hidden under layers of fine linens, layers of silk, brocade, satin, chiffon, muslin. All the colours of the rainbow, materialized by modistes, were here. And rustling quickly hither and thither, in and out of this profusion, with armfuls of finery, was an obviously French maid. [Czech in this case.] Nothing escaped her, and she never rested. She had the air of a born packer—swift and firm, yet withal tender. Scarce had her arms been laden but their loads were lying lightly in one of the many trunks—all painted 'Z.D.' ['R.G.F.', in this case]. She was one of those who are born to make chaos cosmic."

Chaos it was, but there was no extending the deadline. The piles of clothes and stacks of hats, the mounds of presents for friends and relatives abroad, the last scarf and handkerchief had to be stowed in time to meet the sailing date; the ship cast off whether you were aboard or not. This indisputable truth was borne in upon my mother in the late spring of 1928, when we were booked to sail to France on the steamer *Paris,* of the French Line. The ship was to sail at midnight in order to catch the tide—too late for the three of us children to be up. So we and the trunks and the suitcases were loaded aboard in the evening, and the three of us were put in the charge of a stewardess while Mother and Raoul went off to a farewell dinner with friends at a restaurant in town. The stewardess was agreeable but firm (she had children of her own, she said), and we went to bed without fuss.

It was later claimed by my mother that this was the night daylight-saving time came in, something that annually confused her. It seems unlikely, but, whatever the reason, she and Raoul tarried too long at the farewell dinner and missed the boat. They pulled up at the pier in a taxi, without a care in the world—and no S.S. *Paris.* My mother must have come close to expiring on the spot. The ship was still visible in midstream as it made its turn to head down the river, bearing her three children and almost every stitch of clothing she owned. Somehow, Raoul managed to engage a tugboat—maybe he bought it—and he and my mother set off down the harbor in pursuit. But the French captain was putting on speed, and even the stop at the Quarantine to drop the pilot was not enough to allow the tug to catch up.

So there the three of us were—I was ten, Steve eight, and Peter six—off to France by ourselves. The stewardess informed us of our situation the next morning. We were as chipper as birds at first, but it was not to be imagined that three children who had been orphaned in such picturesque circumstances would be allowed to enjoy their lot. Maternal instincts flowered in every female passenger's breast as our story spread through the ship, and almost instantly the nice stewardess was brushed aside in favor of committees of mothers, societies of mothers, which supervised our every waking and, no doubt, sleeping moment from then on. At table, we could not lift a fork without some surrogate Ma coaxing us and crooning over us. Never did we take so many enforced naps. Never had we been driven to bed so promptly. Never before had our toothbrushing been overseen by so many. Never before had our bowel movements been scrutinized by committee. It was a perfectly lousy crossing. Order was restored only at Le Havre, where Aunt Jo was waiting with her chauffeur and her enormous Minerva automobile to take us to her house in Paris.

Back in New York, Mother and Raoul were having a hard time finding passage—the season was at its height—and it was not until two weeks later that they were able, by brute financial force, to commandeer the captain's cabin on a German liner. The captain moved in with the first mate, and Raoul, who hated German ships, had to pay through the nose. Moreover, it turned out that the passengers on the *Paris* were not the only ones who knew of my mother's shame. Somehow, the New York newspapers heard of her children's solo voyage, and we were widely featured, with pictures—I saw the clips later. As a consequence, we kids were treated with some amusement by the household staff when we got home at the end of the summer, particularly by Dan Grady, who pretended that we were now so celebrated and important that he had to take off his cap and bow whenever we passed.

Grady was my hero. He was between coffee-colored and black—very handsome, very big, very strong—and, as I say, he worshiped my mother. On the day he became my hero, he was holding the rear door of the Lincoln town car open for her in front of the Colony restaurant (I was in the front seat), when a cabdriver behind us, who was waiting for us to pull away from the curb, leaned out of his cab and shouted something at my mother as she was getting in the car. I didn't hear what he said, but Grady did. He handed my mother into the car and then walked back to the cab. He pulled the driver out and hit him so hard his feet left the ground. Then he walked back to our car and got behind the wheel without a word, stony-faced.

Grady at this time was about thirty-five years old. He worked for us for maybe fifteen years, as chauffeur, muscle man (there was always furniture to be moved into the house or out of the house, depending on the state of my mother's decorating business), and counsel to the young. He taught all three of us brothers how to play poker, gravely taking our nickels and pennies as we learned not to draw to inside straights. These seminars would take place in the rooms above the Port Washington garage, where he and his wife, Gloria, lived in the summer. (In the winter, they lived in Brooklyn.) The garage was a wonderful, fascinating place—an enormous, sprawling building, dark brown, with cupolas and weather vanes and much Victorian filigree. There were stalls for five or six cows (we had one), and tack rooms and grain rooms and haylofts and rooms of no identifiable purpose. Its smell was an unforgettable mixture of hay, cow, and gasoline. There was room for eight cars on the ground floor, and though we had only five, taking care of them was no sinecure. The head of the line was the Lincoln—dark brown, as heavy and as boxy as a tank, with an open driver's compartment in front (a leatherette roof was buttoned in place on rainy days) and what amounted to a living room in back, complete with two flower sconces (Grady's job to keep them filled), a lap robe, reading lights in the corners, a little rack holding a carafe of water (fresh daily) and two glasses, and a speaking tube, so you could tell Grady where to go if you shouted loud enough. There was a window between the driver's compartment and the passenger salon, which you could roll down if no amount of shouting worked. The rear window was the size of a butter plate, making everything inside very dark and cozy, and on an outside rack at the very back of the car was an enormous trunk—a real trunk, with a lid and latches—for luggage. The Lincoln was the car for formal occasions or distant expeditions; for ordinary city traffic, there was a smaller town car—a Ford—with the same configuration, but on a tiny scale. Then there was my mother's two-seater Pierce Arrow roadster (with a rumble seat), and a Ford station wagon, which we kids were in most of the time in summer, and Raoul's Plymouth coupé. Grady had to keep all these cars polished and functioning, and he did so up until the start of the war, when the whole structure of the family, already rickety, broke up. Then he opened a grocery store in Great Neck and, I regret to say, got fat and drank too much.

My mother and Grady got on famously, although there were times when he strained her affection for him—notably, when she came home one afternoon and found a van from Loeser's, the big Brooklyn department store, parked in front of our house and four men loading our enormous living-room sofa into it. Our dining-room chairs were already out on the street, and inside the house, two other men were disassembling our dining-room table. "Stop that right this minute!" my mother cried. "I'm calling the police!" But there was nothing for the police to do. The Loeser's men had the right address but the wrong furniture. The furniture they had orders to repossess was Grady's, which he and Gloria had bought on the installment plan for their place in Brooklyn and had failed to pay for. Grady had given 151 East Seventy-fourth Street as his address—which, in a way, it was—when he signed the installment contract.

As for Sabine, Grady thought she was demented, and maybe she was; certainly she was temperamental. If my mother had set dinner for eight o'clock and the guests were not on their way downstairs to the dining room on the dot, Sabine would stand in the front hall and bang on a saucepan with a wooden spoon. This always produced results. Not only was my mother shamed but she knew as well as Sabine what a ten-minute delay might do to the ethereal dinner that awaited.

Sabine was the city cook. She didn't go to Port Washington in the summer; she went home to France. There was a cook in the country, of course (I've forgotten her name), as well as a kitchen maid, a luxury denied Sabine. The veteran city staff of Minna, Hedda, Nellie, and the butler du jour would be transported to the country in one big chatty mass in the Lincoln as soon as the city house had been put away for the summer, and they would be augmented by an upstairs maid (Greta, Swedish), who did beds, but not ours, and a combination parlor and upstairs maid (Alice, Alsatian). The outdoors staff consisted of a farmer/caretaker, who lived in a small farmhouse on the property (in my time, there were two successive farmers: George McLaughlin, with whose daughter Martha I used to neck in the backseat of the garaged Lincoln, and Al Wisman, with whose daughter Elsie I fell from virginity in the hayloft of the garage), and a hired man, who came in daily to milk the cow and work the enormous vegetable garden.

The servants' quarters in Port Washington were a lot better than their quarters in town, because the house had been built to our specifications, even to the point of having a servants' sitting room. The Port Washington house was huge. It was built in 1930 to replace a sprawling, rickety Victorian mansion (the garage was its coeval), and it was built big. The living room, for instance, was forty-five feet long and thirty feet wide. It had a single Savonnerie carpet that fitted it exactly; it is even possible that the room was designed around the rug. There was also a library, even though there was no more reading done in the country than in the city, and a dining room containing a Sheraton mahogany table that could seat sixteen, and often did. Less formal dining was done on a screened porch, off a much smaller wrought-iron table with a glass top. Harpo Marx, knowing my mother's edict against coming to table barefoot, and knowing that she could detect any disobedience through the glass top, defied her by showing up at lunch with pansies and cornflowers tucked between his toes. "That won't do, Harpo," my mother said, but it did. Harpo spent a lot of time at our house. He played croquet with Raoul, Averell Harriman, Alexander Woollcott, Herbert Swope, and the rest; he kissed my mother on the sofa in the library (I saw him); and he gave each of us kids a five-dollar gold piece every Christmas. There was always room in the house to put him up—there were twenty-two beds, not counting the servants'.

One of the second-floor guest rooms, with a vast double bed, was known as Mr. Woollcott's room, because, for long periods of the summer, it was. Alexander Woollcott was an odd figure—fat, weak-eyed, mincing, and yet, somehow, forceful; when he was in a room, you knew it. As drama critic of the *Times* and originator of *The New Yorker*'s "Shouts and Murmurs" department, he was a big figure in New York journalism, but he was not yet the fantastically successful radio broadcaster with the stylized, saccharine manner and text that so delighted his listeners and so offended his readers. He was generally thought to be a homosexual, but, as Raoul later told me, his trouble was physiological: He had had a severe and neutering case of mumps in his twenties. He had even wanted to marry Neysa McMein, but, of course, he couldn't, and she wouldn't, and when she married Jack Baragwanath, an almost illegally handsome black-haired mining engineer, he was devastated. He remained Neysa's friend until his death, in 1943. He probably still loved her; in any case, Jack Baragwanath couldn't stand him, just as he couldn't stand Charlie Chaplin—for better-founded reasons of sexual jealousy. In a petulant, prissy way, Woollcott also loved my mother, but he sometimes turned on her as he never would have turned on Neysa. In a gossipy *Times* piece he wrote about poker-playing among the haut monde, for instance, he added a characteristically waspish and gratuitous parenthesis: "Both Neysa McMein and Mrs. Raoul Fleischmann (known to the Middle Western press as 'Quincy's talented daughter' and 'Quincy's untalented daughter,' respectively)—both of these fair visitors played shrewdly, pocketed their winnings, and refused ever to sit in the game again."

Most of the time, my mother found Woollcott amusing, but she, too, had a bite. They played endless games of cribbage and two-handed bridge on the screened porch off the living room, gossiping and scandalizing together in great good humor, but once he said something more than scandalous—downright bitchy—about Emmy Ives, who was one of my mother's best friends and, as I can attest, just about the nicest, straightest woman around. She was also a beauty. She was the managing editor of *Vogue* (and the sister of the actor Louis Calhern), and Woollcott intimated that she had used some sexual chicanery to land an advertisement in her magazine. (I heard all this from a corner of the porch, where I was getting my weekly fix of *Collier's*.) My mother went straight up in the air. She and Woollcott were playing cribbage at the time, and she threw the scoring board on the floor and said, "Alec, you can leave this house right now. I'll have Grady drive you to the station. I want you out of here in ten minutes. If there's no train, you can wait on the platform." She meant it, and he knew she meant it, and he left. They did not speak for more than five years, but it was too late to do anything about changing the name of his room.

Another regular at the Port Washington house was George Abbott, who was sharing a house with Neysa McMein and Jack Baragwanath on Sands Point, nearby. He died in 1995, at the age of 107. In 1987, when he was one hundred, he directed a revival of *Broadway,* a play that he directed (and wrote, with Philip Dunning) in 1926. In 1932, when he was forty-five and I was fifteen, he directed me in a movie. It was shot at our place in Port Washington—the movie script called for a classy, affluent setting—and the star was Tallulah Bankhead. Abbott was already a big name on Broadway, and went on to become an even bigger one, though not with this picture. (*The Boys from Syracuse, Damn Yankees, On Your Toes, Pal Joey,* and at least a hundred other shows were written, directed, and/or produced by him.) While I didn't care one way or the other about Abbott, I was entranced by Tallulah, particularly by her husky, deep voice. Also by her language; she was the first woman I ever heard say "shit." Abbott, who was an austere and New Englandish sort of man (he was born in upstate New York), had a lot of trouble directing her. Her mind always seemed to be on something else. He would spend ten minutes showing her how he wanted her to walk stiffly into a room (the room was our library, all lit up for the occasion), like a woman expecting a rebuff, and then, with the cameras rolling, she would walk in any old way, with a big smile. He would protest, she would plead, "George, darling, can't we just get on with it?" he would say no, and they would do it again.

I was much easier to direct. My part consisted of sitting on the porch steps and bouncing a tennis ball; there were some possibly more important actors on the lawn in front of me, but I was concentrating on my role too hard to notice. Unfortunately, my art (and Tallulah's and George Abbott's) was wasted. The picture was a bust—its title, *My Sin,* could have been the reason—and it was withdrawn from the movie theaters almost overnight. I never saw it even once. But Tallulah was in it, and that was enough for me. All during the week or ten days she worked at our place, my enslavement grew, but eventually, of course, the black day came: the shooting was over, and Tallulah would leave. I ran into her in the living room. Be debonair, I told myself.

"So it's all over," I said. "You must be terribly lucky."

"Yes," she said, looking at me in some puzzlement. "Good-bye." And she shook my hand and walked away.

I could hardly believe my own stupidity. "Lucky!" I yelled at myself. "What kind of sense does that make? 'Pleased' is the word! 'You must be terribly pleased.' Then she would have said, 'The only pleasure was meeting you,' or something like that." It was quite plain to me that if only I had said "pleased" instead of "lucky," she would be known as Tallulah Botsford today.

From the Beasley School I should have gone to high school, which in our house meant prep school, but my mother had a new worry: I was too short. This time, she decided that a vigorous outdoor life was the remedy, and off I was shipped to the Fresnal Ranch School, about fifty miles from Tucson, Arizona. It was the fall of 1931; I was fourteen years old. I have no idea how my mother heard of the place, but it was certainly not what she had in mind. It was a parent's dismay and a schoolboy's dream, since it was only nominally a school and in actuality a working ranch, with many thousands of acres of range and about six hundred head of cattle. What my mother and the mothers of the ten or fifteen other students were unwittingly paying for was the indenturing of their sons as cowhands. There was a bare modicum of scholastic instruction—in those days, college-entrance exams were given at the end of every high-school year, and the headmaster/ranch owner had to at least pretend to be concerned about them—but our real role was with the cattle. The school year started with three weeks of pedagogy, but then it was time for the fall roundup, and we were transformed into cowhands. One Mexican professional could have replaced the lot of us to advantage, but we came cheaper. Free, in fact. And when the Fresnal herd had finally been tallied, we moved on to our neighbors' ranches to help do the same thing for them.

It was a marvelous life, but the piper had to be paid. In my case, the piper was the College Entrance Examination Board, and I paid his fee that spring on a hot June morning in a classroom at Columbia University, where I and maybe a hundred other high-school freshmen were examined in algebra. It was a nightmare; I knew nothing. Never before had I sat for two hours in an examination room and not known one single thing. I'm sure the 13 I got for a mark was charity; I certainly didn't know 13 percent of what I was asked. Fortunately, the practice of annual college-entrance exams was abandoned a bit later, and my shame was forgotten.

Because I had grown half an inch a month during my stay in Arizona, my mother pronounced me fit for more conventional schooling. (She also knew about the 13 in algebra.) So off I was shipped to Hotchkiss. Why she chose Hotchkiss over Andover or

Choate or Groton, I don't know, but if she was looking for academic rigor, she got it. The work was hard; it was endless; it was impossible. For the first time in my life, I really had to study, and study I did, for three years. At the end of my senior year, I took my final school exams and the now-consolidated college-entrance exams; the school exams were the harder by far, and I did fine.

The year was now 1935—five years into the Great Depression. Breadlines. Gangsters. Speakeasies. Though Prohibition had been repealed two years earlier, speakeasies were still part of the fabric of New York life; the only difference was that they now operated as legitimate nightclubs and restaurants. All the jazz joints on West Fifty-second Street—Jack White's, Leon & Eddie's, the Famous Door, the Onyx Club—were former speakeasies. Sherman Billingsley, who owned the Stork Club, on Fifty-third, was that rarity, a WASP bootlegger. At 21 West Fifty-second was "21," originally the retail outlet of a pair of bootleggers named Jack Kriendler and Charlie Berns. It had a trick bar to defeat snooping Prohibition agents; at the push of a secret button, the shelves behind the bar would tip forward and dump all the illegal bottles of booze into a concrete pit that opened up in the floor below. After Prohibition, "21" became the trendiest restaurant in New York. It was also one of the most difficult of entry, but not for me, because Murray Seiderman, the man on the door, used to sell me Baby Ruth peanut bars when I was going to school and he was the pharmacist at the Whelan's drugstore on our corner.

Equally difficult of entry was another former speakeasy—the Colony, on East Sixty-third Street. Its owner, Gene Cavallero, who once welcomed all sorts of raffish lawbreakers, now made outrageous use of his reservations book to keep out inferior persons. It was in an upstairs private room at the Colony, at a regular meeting of the Thanatopsis Marching and Inside Straight Club, that Raoul Fleischmann met Harold Ross, over a poker table. Raoul was an ardent gambler. He played high-stakes poker and was busy at the racetracks. In 1926, when the struggling *New Yorker* was about to go under and he had exhausted his own finances, he raided his sisters' trust funds, of which he was the custodian and trustee, gambling that the magazine would succeed and he would be able to put things right. He won that bet, but by law he should have been indicted.

The Colony was also my mother's favorite restaurant, both because it was unquestionably the best restaurant in town and because it was close to the office of her decorating business, on Fifty-eighth Street. She was a serious decorator. She took courses at some school downtown (I imagine she was the only scholar there who was driven to class by her chauffeur), where the curriculum was exacting, with periodic exams. When she graduated, she apprenticed out to a well-known decorator named Isobel Shotter, and then set up her own business, under the name Chez Vous, with offices and showroom on the second floor of 20 East Fifty-eighth Street. Some of her jobs took her out of town for long periods—to South Carolina, for instance, where she redid Bernard Baruch's house, Hobcaw Barony, from top to bottom. Whenever she had a big job in hand, she would use our house on Seventy-fourth Street as a test site for the furniture she was considering; if it satisfied her when in place and in use, it would be sent on to the client. If it didn't satisfy her, it would be returned to the dealer, and if the dealer wouldn't have it back, it was used to furnish the brand-new offices of *The New Yorker*. These tidal changes in domestic decor meant that our furniture was always in transit—whole rooms at a time. Every so often, when I came home from school, I would think I was in the wrong house.

Being home from school always meant at least a couple of lunches with my mother at the Colony, where she went two or three times a week. One of the things about the Colony that appealed to her was that no money ever changed hands there; in fact, the waiter never even presented a check. The charges were simply and silently carried forward, along with a percentage for the tip, until the end of the month, when a thick engraved card, bearing a single figure in a copper-plate hand, would arrive in the mail. Nine times out of ten, my mother would not have had enough money to pay the bill anyway. (Credit cards, of course, did not yet exist.) Her financial habits were extremely erratic; some days, she would have as much as a thousand dollars in her purse (I counted it once), but most of the time she was penniless and had to borrow a dollar from me or Steve, or even from Gene Cavallero, to tip the ladies' room maid. The Colony's ladies' room was the only public bathroom in the city that she would use. When she was going around town on business, she would have Grady drive her home from Macy's or an auction gallery or wherever so she could sit on her own familiar toilet; then he would drive her back.

After I graduated from Hotchkiss, my mother, for the first time in my life, had nothing to say about my further education. In the absence of a directive, I, of course, did nothing. I had ties at Williams, where my father had gone and where various Botsfords had been going since the Bronze Age, but Williamstown was much too far from New York, where the action was. Eighty percent of my class at Hotchkiss had signed up for Yale, so when my mother asked me my plans, I said I thought I would probably go to Yale. But it never occurred to me to *do* anything about any of this—I sent no applications, I made no inquiries. Instead, I went to France with the family. In the middle of August, we were back, and my mother, noting the date, asked me if I'd heard from Yale. Well, no, I said. I did not add that Yale had not heard from me, either. I could see from her attitude, however, that I had better get hopping. So I hopped. I had no application papers, and I didn't know the dean of admissions from Herbert Hoover, but the Depression was still on, and getting into college (if one was academically up to the mark) was about as difficult as getting on the Staten Island ferry. In any case, I hopped so well that within three weeks I was an accredited member of the freshman class, and in six weeks I was in New Haven, for the first time in my life, moving into Durfee Hall.

For anybody who had graduated from Hotchkiss, the freshman courses at Yale were laughably easy, and I consequently laughed my way down to New York with regularity. My mother was not all that glad to see me, but I was not there to see my mother. I was more likely headed for Café Society, on Sheridan Square, or the Ubangi Club, on Seventh Avenue around 130th Street, where an enormous black woman named Gladys Bentley would visit among the tables, singing dirty lyrics to "You're the Top." Or Dickie Wells's after-hours place, where Choo Berry played the saxophone against Wells's trombone, and the rest of the band played kazoos, presumably for reasons of economy.

Café Society. Dickie Wells. The Ubangi. I now wonder how I I was able to afford all that. I certainly wasn't overburdened with cash. In the fall of 1935, when I started Yale, I was put on a monthly allowance of $125, out of which I was to pay for everything—tuition, books, room and board, clothes, frivolities. Only medical bills were on the house. My mother opened a checking account for me at the Guaranty Trust Company that year (I am now their oldest private customer), and she paid in the $125 monthly. There were no extras. Tuition at Yale was about $450 a year, and room and board about $600. This left me around forty dollars a month for clothes, books, midnight snacks, movies at Loew's Poli, drinks, and the Ubangi Club. I managed to make do; in fact, I made do so well that in my sophomore year, my mother invited herself to New Haven for the Brown football game and passed the afternoon in my room cutting my allowance. She was so draconian that I was hog-tied for weeks—even Loew's Poli was out. She relented when I got on the dean's list at the end of the term, no doubt as a result of my unaccustomed steady presence in New Haven.

My family—as I came to realize in later years—was undeniably rich. Because of the Fleischmann name, everybody assumed that we were rich solely on yeast money, and it is true that Raoul had inherited barrels of the stuff. (His father, however, was a cadet in the Fleischmann hierarchy and in the second tier of Fleischmann affluence. Raoul could not have emulated one of his cousins in the first tier, who built himself the largest private oceangoing vessel in the world right after the war.) Yet I would not be surprised if my mother's family was just as rich as Raoul's, even though nobody outside Quincy ever heard of them. If the center of your family's being is deep in Illinois, and if what you do is make pumps, your name hardly resounds in the big world out there. However, those pumps pumped cash, and they must have eased Raoul's mind when it came time to draw up his will. He was an uncommonly generous man, but he was also a strong believer in the perpetuation of one's family name and fortune. Because his two stepsons were so well provided for by the busy pumps, he could in good conscience leave everything he owned—cash, stock, and barrel—to his own son, Peter, and he did so.

For the Gardner family, everything started with the Gardner governor, a device invented in 1859 by my great-grandfather Robert Gardner to control steam engines. He was a Scot and had a degree in engineering from the University of Edinburgh, and I have no idea how he got to Quincy. But he did, and opened a bicycle shop there, from which emerged, in time—he was an indefatigable tinkerer—the celebrated governor. Until then, steam power—which ran everything from railroad locomotives to threshing machines to oil-well drilling rigs—would all too often run away with itself at the moment the load on it was lifted. A locomotive hauling a freight train up a mountain pass might crest the rise and then race uncontrollably down the other side. The danger of sudden release was particularly acute in the oil fields, where the risk of fire was always present. Great-grandfather Gardner's invention somehow cured all that, and soon a Gardner governor was de rigueur on steam engines all over the world.

Robert Gardner's son, J. Willis Gardner, my grandfather, expanded the Gardner Governor Company enormously, and branched out into pumps, mining machinery, and air compressors.

He and my grandmother (née Gifford, the daughter of a railroad conductor) lived in an imposing house on Quincy's Maine Street: red brick, with wings, dozens of rooms, and an apple orchard out back. There were five or six resident servants, even a resident seamstress, who was actually called "Tweenie"; the coachman, later chauffeur, was Henry, who taught me how to ride a bicycle, giving me a push down the ramp of the garage. The most interesting car in the garage was Grandmother's Baker Electric, which looked exactly the same front and rear, and went just as fast (about eight miles an hour) in either direction. It was steered not by a wheel but by a tiller, and on the Fourth of July, Henry would weave strips of red, white, and blue crepe paper through the spokes of its wheels. Grandmother actually drove this thing around the streets of Quincy; she had the look of riding in a sedan chair. She was an indomitable woman; when she was fourteen, she shot a burglar in the shoulder with her father's pistol (Illinois railroad conductors were armed in those days), and then tied him up to await the police.

There were three Gardner children—Marion, a solid 160-pounder, all bosoms and corsets when I knew her; Ralph, a wimp; and my mother, the youngest, born in 1894, and the only one who left Quincy permanently. There were ten of us cousins in the next generation—three by Marion, sired by Archie Rogers, one of the 500,000 Americans who died in the flu epidemic just after the First World War; four by Ralph; and three by my mother. In my teens, we of the eastern branch would often go to Quincy for Christmas. It was not a simple journey. It meant taking the overnight Twentieth Century Limited from New York to Chicago; using up half a day in Chicago while waiting for a train to Davenport, Iowa; and then, in Davenport, taking a train that followed the west bank of the Mississippi down to Quincy and Tom Sawyer country. Quincy, a few miles upstream from Hannibal, Missouri, was the Illinois town that Tom and Huck Finn crossed to, dressed as girls, while hiding out on the island in the river; in our day, the locomotive of the Davenport-Quincy train was called "Engine Joe."

Quincy was a dead end; the train had to back across the river bridge to reach the station, since there was only one way in and one way out, and nothing improved over the years. In 1950, when Steve and Peter and I took our mother's ashes to Quincy for burial, we still had to lay over for half a day—a Sunday at that—in Chicago, and back into the station at Quincy. That layover almost lost us our mother. Chicago is not a great place to spend half a Sunday if you have nothing to do. We dispiritedly wandered the streets for a while, carrying Mother in her urn, and when we came across a movie theater where the stage show was just about to start, we bought tickets and went in. It was eleven o'clock in the morning, and the theater was empty except for the three of us and maybe five other people, all of whom seemed to be asleep. The lights went down, the curtain went up, and there onstage was Orrin Tucker's sixteen-piece orchestra doing its stuff. The MC, wearing a dinner jacket and throwing smiles all around the empty house, loped in from the wings to introduce the star attraction—Wee Bonnie Baker, who would sing her top-o'-the-charts hit, "If I'd Known You Were Coming I'd Have Baked a Cake." And out sailed Wee Bonnie, in a bouffant evening dress and outsmiling even the MC. Orrin Tucker, frantic with joy and energy, waved his baton at his employees, and Wee Bonnie, now flirtatious, now adorable, sang her wee heart out for her audience of eight, most of them asleep. The whole thing was so disorienting that when we left (we skipped the movie), we forgot Ma in her urn under one of the seats, and we had almost got back to the station before somebody remembered.

In earlier times, the focal point of our Christmas visits to Quincy was the family breakfast on the day itself, nine o'clock sharp. Grandmother would command the presence of every family member in the region, whatever the degree of consanguinity, and every one of them would come, and be on time: Grandmother was not a person to be crossed, especially with the dreadful presence of Grandfather behind her. He was a tough, hard man, a classic midwestern Republican businessman, whose view of the world was limited to what could be seen through the window of his accounting office. His adversary to the death was the tax collector—the tax collector and government profligacy. When it came to business matters, he was all business, even when writing to his own daughter. "Sincerely yours, J. W. Gardner" is the way he ended a letter he wrote my mother on the subject nearest his heart in the fall of 1942.

Dear Ruth:

I do not know to what extent your children profit by your financial advice, but I feel it is your duty to call their attention to the probable decrease in your income.

. . . It is so easy to slip into extravagant practices, and nearly every one of your children [there were only three] is driving an automobile that cost as much, or more, as the one that you drive. They are so spoiled that they can't even cross the street without hopping in their automobile to make the journey. [At the time he wrote, all three of the feckless children were in the Army, on foot.]

You know already what the government has done with its tax program. Taxes are bound to increase a great deal more, and unless you and your children put into effect the most drastic economies, you are all going to be forced to retrench.

The government is practically spending two or three dollars for every one it collects, so you can see there is no exaggeration in my statement when I speak of economy.

I think you should read this letter to your children at occasional intervals, and if they won't heed it, they will be the ones who will have to suffer.

Sincerely yours,
J. W. Gardner

Grandfather and Grandmother owned Quincy, and they knew it. So, as the carriage clock on the mantel struck nine on Christmas morning, some forty or fifty people would sit down to breakfast. The sliding doors between the dining room and the parlor would have been opened, and the dining room table extended by means of boards and trestles to the full length of both rooms. Breakfast was gargantuan: ham and bacon, kippers and sausages, hot biscuits, jams and rhubarb, fried eggs, scrambled eggs, boiled eggs, smoked Mississippi River catfish, waffles and maple syrup, cut-up fruit, hash brown potatoes, pitchers of coffee, cream, tea, cocoa, and milk. Everybody ate; few enjoyed. I certainly didn't. For one thing, I generally had a hangover, the product of an evening spent at a local bar called the Oil Can with my cousins Helen and Eleanor Rogers—Marion's children. The seasonal special there was the Tom and Jerry, an eggnoggish sort of drink, heavy with bourbon. Delicious and lethal. Helen was about three years older than me, so she was welcome at the Oil Can, and Eleanor and I got in under her chaperonage; the fact that she was an incandescent sort of girl who exerted an electrical charge on every male within range didn't hurt, and neither did the fact that we all were grandchildren of J. Willis Gardner, proprietor of Quincy.

After breakfast came the central set piece of the day: Grandfather's annual distribution of Christmas dollars. He would take up his position in an armchair in the living room, with a foot-high stack of brand-new dollar bills on a table by his side. One by one, each member of the revel would come forward and be wished a merry Christmas and given one dollar for every year of his or her acknowledged age—"acknowledged," because vanity was very often balanced against greed, causing a good deal of whinnying and tittering among the ladies present. Since every single person in the house, from Tweenie on down, was eventually accorded the dollar benediction, this ceremony took a long time, and I yearned to be back in the Oil Can with Eleanor and Helen.

* * *

My sophomore year at Yale was the standard disaster. I signed up for all the wrong courses, taught by instructors I grew to loathe. Furthermore, I had spent the summer after freshman year as a horse wrangler on a dude ranch between Reno and Carson City, Nevada (my apprenticeship as a cowboy at the Fresnal Ranch School helped me get the job), and I had fallen in love with a prospective divorcée named Nell Hastings, who was putting in her six-week Nevada residency at the ranch. She was two or three years older than me, but that meant nothing—not to me anyway—and we spent a lot of time in Reno, staying up too late at the gambling palaces and bars (I had to be out rounding up the guests' horses at seven in the morning), and in Carson City, where there was one solitary bar, with the obligatory slot machines and roulette wheel. The owner of the place was a very tough man named Sid, who had a badly scarred face. ("Knife fight," he said electrifyingly.) To Nell and me, however, he was nothing less than amiable, mostly because there was never anybody else in the place. The two of us spent a lot of time there, playing the jukebox (Vincent Youmans's "Time on My Hands," over and over), and listening to Sid's stories of his gambling days. He showed us how to double-deal at blackjack and advised us never to play the game. One evening, out of boredom, he invited us to play a few spins of the roulette wheel. Nell said she wouldn't think of playing roulette with a man who had just showed her how to cheat at blackjack. "No, no," Sid said. "This is on the level, among friends." So we sat at the table and played for dollars. On the first spin, single zero came up, and we were cleaned. On the second, double zero. "Goddam!" Sid said, and kicked the table. On the third spin, double zero again. "That's all," Sid said. "Game's over. Take your money back. Something's gone wrong with the wiring." I never again played a roulette wheel in this country, and sometimes I wonder about the French wheels.

When I had to go back to college, Nell was still a couple of weeks away from her divorce hearing, and she stayed on. New Haven seemed very drab. Then Nell got her divorce and instantly married a guy she had never once mentioned to me.

It was a poor year all around, and it didn't improve in the summer, when John Reed and Bill Sweney and I decided to go on a bicycle trip through Europe. At the last minute, John Reed's mother said that we would have to take along the son of a great friend of hers, who was also a classmate of ours—Charles ("Rose") Hulburd, whom I had known since Hotchkiss and thoroughly detested. But he came, and ruined the trip. This was the summer of 1937, and Hitler was in full cry in Germany. We went there anyway, after touring through England and France, and Rose loved the country—all the daggers and uniforms and discipline and guns. He got a special frisson from the stony SS soldier who stood at attention, as if a statue, under a plaque marking a spot in Munich where some Nazi thug had been killed in a failed putsch; everyone who passed by, whether on foot, in a car, or on a bus, was supposed to raise an arm in the Nazi salute. Rose saluted like an automaton; we three didn't, and got shouted at. He almost wept with emotion the night we went to a Nazi rally in a gigantic open stadium outside Munich. Hitler was there, standing on a brightly lit elevated tribune at the end of the stadium while battalions of torch-bearing SS and SA troops paraded in front of him. Giant searchlights swept their beams around the packed stadium and the night sky, reflecting off the roiling smoke from the torches. Drums and swastika banners were everywhere, huge drums en masse, pounding in unison, slowly, and the crowd kept to the beat: *"Sieg Heil! Sieg Heil!"* Rose was in a trance. We were so far away that we could barely see the speck that was Hitler on the podium, but we could hear him, deafeningly amplified. I couldn't understand anything he said, but what he meant was clear enough. John and Bill felt as I did, and the next day the three of us threw our bicycles into the luggage van of a train and headed back to France. Rose stayed on, enjoying.

Back in genial France, we toured around a bit and then split up. Sweney and Reed went home, and I went to Normandy to spend ten days with my friend Peter Dewey at his place on the Channel, not far from Bayeux. The Deweys were from Chicago and had a lot of money. When Mr. Dewey, an amateur medievalist and a former U.S. ambassador to Poland, bought the property, many years earlier, it was an impoverished farm, but he was convinced from his studies that the farm was a present-day mutation of a thirteenth-century abbey—the Abbaye Sainte-Marie. After a lot of research and archaeological earth-moving, this theory proved to be true, and when I was there a French artisan was at work gently scraping the walls of what had once been the monks' refectory and more recently was the henhouse. Scraping and dusting and scraping, he was slowly, slowly, bringing forth a remarkable wall painting depicting a Crusader (possibly the patron of the monks, possibly the abbot himself) accoutred for his expedition to Jerusalem. There was much scraping and dusting yet to be done, but one could already see that Peter's father had fallen upon a treasure. In fact, the whole place was now a treasure, nicely balanced between its antique past and its modern comforts. Sitting on the terrace during the long twilight summer evenings, looking out over the same Normandy fields that had sustained the monks seven hundred years ago, one could envy them their uncomplicated lives, but envy stopped short as one climbed into one of the Deweys' luxurious guest-room beds, with a fine bathroom hard by. Altogether, it was not a bad spot to spend a gorgeous ten days in August.

That was the summer of 1937; by the summer of 1940, the Abbaye Sainte-Marie was a German regimental headquarters. Then in June of 1944, the First Division landed on Omaha Beach, only a couple of miles away. About a week after the landing, I was in Bayeux on Army business, and I decided to look in at the abbey, only a step farther on. To my surprise, two of the Dewey maids were still in residence—women in their fifties, natural-born family-retainer types. They were deeply suspicious of me at first—they had little use for soldiers after four years of the Wehrmacht in the house—but when I uttered the magic name Dewey, they fell upon me joyfully. They even said they recognized me, but they were in such a state of nerves after the confusion, noise, and fright of the invasion that I think they would have said they recognized the president of Turkey.

They had not had a happy time of it. The senior Deweys had gone back to Chicago in the summer of 1939, when war seemed imminent, and for a while letters came through regularly. But then, in the summer of 1940, the Germans moved in to stay. The other members of the household staff quite sensibly disappeared, leaving only the two of them in place; they could not desert the Deweys, who would someday come back and expect to find the abbey in good condition. The Germans had kept both of them on as servants, and life had been bearable—but what animals the Germans were! They had carted off all Mr. Dewey's books, drunk the cellar dry, and left a mess everywhere. I asked after the Crusader, and they took me to him. The Germans had used the refectory as their mess hall, and after dinner, from the look of things, they must have hacked away at the wall painting with their knives and forks. Not only that: they had laid on their own paint, adding mustaches and such to the old boy. That, of course, was the end of him—another victim of the war.

In fact, the war was the end of everything for the Deweys. Peter's father died shortly after his return to Chicago, and Peter himself, who was in the OSS, was killed in Indochina at the very end of the war; he may have been the last American soldier to lose his life in that theater.

The winter of 1937–1938, my junior year at Yale, was the winter I didn't go to Brenda Frazier's coming-out party. She was the ultimate debutante, with her picture on the cover of *Life* and clouds of press agents and photographers trailing her wherever she went. Wherever she went, I sometimes went, too, but my brother Steve's treachery caused my name to be stricken from society's rolls, and I wasn't asked to her party. Until he put an end to my social career, I went happily to dozens of deb parties, each one bigger and more elaborate than the last. They were like dinosaurs: the bigger they got, the closer they drew to extinction. Nowadays, they seem like the stuff of myth, and even then they were hard to believe. The fact that a perfectly rational businessman from Toledo or Harrisburg or Chattanooga would rent an apartment in Manhattan (necessarily of considerable size and consequence) and send his wife and daughter to live in it for five or six months, with absolutely no aim beyond producing a single evening of great expense and deep boredom for himself and of social anguish for his daughter, was, and is, simply incredible. But it happened. Mother and daughter would move in during the early fall and go shopping. The immediate requirement would be dresses for the "little season," in October—tea dances, generally, and at the Plaza, preferably. Then they would lay in the heavy artillery—eighteen full ball gowns for the big season, which stretched from December 16 to January 7, with only Sundays and Christmas Day off. I am knowledgeable in these matters because of Patsy Foss, a Brearley senior I was much interested in. It was her season for a coming-out party, and she had added up what the event would cost in order to persuade her father to forego the party and buy her the car she wanted instead. No such luck: no car, and no party either, since, as he pointed out, she was already a New York girl, and so not in need of artificial stimuli. New York girls would be invited to the dances, since they were New York girls, and the point of the whole operation was to give the party a New York cachet. More important, of course, was the fact that the New York girls acted as bait for the New York boys, who were what the whole operation was *really* about. We New York drones drank and danced entirely at the expense of out-of-towners, not one of whom we had ever heard of before.

With as many as 150 guests, a proper coming-out party was no small affair. Mrs. Harrisburg, if she was energetic and dictatorial, could no doubt have brought it off by herself; what she couldn't do was supply the necessary boys. There she was entirely dependent on two sources: Miss Juliana Cutting and the firm of Mesdames Tappin and Tew. They had lists upon lists of arrogant, spoiled, unprincipled young men (like me), who could more or less be counted on to show up in white tie and tails. It was one of these lists that caused my social banishment. Early in the fall, the ladies would send out questionnaires to names culled from class yearbooks of the haughtier prep schools, from the freshman-enrollment records of the haughtier colleges, from the *Social Register,* and so on. Each young drone was asked to set forth his name, his address, his age, his school or college, and his nickname—"because so many girls ask for boys by their nicknames." (The ladies never faltered in their insistence that their young drones were bona fide friends, or at least acquaintances, of their clients.) On this occasion, my questionnaire for the coming season arrived when I was away. However, Steve wasn't away, and he undertook to fill it out for me. He was cut-and-dried when dealing with my name and address and school, but when he got to my nickname, he allowed his thoughts to roam, and then wrote in "Prick." His success was total. I never got another invitation.

Of all the tribulations I inflicted on my mother, I think my career as a debs' delight and lounge lizard was the most testing. She looked upon the deb-party scene with derision and hilarity, and since there was no hope of getting her to contribute financially to my adornment, I had to buy everything myself, which I did, on the cheap. I got my tails from a New Haven tailor for forty-five dollars; they didn't fit, but when he offered to throw in a tuxedo jacket as well, I couldn't say no. My roommate sold me his opera hat for six dollars; it was half a size too big, but it collapsed nicely. Starched-front dress shirts cost a fortune, so I had only one. Nellie, the laundress, refused to wash it more than once or twice a season, and by the time the season was half over, it had black bull's-eyes around the three buttonholes on the shirtfront. Raoul, in his efforts to make a gentleman of me, kept telling me to wash my hands before I put the studs in the shirt, but I kept forgetting.

It says a great deal for my mother's and Raoul's tact and social skills that they could maintain their composure when I stopped by to say good night in my droopy tails and bull's-eye shirt, with my opera hat held up by my ears.

The deb-party drill was that Alice, the commodity on display that evening, would stand in a receiving line with her father and mother and greet the family's throng of friends, few of whom they had ever seen before. For identifications, they were dependent upon a stentorian butler who announced each guest—just as in the movies. He would bend his head to me as I came up, and I would tell him my name. "Mr. Garner Buffer," he would intone, and Mrs. Harrisburg would brightly shake my hand and say, "We're so glad to see you, Mr. Buffer. I think you know my daughter Alice?" "Yes, of course," I would lie. "How are you, Alice? Wonderful party." And Alice would shake my hand speechlessly. What, after all, could she say? I was a complete stranger to her, and right behind me was an endless Indian file of other complete strangers. She may have wondered about the bull's-eyes on my shirtfront, but she was too well brought up to ask questions, so she said nothing and smiled, and I said nothing and smiled, and then I moved on to shake the hand of the poor boob who was paying for all this.

In the fall of my junior year, I started writing a humor column for the *Yale Daily News*—"Once Over Lightly" (I don't know who picked the title)—three times a week. It was a lot of work, but it was also a great success. I became a campus celeb. I was asked to join the Pundits, a literary and eating group started by William Lyon Phelps, which met once a week at Mory's for determinedly intellectual lunches, and also the Elizabethan Club, which I liked, and also a cheerful, informal group called the Phoenix, which met every Thursday for dinner in one or another of the private dining rooms of the second-rate hotels on Chapel Street. The food was invariably dreadful, but the wine never ran short.

One of my fellow Phoenicians was Bill Verity—Calvin William Verity, Jr.—the business manager of the *Yale Daily News.* When the *News* divided up its profits toward the end of our senior year, he and I both made a nice bit of money—he from selling advertising, I from writing my column. It was, I thought, well-earned money, and I was determined to do something satisfying with it. Verity, one of the freest of free spirits, was of like mind. Not for us the banks and brokerage houses and manufacturing companies that would soon be swallowing up our classmates. I wanted to be—though not just yet—a journalist, like those funny, sardonic reporters in *The Front Page.* Verity wanted to be—who knows what Verity wanted to be, but it was not a company man in the Ohio steel town he came from. The only project that seemed to fit our immediate needs, we decided (I cannot explain why), was a trip around the world.

There were two obstacles. The first was the inevitable parental injunction to stop fooling around and get a job. Verity's father was insisting that he go to work at the American Rolling Mills, a steel company in Middletown, Ohio, founded by Bill's grandfather. My mother was insisting that I get a job anywhere, as long as it was right away. The second obstacle—and it was indeed in second place—was the war looming in Europe. In those innocent times, the event that was going to turn every one of our lives upside down was as nothing compared to the ogre of parental displeasure. In the end, we couldn't find the nerve to face the ogre, so we simply stole away in the night without telling anyone of our plans (except Steve, who promised *omertà*). First stop Honolulu, then on to Japan and China.

Our unprecedented act of defiance was noted, of course, at the first bed check in Middletown and New York. Bill's father grumbled and snarled and promised reprisals, but my mother's response was not so Neanderthal. She saw a game in prospect. If I thought I could flit about the world without her knowing where I was or where I was going, I could think again. She relished any sort of game or contest, and I had presented her with a fine one.

She was good at games—a first-class bridge player, and the best bluffer I ever encountered at poker. She would bet on anything. One evening at dinner in New York, she bet Raoul forty dollars—every penny she could find in her purse—that the sound we heard outside was not rain but the rustle of leaves in the backyard, and she won. Her first move in her contest with me was ingenious. By the end of the week, using her unimpaired talent for charming public and private servants, she had acquired what amounted to a personal overseas telephone operator, charged with finding me for a person-to-person phone call. The operator's name was Geraldine (Steve reported later), and during the six months we were gone, she became almost a member of the family. She would check in regularly with my mother to discuss strategy, and together they would go over my letters for clues. I wrote home regularly (bad conscience), but, as my part in the contest, I wrote like the backward-flying bird: I reported extensively on where I had been but never on where I was going. Every now and then, I incautiously mentioned a hotel I had stayed at—Frank Lloyd Wright's Imperial Palace in Tokyo, Raffles in Singapore—and Geraldine would get the hotel on the line to see if anybody there knew when and where I had gone. That was how she finally nailed me, in Sydney, at the very end of our trip. We were living in a rented apartment we had found through a Sydney acquaintance of Fred Koch, our previous innkeeper, in Bali. Koch had put Geraldine on the trail, and before I could think of a single dodge, she had my mother on the line. Ma had homered in the ninth.

I don't know what I expected to hear from her—a crow of triumph? A mock-serious wigging?—but what I got was neither. Something had changed, and what I got was tearful entreaty.

"Please come home," she said almost timidly. "Now—while you can. All those Russian submarines . . ."

What had happened to her? *Please* come home? Russian submarines? Where was the old bubble and spirit, the old delight in a game? Well, I knew what had happened. It was the war in

Europe—not the war as it was but the war as she saw it through the filter of Peter Vischer. In world affairs, she was a complete innocent, and when he told her what to think, she thought it. Although he was not an out-and-out Nazi (his line was "Adolf Hitler is a disgrace, but we must take a long view of history"), he was certainly a thoroughgoing Teuton. He never let up on the glories and destiny of the German people, or on the power and majesty of their arms. (His sister, Rotraut, who worked at one of the big New York publishing houses, apparently *was* an out-and-out Nazi: according to her brother, she sent a tithe of her monthly paycheck to the party in Berlin.) To my mother, politics and world affairs were about as interesting as old motor oil. While she was married to Raoul, their *vie* was the sort of moneyed *vie de bohème* practiced in New York and London and Paris—summers in Le Touquet, winters in Jamaica, weekends at Antibes or in Surrey. (I have a wonderful picture of her earnestly reading *Vogue* on the beach at Antibes.) This was the life she was made for, and the charm started leaking out of it when she and Raoul were divorced. And on September 1, 1939, the outbreak of war blew away everything that was left of it. She never adapted to the new world, and she never fit in. If my mother had hit the apogee of her life and times with Raoul Fleischmann, Peter Vischer, who found in her an unresisting sponge for his *realpolitik,* was the director of its downward skid. On the other hand, it must be said that she would have been an equally easy mark for a devotee of *New Masses* or the *Daily Worker.* Politics held no meaning for her (neither did history or any part of science). She was undoubtedly a liberal—an instinctive liberal, uninstructed and without an agenda, who, as far as I know, never voted in her life. Dorothy Thompson and Walter Lippmann would have despaired of her. She and her colorful friends were serious enough about their art or craft—writing, painting, composing, editing, acting, decorating—but their world stopped there. Up against an ideologue like Vischer, my mother didn't stand a chance, and when he told her that the Nazi-Soviet pact had made the German cause invincible, and scared the wits out of her with talk about the Russian submarines in the Pacific, she believed him. So *please* come home.

As it happened, Verity and I already had our tickets home. We had no place else to go; the war in Europe had shut down the possibility of visas. Yet there *was* no war—or no real war. Instead, there was a Rover Boys sort of conflict, exciting rather than dangerous. ("Royal Air Force planes carried out reconnaissance flights over enemy positions in the Saar. All our aircraft returned safely.") The French, who were in it, called it *"une drôle de guerre."* True, things had gone badly in Poland, but the common view—my view—was that while Hitler might have succeeded against the antiquated Polish cavalry, he would be a dead duck when he came up against the British and French heavyweights on the Maginot Line. Nor could he push east against Russia (everybody knew the Nazi-Soviet pact was a sham), because the German and Russian railroad tracks had different gauges, which made the Russian tracks useless to an invader. Meanwhile, the British naval blockade would reduce Germany to starvation.

I believed in this comforting fantasy as firmly as I believed in the first day of spring. The possibility that Peter Vischer's view of events might be closer to the truth than mine never occurred to me. Nor was I alone in my unthinking confidence. Only the Vischers and the other supporters of the America First position failed to accept this happy scenario as an article of faith. *The New Yorker* ran an admiring Profile of Field Marshal Gamelin, the commander of the impregnable Maginot Line. Every New York cabdriver, now an overnight Clausewitz, told you about the Russian railway gauges. Radio commentators expressed their strong personal confidence in the British naval blockade, exemplified by the British battle cruiser *Hood,* the deadliest killer afloat.

Looking back on the naïveté of the times (the *Hood* was almost immediately sunk by the German battle cruiser *Bismarck,* with a loss of fourteen hundred men), the historian Hew Strahan wrote:

> In the nineteen-thirties, Britain was persuaded that it had eventually won the First World War thanks to the use of the blockade—pressure on the German civilian population had led to revolution and internal collapse. There is little real evidence for this, but the point was at least arguable. Therefore, the conviction in 1939 that Britain would win the Second World War rested on the renewal of a blockade. . . .

Everybody knew how the Allied victory would be achieved. A British member of Parliament (quoted by Evelyn Waugh in *Men at Arms*) gave the blueprint:

> No one in his senses would try to break the Maginot Line. As I see it, both sides will sit tight until they begin to feel the economic pinch. The Germans are short of almost every industrial essential. As soon as they realize that Mr. Hitler's bluff has been called, we shan't hear much more of Mr. Hitler.

Thus, in perfect confidence, Verity and I took passage home on a passenger/freighter running between Sydney and Los Angeles—thirty-four days, with stops in Auckland, Pago Pago, and Honolulu. Our fellow passengers included a stable of professional wrestlers who had just finished their Australian winter tour and were heading home for an American winter tour; and a troupe of carnival sideshow freaks—a fat lady, a sword-swallower, a leopard man, a juggling team, a half-man–half-woman—who were doing the same thing. The wrestlers were better company than the freaks. There were eight of them, and they were huge, averaging out at well over three hundred pounds apiece, all muscle. One of them—a gigantic, morose Ukrainian—was even bigger. Their keeper was a little yapping terrier of a manager, whom any one of them could have eaten for lunch. According to the manager, the Ukrainian was the only one who really knew how to wrestle. The others, he said, were all muscle and no brains—okay for the tour, which was showbiz anyway, and big enough to put down any tank-town tough guy who wanted to show off in the ring. But if one of the showbiz wrestlers started to get discontented ideas about his station, the manager would put him in the ring with the Ukrainian—"the enforcer," the manager called him—and the Ukrainian would damn near break every bone in the miscreant's body. There was something fascinating about being in the company of people as big as this. On land, in a city, they might have been more or less absorbed into the background, but on a ship, where everything is small, tight, and constricted, they seemed shockingly out of scale. Even after weeks of living among them, I was regularly startled by their immensity. Getting past one of them in the ship's narrow corridors required a feat of engineering, and four or five of them gamboling together was a scene from science fiction. The freaks, on the other hand, were a bust. They played bridge incessantly and told one another the plots of every movie they had ever seen. This was too bad, because there were a hundred things I wanted to know about carnival life and (if I could phrase the question delicately enough) about a freak's life. But I got nothing. This was a road-company outfit, far from the big time. Even the fat lady wasn't all that fat—she had to hold her appetite down, she said; if she put on more weight, she would have trouble moving from place to place, and moving from place to place was what carnival life was all about, wasn't it? The leopard man was nothing more than a partly albino black man, and I could never figure out the half-man–half-woman at all. He (or she) dressed as a man the entire trip, and was a devotee of the Detroit Tigers.

Thirty-four days is a long time to spend on a ship, and by the time Verity and I finally got to Los Angeles and then to New York, I was through with traveling. It was now the middle of winter, and my mother was about to leave for Jamaica. I didn't know what to expect at our first meeting. Was she going to be the plaintive and pleading Ma of the Sydney telephone call? Or the lively spirit I had left six months before? I hoped for the second, but I got the first: the change I had sensed in Sydney was permanent. She simply said she was glad I had come home, then added sadly that she wished she had been born a boy so she could have done the same thing when she was my age. It was disheartening. The fun, the *life,* had gone out of her. Still, she was able to rally for a moment. "When are you going to get a job?" she asked.

The next day, she left for Jamaica, and Verity and I moved into her house. This was a serious act of defiance for Verity. He had gone home to Middletown after our trip, and his father had told him to show up for work at Armco on Monday morning. He had said he couldn't oblige and taken a train for New York. This meant that he now really did have to get a job, and so did I. We decided to take advantage of our *Yale Daily News* experience: he would hit the Madison Avenue advertising agencies, and I the metropolitan newspapers.

Verity made out better than I did. At one of his first stops—Young & Rubicam—he was interviewed by a certain Chet LaRoche, and came away not as a junior adman but as the new manager of a restaurant on East Fifty-fifth Street called the Hapsburg House. LaRoche and a Young & Rubicam partner of his had been such steady customers of the place that they finally bought it. (In the thirties, admen were the Wall Street spenders of the eighties, the dot-com entrepreneurs of the nineties.) The place came with a maître d'hotel who could take care of the technical side, but they needed a front man.

Verity turned out to be a natural-born front man. Within a month, he was calling himself Monsieur Calvini and supplying the New York papers with gossip centered on the place; he practically owned Lucius Beebe, of the *Herald Tribune*, and Leonard Lyons, of the *Post.* Actually, the hype was justified: the Hapsburg House was a good restaurant. Ludwig Bemelmans had filled it with dozens of murals, and had even painted a trompe-l'oeil blindfolded violinist melting lovers' hearts in an intimate upstairs private dining room. Echoes of Old Vienna resounded everywhere: bent-wire café chairs, voluminous swags of red velvet, marble-top tables, highly polished brass chandeliers. Not only that: the food was good.

As for Monsieur Calvini, he was everything a restaurateur should be. He deferentially seated ladies at table and clapped their escorts on the back and told them little jokes, whispered in Lucius Beebe's ear, and generally had a high old time. But he wasn't able to stay the course: when his father eventually lost patience and ordered him home to take up his proper position at the American Rolling Mills, he went. It was the dumbest thing he ever did. It changed his character completely—slowly but completely. With every step he took up the corporate ladder, he became more stone-minded, and by the time he reached the pinnacle of corporate America's dream—appointment as Ronald Reagan's Secretary of Commerce—he was lost forever.

Not long after Monsieur Calvini got his job at the Hapsburg House, I got a job as a reporter at *The New Yorker.* Raoul had discouraged me from applying there—he said that he and Harold Ross had drifted so far apart that anybody with a Fleischmann connection wouldn't be allowed on the editorial floor. Nevertheless, *The New Yorker* was the one place I wanted to work, so I applied anyway, and succeeded. I later learned that Raoul had been right: The only reason I got the job was that Ik Shuman, the executive editor and office manager, had come across my stuff in the *Yale Daily News* on one of his regular talent hunts through the college newspapers and had persuaded Ross to take me on. So I was given a desk, a lot of pencils, and a couple of assignments, and in two weeks Ik Shuman called me in. Mr. Ross felt that things weren't working out, he said. Perhaps if I acquired some experience, preferably on a newspaper, I might apply again.

Any such experience was hard to acquire. I made the rounds of almost every paper in New York and got nowhere until one day when Walter Lister, the famous hard-edged city editor of the *Post,* said okay, report on Monday morning.

At 7:00 A.M. Monday morning, I arrived, brisk as a squirrel, and by 7:30, I had had my initial lesson in the shamelessness of New York daily journalism. My assignment, given me by one of the deputy city editors, was to rewrite a sheaf of short news stories clipped from that morning's edition of the *Daily News* and make them sound as if they were fresh stories written by *Post* reporters. (Undoubtedly, the *News* was doing the same thing with *Post* stories.) Only one of my rewrites appeared in that day's editions—an inch and a half at best—but it was enough: I saw a glittering career ahead. The next morning, Walter Lister himself came over with a *News* clipping that he said needed a little extra attention in rewrite—more human interest. It was about a high-school student in Queens—the leading scholar in the senior class, the captain of the football team, slated for Harvard in the fall. He was now in Jamaica Hospital after trying to commit suicide by cutting his throat at a school dance. The story took up four inches of type. "More details," Lister said to me. "Why does a school hero try to commit suicide? Is suicide the price of success—that sort of thing. Talk to his teachers and friends. We can use it in tonight's late edition. Deadline two-fifteen."

In the movies, a reporter on assignment sticks a pencil behind his ear and races out the door. I was ready to race, but where to? And how was I going to get there? A subway to Queens would take forever, and I knew without asking that a cab fare would be on me. And where was the high school anyway? This was the start of a bad, bad day. I ultimately got to Queens (subway), but by the time I found the high school and persuaded the principal's secretary to talk to me, the late edition of the *Post* had gone to press, and by the time I found the girl who had been the football hero's date (named in the *News* story), Walter Lister was home in bed. To cap it all, the Harvard-bound golden boy turned out to be nothing but creative writing by the *News* reporter, an embellishment of a lackluster ambulance report from Jamaica Hospital. The girl told me that he had never played football or anything else, was always close to flunking out, and certainly wasn't going to Harvard. He had got drunk at the dance, fallen down while carrying a drink, and had cut his neck on the broken glass. "He got blood all over my brand-new formal, the creep," the girl said.

The next day, when I told Walter Lister that there had been no story at the high school, he just looked at me with his famous cold stare. It was clear that nothing I could say would dent the veracity of a story that had actually appeared in print. I was fired at the end of the week.

Getting fired left me not only unemployed again but at a dead end, since I had now been turned down by every daily newspaper in New York. Furthermore, my mother was home from Jamaica, and for me to go on living in her house when I had no job was not a good idea. So in late April I reluctantly took a train to Jacksonville, Florida.

Ever since college, my old Yale roommate, John Perry, had been badgering me to go to work on one of his father's newspapers—the old man owned several, in Florida and Pennsylvania. Lowell Clucas, the managing editor of the *Yale Daily News* when I wrote for it, was already working for Perry on the *Jacksonville Journal,* but I was not eager to join him. I had already worked for the old man on the Reading, Pennsylvania, *Times* during the summer after my junior year, and I knew him to be a right-wing bigot. But now, with no possibilities left in New York, I took the train to Jacksonville.

It was a very good move. If Perry Senior was right-wing, his staff on the *Journal* was anything but. Before I had been there a week, Harold Cohn, the managing editor, bullied the entire reportorial staff into taking lunch daily at a nearby restaurant whose proprietors were card-carrying Communist Party members. They were friends of his, down on their luck. The place was not really a restaurant at all; it was actually the flyspecked kitchen and living room of a second-floor apartment in a grungy, run-down building, and the proprietors were a middle-aged intellectual Jewish couple from Long Island, letter-perfect in Karl Marx but illiterate in Escoffier. The food was even worse than the setting—so bad that even Harold soon had to give up.

Harold, without knowing it, was an extraordinary teacher—better than anybody I had had at Yale. He knew exactly what he wanted, where to get it, and how it could be got, and he could, and did, take strips of skin off anybody who failed to deliver. Jim Massey, the city editor, was a good reporter and an even better writer, but he was a miserable city editor. He couldn't give orders properly. As a result, he busied himself with the quality of the writing that came across his desk, and Harold gave the orders. Harold had no trouble giving orders. He was an intense, mercurial man of about forty-five, not very big, with curly black hair and eager black eyes. He had a good voice, with a brisk, rather than languorous, Southern accent, and a great laugh. He could sell anybody anything—an idea, a project, a new place to eat lunch—and he was endlessly busy raising money for his beloved Jewish charities. He once sent me down to the Federal Office Building to register "Anti-Nazi" as a trademarked brand name, with all rights to be held by the local chapter of B'nai B'rith. "Just think!" he said. "Anti-Nazi peas! Anti-Nazi plumbing fixtures! Anti-Nazi dog food! Every Jew in the country will switch to the Anti-Nazi brand. There's a gold mine waiting here." He may have been right, but the federal people said nothing doing.

Harold had been managing editor of the Memphis *Press-Scimitar* until the senior Perry lured him to Jacksonville with an irresistible salary. Once Harold had settled in, acquired a mortgage, and put his children in school, Perry began cutting that salary until it was below what it had been in Memphis. Jim

Massey had the same history: he had been lead reporter at the Nashville *Banner* when he heard Perry's siren call. Most of the other reporters on the paper were roughly my age, but far more competent than I was, having started their newspapering as high-school correspondents. My first assignment at the *Journal* was as second-string police reporter behind Douglas Danford, who was a year or two younger than me but way ahead in experience; as soon as I was competent, Doug would move up to the county run. I was also to write my *Yale Daily News* column, "Once Over Lightly," three times a week.

For anyone brought up, like me, on the newspaper movies of the thirties, the police beat was the real thing, what newspapering was all about. No more nonevents at Queens high-school dances; I could now saunter through sunlit fields of honest crime. I buddied around with real-life detectives and drank beer with coroners. I became knowledgeable about police department politics, whorehouse management, sleazy lawyers, and municipal corruption—a world of jaunty reprobates and warmhearted whores, all so satisfyingly sordid, so different from everything I had grown up with. It came as a great shock, therefore, when a truly brutal crime broke into my Damon Runyan view of misdemeanor. It was the kidnapping, raping, and butchering of two girl hitchhikers by a traveling salesman and sometime con artist, a personable young man from New Jersey named Jefferson. I covered the gruesome trial, which ended in a sentence of death by electrocution. Florida law then required that a member of the press, representing the public at large, be present at every execution. Since I had covered the trial (and was the least-senior member of the staff), I drew the assignment.

The execution was to take place at 8:00 A.M. in the state prison in Raiford, forty miles from Jacksonville. Early in the morning of the appointed day, I drove to the prison. At its front gate, I was added to a group of about ten other witnesses—representatives of the girls' families, sheriff's people, prison officials—and at quarter to eight we were led into the execution chamber itself, a small, square, bleak room with the unmistakable Chair near its center, facing a sort of wooden bleachers. We witnesses filed into the bleachers and silently waited. At Jefferson's trial, his porous, almost negligible defense had been buried under a mountain of ironclad prosecution evidence, and the jury was out for less than two hours. I agreed with its verdict, but now, sitting in these bleachers, confronted for the first time with a realization of what police work and the law can lead to, I was getting uneasy. A minute or two later, Jefferson himself, silent and (fortunately) composed, was led in, handcuffed and shackled. He was maneuvered into the chair, and two guards, with a great deal of muttered bickering about how to do things right, finally got him strapped in. They stood back, and again there was complete silence. Jefferson, a good-looking, well-spoken young man, raised his head and looked us witnesses straight in the eye, one by one. Then he said, quietly and compellingly, "You are killing an innocent man." It was shattering. I *knew* Jefferson had killed those girls. I had seen his busy record of rape in other states, his conviction of butchering a neighbor's dog in Trenton and mailing the severed head to its owner. But that was yesterday, and what you saw and knew yesterday cannot stand up to what you see and hear today—rationality has nothing to do with it.

A guard came forward and put the black hood over Jefferson's head. Florida law also required that the sheriff of the county in which the crime was committed throw the switch. The appropriate sheriff, a paunchy good-ol'-boy sort of man, like most Southern sheriffs, moved to a panel behind the chair. "Now, son, you gotta be sure I throw the right switch," he said to the guard in a big voice that everybody in the room, including Jefferson, could hear. "This one? No? Then this one . . ." Jefferson convulsed in the chair, proving the sheriff right.

The whole thing was so upsetting that when I got back to the office I wrote about a yard and a half of emotional copy, full of outrage. Harold Cohn threw it all away. "I want maybe two inches saying that it happened. That's all you were there for. Capital punishment may be a sin and a shame, but what I want now is a news story and not a lecture. Two inches." So I wrote him his two inches, and by the next day, what I knew had reasserted its primacy over what I had felt the day before. I knew, if nothing else, that they at least had not executed an innocent man.

Whorehouse management: Everything I learned about whorehouse management I learned from the mayor of Jacksonville's bagman, who collected the mayor's daily extortion money, and from various of the town's madams, who paid in every Tuesday. The bagman was an affable old coot named Artie, who hung out in the police station when he was not out filling his bag. The town's madams managed about a dozen houses in the red-light district—rambling old Victorian elephants, each on its own plot of green. Artie covered them all, and it was through him that I got to know the madams. Almost every one of them came from a big city in the Northeast—Boston, New York, Providence. They were busy at night, but in the hot and tedious afternoons they liked to schmooze with a fellow northerner over a glass of ice tea. A couple of them even read my column. On Tuesday afternoons, Artie would show up to accept a glass of tea and collect his money. There were about a hundred prostitutes in town. Artie knew the exact number, because they were all required to register with the city Health Department as meat handlers. (Was this somebody's coarse joke? I never found out.) To avoid being bounced by the police, each girl was required to contribute ten dollars a week, through her madam, to the mayor's welfare fund. The cost of a trick being two dollars, this meant that every week five clients were unwittingly doing their bit for the mayor. The girls were strictly held to a maximum of fifteen minutes with each client, and they put in an eight- to ten-hour day, starting at 5:00 P.M.; on a weekend, a girl might do twenty or thirty tricks. Artie and the mayor, full of compassion for the fallen, allowed the girls to keep their tips, which could run quite high. Jacksonville alone—pop. 150,000—could never have supported such a high number of prostitutes, but Camp Blanding, the huge Army base nearby, and the Jacksonville Naval Air Station, where Navy pilots were trained, could and did.

Municipal corruption: Even though Jacksonville was very likely the most corrupt city in the South, the mayor's thousand dollars a week (minus a slim cut for Artie and a medium cut for the chief of police) still seemed a bit excessive to me (I was making one-fortieth of that), and I was not surprised that the *Journal* was supporting the mayor's opponent, Zeph Gordon, in the coming election. In fact, I even went to Harold Cohn and proposed that I write a full exposé of the mayor. Artie, I said, would be a perfect source, and my friends among the madams could spill a lot of beans—it would be a big boost for Zeph Gordon. Harold looked at me with the suppressed exasperation of a man trying to teach his awkward son to ride a bicycle. "Don't be silly," he said. "Artie is seventy-two years old [Harold knew everything about everybody], and you really think he would risk his job, and maybe his knees, by testifying for us when the mayor sues for libel? Or those madams? They're businesswomen. They know which end is up. And who would believe anything their girls might say, even if they put on some clothes? Grow up. This isn't boola-boola anymore." To Harold, Yale and boola-boola were synonymous and equally ludicrous. "And if you think you'd be doing Zeph Gordon a favor, think again. Gordon's an even bigger crook than the mayor." I knew that Gordon, a city councilman, owned an insurance agency, but what I didn't know, until Harold told me, was that every dime the city spent on insurance—from liability insurance to floodwater insurance to automobile insurance on its trucks and buses—was funneled through that agency, where it was skimmed. The skim made the scourge of the meat handlers look like a piker. Why, then, was the *Journal* supporting Gordon? I was still too boola-boola to ask. I didn't want to know the answer.

In the face of Harold's withering realities, my vision of myself as a fearless investigative reporter faded, and I went back to ordinary police reporting—*too* ordinary to suit Harold Cohn. Once again, it was my scarlet women who set him off. A new federal law—the May Act—had been passed by Congress to protect Our Boys from sin. Among other pious provisions, it prohibited prostitution within X miles of a military base, and Jacksonville was one of its targets because of Camp Blanding and the Naval Air Station. I wrote an ordinary story about this, and Harold rejected it out of hand. "You're missing the boat again," he said. "Are you never going to learn? If you were any kind of reporter, you'd know that the injunction in the May Act must be read out loud in every whorehouse in town before it becomes effective." He was right, of course, and I should have known about it. "That's where the story is. The reading starts tomorrow at eight A.M. Be there."

So I was there. At eight o'clock, the federal guy marched into the first house and told the madam to wake up her girls and get them assembled in the bar parlor for the reading. He acted and sounded like a drill sergeant, but he had a lot to learn. The girls had had a long night and were not in a mood to be read to by anybody. Many of them were fast asleep with their "sweetbacks"—their personal lovers. Getting them downstairs for a bedtime story they didn't want to hear took a lot of doing. In time, though, they were assembled in the bar parlor, yawning, straggle-haired, and full of bad language. Two or three of them were in nightgowns; the rest were as bare as eggs. The federal guy took a head count and read his injunction—nobody paid the slightest attention—and then we moved on to the next house.

It was a tedious procedure, and after a while I cut out and went back to the office, where I wrote an equally tedious story. I thought Harold would go up in smoke. "Every goddam woman in Jacksonville wants to know what goes on in a whorehouse—what the place looks like, what the girls look like, how the madam keeps order—and what do you give me? A goddam boring story about law enforcement!" With this encouragement, I wrote him a new story, with everything in it that the ladies of the city wished to know.

* * *

At the end of August, I took a week off from my crooks and fallen women and went back north to get married. Katharine Chittenden (or "Tass," as she was known) was a singularly good-looking girl with coal black hair, green eyes, and an inspirational figure—a sister of my Hotchkiss and Yale classmate George Chittenden. The Depression had hit the Chittenden family hard, and when it became Tass's turn to go to college—she had two sisters ahead of her—there was no money left. When I first knew her, she was a salesgirl at Macy's, at eleven dollars a week, and a night student at secretarial school. (At the time of our marriage, she was secretary/assistant to the fiction editor of *Harper's Bazaar,* making more money than I was.) I had liked Tass from the first, back in her Macy's days. She was funny and quick, and she liked me a lot, which always helps. And her father, Horace, required his wife to remove the lining from all his neckties; a necktie with a lining gave him a toothache. That was pretty irresistible, too. In fact, she was periodically my favorite girl—until a Martha Stevenson (later Mrs. St. Clair McKelway) or a Genevieve Scott or a Nell Hastings came along. In the usual male fashion, I was entirely satisfied with this arrangement—up to the point when John Hersey and, in particular, Oliver Lombardi appeared in Tass's life. Just friends, she said, but I wasn't so sure. It came to me as a sudden revelation that I liked her just as much as she liked me, and that we ought to get married. I knew I was too young (twenty-two), that I was intending to leave the only job I had ever had in favor of a magazine that had already fired me once, and that I was likely to disappear into the draft at any moment—but we ought to get married anyway. She agreed.

To this end, I presented myself at the Chittenden family house in East River, Connecticut, at the appointed time on August 31, 1940. Tass and I had endeared ourselves to our friends by having the wedding on the Saturday of Labor Day weekend, thus spoiling holiday plans up and down the East Coast. I arrived in New York from Jacksonville on Friday, was berated by my mother for inattention to the sort of details important to a bride (failure to arrange for a proper wedding bouquet), and went off to a bachelor dinner at Hapsburg House, where Verity had laid out a great spread for six or eight of us in the private dining room of the blindfolded violinist. The next day, I drove to East River. My mother and Steve and Peter were already there; Peter Vischer did not attend. I didn't think my mother would find much in common with the small-town, high-WASP wedding guests who bore the Chittenden label—minor academics, dry lawyers, Yale-dipped businessmen. But I underestimated her, even in her new, subdued state. She knew all about their kind. She had grown up among them—or, rather, among their cousins in the Midwest. Without a twitch, she shifted gears to Quincy's Maine Street, and in no time they were being roguish with her and practically chucking her under the chin.

Back in Jacksonville, Tass got a job as a bookkeeper and general manager in an expensive dress shop, making ten dollars a week more than I made. My column in the *Journal* was prospering, however, to the point that cops and politicians were deferential to me, and every week one of my three columns was picked up by the Western Newspaper Union, a company that supplied boilerplate to fifteen hundred weekly newspapers across the country. If a small-town weekly could not fill its four or six pages on its own, it could run a page or two of canned stuff (including my column) from the WNU. The pay for my share in this intellectual enrichment of America was five dollars a week—a third of a cent per paper.

Altogether, the sun shone brightly, but there was always a black cloud on the horizon: the war in Europe. It was going badly. The Russian railway tracks and the British naval blockade had betrayed the Clausewitz cabdrivers and the oracular news commentators. (On the day the Germans crossed into Russia, the *Journal* got out an extra, tearing up the front page of the regular edition to run an Associated Press story headed GERMANY INVADES RUSSIA! Also on the front page, forgotten in the rush, was an interview I had had the day before with H. V. Kaltenborn, the Henry Kissinger of his day. This one was headed WHY GERMANY CANNOT INVADE RUSSIA.) The war colored everything you did, or decided not to do. It was always a presence, and on no one did its presence weigh more heavily than on my mother. Two of her many friends in England had already been killed—one, Esmé Cotterell, by a bomb, and another, Archie Crabbe, in the RAF. Although she was no longer married to Raoul, she was still friends with his two sisters, Jo and Anne, both living in Paris. Jo had made it back to the States, but Anne had simply disappeared. She had not been heard from, or even of, since the fall of France. Raoul had followed every lead, pursued every contact, to no avail. Then, out of the blue, a mysterious postcard was forwarded to him by the Red Cross in New York, having presumably traveled through a neutral country. The card had originated in a small village about fifty miles south of Paris, along the main route to Nice, and it recorded the burial in the village cemetery of one Anne Fleischmann Anderson, killed in a German dive-bomber attack in late May 1940. It was signed by the village mayor. How had the mayor got Raoul's address? How had the card reached the Red Cross? Nobody in New York could (or would) say. As soon as travel was permitted after the war, Raoul went to France. He found his sister's grave all right, but the card remained a mystery, because the village mayor himself had been subsequently shot by the Germans.

If all these bleak facts were not enough for my mother, she had to endure Peter Vischer's extolling of the merits of the German cause. She didn't know where to turn—an innate but muddled liberal sharing a house with an articulate and ardent Teuton. To cap it all, she had three sons of the right age to be killed (as she was convinced) in battle.

I had drawn a fairly high number in the draft, which meant that I would be a civilian for several months—safe but full of guilt. The war was no longer being fought by nameless, faraway figures but by people I knew myself. A number of my classmates at Yale had skipped over the border to join the Royal Canadian Air Force, and, closer to home, Doug Danford had signed on to train as a Navy pilot. A Yale classmate named Foster Fargo, also scheduled to start pilot school in Jacksonville, showed up on our doorstep with his bride of six days—a girl named Ruth, whom Tass knew slightly. Could they stay with us for a couple of days, until their quarters at the Naval Air Station were ready? We put them in our spare room, and three days later, he was dead in a crash. I have never seen anybody in such a state of shock, incomprehension, and paralysis as Ruth was. For days, she couldn't eat, sleep, move, or think. We had to get neighbors to watch over her while we were at work. Then her mother finally came down from New Jersey and took her home. It was a terrible business; and it fed my guilt. Here was I, still the Herodotus of the Jacksonville police department and vocal hawk, with never a thought of *doing* anything.

In the fall of 1941, Tass and I moved back to New York. By then, lines had been drawn in the sand between the pro-German groups (generally disguised as simply noninterventionist) on one side, and all of us right-thinking interventionists on the other. The atmosphere had become nasty. "There was quite a bit of rowdy activity in the streets, incited by Fascist and anti-Semitic agitators," Richard Rovere wrote in *Final Reports.* "Rallies of one sort or another were being staged by Fritz Kuhn's German-American Bund, by Father Charles Coughlin's Social Justice movement, by a coalition of Fascist groups known as the Christian Front, and by a good many others. There was a particularly inflammatory Fascist rabble-rouser named Joe McWilliams, whose meetings had a way of turning into riots in which blood, generally Jewish, was spilled."

Within a week of my arrival from Jacksonville, the America First people announced that they would take over the old Madison Square Garden for a speech by Charles Lindbergh on the formidable German air force, which he had recently visited. My brother

Steve, who had just received his draft summons, and I decided to attend, to show the flag for the other side. We couldn't get in. The Garden was filled to overflowing, and loudspeakers had been set up in Fiftieth Street to carry Lindbergh's message to the crowd outside. Ominous-looking men in dark suits and with no smiles—Joe McWilliams's or Fritz Kuhn's men, I assumed—were circulating through the crowd to ensure that proper attention was paid, and the crowd was remarkably silent. Lindbergh, in a light, unprofessional voice, was saying that the Luftwaffe was so powerful, so well trained—so beautiful, in a way—that it would be suicidal to tangle with it. At that moment, I heard a long and loud Bronx cheer from Steve. It rang out in the silence, and people started muttering at us angrily. It was clearly time to get out of there, and we sped our departure when two or three of the Joe McWilliams thugs started shouldering through the crowd to get us. They were right behind us when we reached the subway station and ducked in.

When Tass and I had arrived in New York, I wasn't precisely jobless, but close to it. I was still writing a column a week for the Western Newspaper Union, and a different column a week for a chain of Florida newspapers, including the *Journal*. Then I got a sort of a job at *The New Yorker*. I wasn't exactly on the payroll, but Ik Shuman had said he would pay me two dollars an inch for anything of mine that was printed in "Talk of the Town." I went to the magazine every Tuesday and got a handful of assignments from William Shawn, the new managing editor, succeeding St. Clair McKelway. They weren't assignments so much as proposals. A typical one was "An article in this month's *Figure Skating* says that sharpening skates requires a skill and a knack as delicate as tuning a piano. The country's leading skate sharpener, or tuner, is a man named Magruder, who has a workroom on West 49th Street, near the Garden. Figure skaters from all over send him their skates for sharpening. He also does all the hockey players. We could drop in and pick up some lore." I did a couple of these reports every week and turned them in to Shawn. None of them ever appeared; therefore, no pay. My weekly column for the chain of Florida papers brought in twenty-five dollars, and my column for the Western Newspaper Union was still paying a dispiriting five dollars. I had also engaged to write a novel. This came through an acquaintance of my father's, a producer of B pictures. Movies always did better at the box office, it was thought, if their advertising could claim "Taken from the scintillating novel by [anybody]." I was to be the anybody for this man's latest picture: Since there was no novel for it to come from, I was to create one out of the screenplay—two hundred dollars for an outline, three hundred more upon completion. I foundered on that project after a week. I suppose I could have applied for a handout at home, but I would have died, or gone to work in a brokerage house, first; penury was better than having to admit to my mother that I couldn't make it on my own.

Fortunately, Tass got her job back at *Harper's Bazaar,* at fifty dollars a week—more money than I could make, no matter how hard I worked. Obviously, I needed to rationalize my work load and renegotiate the nonperformers. The first target was clearly the five-dollar column for the Western Newspaper Union. Oddly enough, I had never spoken to my editor there—I had been hired by mail, and he printed whatever I sent him without changing a comma. Once a week, I would drop my column in the mailbox, and once a month he would send me a check and a copy of a four- or six-page paper in Kansas or West Virginia or somewhere, with my column on an inside page, surrounded by a mélange of gardening tips, cooking recipes, medical counsel, crossword puzzles, and comics. I had imagined the editor of so vast an enterprise to be a tycoon walled in behind English secretaries, but the Western offices turned out to be a single dark and grimy room in a run-down building in New York's garment district, and the intimidating editor was an old guy in a stained sweater. I started telling him my troubles, and before I finished the first sentence he was shaking his head. "No more money," he said. "We're even thinking of dropping the column. Too glossy." This was a hard blow. All that gloss not worth even five dollars? "But I'll tell you what I'll do," he said. "You can write the medical column for the same money. It's a lot less work." I said I wouldn't write anything for five dollars a week, and, anyway, I wasn't a doctor. "So who's a doctor?" he said. "All you need is a medical book—you make up the questions and then you answer them. But suit yourself." As of then, I had one less commitment—and five dollars less a week.

On Sunday, December 7, Tass and I we driving back to town from a weekend in Lambertville, New Jersey, where my mother now lived with Peter Vischer in an old farmhouse she had beautifully remodeled and decorated. Along the way, Tass turned on the car radio: Pearl Harbor. I was on jury duty at the time, and on Monday morning, in Foley Square, standing in a crowd around a cab with a radio, we heard that the United States was now formally at war. The crowd around the radio went totally silent and then slowly broke up. There was a lot of private, personal assessment going on. I must say that I was of two minds about the news. I thought it right and good that we were now in a war that others had been fighting on our behalf, but I had some ignoble feelings about the timing: Ik Shuman had just told me that *The New Yorker* was going to take me on full-time, starting in January.

In the first week of January 1942, I went to work at *The New Yorker* for the second time. Fifty years later, Ben Yagoda, who was writing a cultural history of the magazine, found in the archives a memo from Shawn to Ross that preceded my hiring. It was dated December 4, 1941, and it read:

> Mr. Ross:
>
> Attached are two Talk of the Town originals by a young man named Botsford. There are things the matter with

> both pieces—the one on the ship refloater is tenuous, because of the idea itself, and the one on the skate-sharpener is far too long. Also, there are rough spots in both. On the basis of these two stories, however, I'd like to recommend that you put Botsford to work on some sort of drawing-account or small-salary arrangement. ["Small" is right. I was put on a drawing account of twenty-five dollars a week—five dollars less than I had finally been making in Jacksonville.] It's the most promising Talk writing that has come along in the last two and a half years, I think. He seems to have the touch, and he is not merely imitative. We don't need any additional men on Talk right now but I'm against passing up talent; we can certainly find plenty for him to do. Botsford, unfortunately, is a Fleischmann ex-stepson [the old bugaboo!], but I don't see why that should be a consideration. If the man is a good writer, and funny, that's all that matters; and he appears to be both.
>
> Shawn

Across the top of this memo, Ross, who had clearly forgotten that I had already worked for him—briefly—scribbled "I'm not so hopeful. He's got to learn a lot." And, at the bottom: "He might learn more on a newspaper. How old is he?"

Shawn, swallowing his "unfortunately," prevailed.

On my first day at work, Ik Shuman had no desk for me. The magazine then occupied two floors at 25 West Forty-third Street—the nineteenth (editorial) and the twentieth (business)—but there were little editorial enclaves all over the building. While Ik looked for a spot, he parked me in Joseph Mitchell's office, on the nineteenth floor, where the big-time writers lived. I had been reading Mitchell not only in *The New Yorker* but, earlier, in the *World-Telegram,* and I admired him enormously. To sit where he had sat should have been somehow meaningful, but it wasn't; I might have been sitting in a dentist's waiting room. The office contained no trace of its tenant. There was a neatly covered typewriter on a stand and a glass tumbler full of needle-sharp pencils on the desk, and nothing else—no papers, no files, no foolish souvenirs, no telephone numbers scrawled on the wall, no ashtray, no yesterday's coffee cup. Joseph Mitchell was obviously a monk.

At the end of the day (I had done absolutely nothing), Shuman moved me down to a *New Yorker* enclave on the fourteenth floor, where Mark Murphy, Marion Miller, Sally Benson, Seymour Krim, and Robey Lyle were already installed.

Mark Murphy, who came to have a sharper effect on my life than any of the others, was one of those good-looking black Irishmen—dark-haired and dark-complexioned, with brilliant blue eyes. He had been a police reporter on the *New York Post,* and Ross was very high on him. Quick and witty and excellent company, he could charm the birds off the trees and wring confidences from a stone. He was about my age, and in about my position in the draft, but his plans were larger than mine. He wasn't going to wait to be called up, he said. He was going to volunteer first, and the more hazardous the duty, the better—it was just a matter of choosing. Periodically, he would tell me of the new danger du jour—this week, the Daring Merchant Seaman, carrying supplies to Russia on the suicidal Murmansk run, next week the Fearless Commando Paratrooper, dropping behind enemy lines to blow up bridges and derail freight trains. Mark's powers of persuasion were such that I half-believed every one of these Tom Sawyer projects, seriatim. Three years later, however, his flamboyant imagination, coupled with his almost irresistible powers of persuasion, put me in a terrible mess that could have got a lot of people killed. It happened this way, in the Hürtgen Forest, that appalling quagmire of mud, misery, and death: I was trying to catch a nap in an abandoned cellar one morning when I got word that Colonel Carson was looking for me—a new correspondent who said he knew me had arrived at headquarters. It was Mark, but a far different Mark from the one I had so admired on West Forty-third Street. The Daring Merchant Seaman and the Fearless Commando Parachuter had now become the Intrepid War Correspondent—a *draft-exempt civilian* correspondent, it turned out—working for a slick-paper Air Force magazine quartered in New York. He was, however, the most warlike correspondent I ever saw. The Irish charm had changed into Irish belligerence. He swaggered and talked tough, and even had a trench knife stuck in his belt. He was writing an article for his magazine on how the other half—the infantry—lived, and he had come to the First Division to find out. I couldn't help much, because Colonel Carson almost immediately sent me down to a crossroads hamlet called Hamich to see if we could get a unit identification on the German tanks down there.

The tanks, I found, were not from a new unit in the line, as feared, but our troops couldn't move anyway: German machine guns, mortars, and artillery had complete control of the Hamich crossroads. Back at Division Headquarters to report, I found Colonel Carson deep in another cellar, conferring with the division's commanding general, its artillery commander, and, of all people, Mark Murphy. Obviously, Mark's enterprise and powers of persuasion were still strong. I gave my bad news about the Hamich crossroad, but Mark refused to accept it. "That crossroads is open," he said. "I drove through there this morning. A little spatter of machine-gun fire but nothing too much for our guys to handle." I could have been back on West Forty-third Street, listening to the almost paratrooper, the not-quite Murmansk seaman. The general, however, had never been on West Forty-third Street, and what he heard was the Intrepid War Correspondent, the trained observer, the bearer of high credentials. He looked at me the same cold way Walter Lister had looked at me when I told him there was no story at the Queens high-school dance. This was getting serious; the Intrepid War Correspondent could cause a lot of damage, and the fault would be mine.

"That's not so," I said. "There's no way Mr. Murphy could have been in Hamich."

Now it was Mark giving me the baleful eye. "What do you mean, soldier?" he said. (Soldier! Where did he pick that up?) "Of course I was there, and that crossroads is open."

"Not possible," I said.

The general's aide, sensing trouble, slipped out of the cellar and had a word with Mark's jeep driver. He came back and clinched the matter: Mark had not been one inch closer to the front than he was at that moment. With this, Mark stormed out of the cellar and drove away. I never saw him again, on either side of the Atlantic. He died of cirrhosis of the liver in South Africa at the age of forty.

Let us return to West Forty-third Street and Marion Miller, another tenant of our fourteenth-floor warren. She was Lois Long's assistant in the fashion department—a nice Catholic girl, in no way a writer, who would have made a good secretary to a life-insurance executive. She was very proper and very conservative, and she was in constant battle with Seymour Krim, who was a "Talk of the Town" reporter, like me. Seymour was a thorny Jewish boy, in every way a writer, far from proper, and anything but conservative. When the weather got hot (no air conditioning, of course), he would take off his clothes and sit at his desk naked except for his jockey shorts, and this drove Marion wild—so wild that she eventually marched in on Ross and said she would quit if Seymour didn't put his clothes back on. Ross sent down a memo saying that "Talk" reporters were to remain dressed while at work.

Figuratively speaking, Seymour continued to take his clothes off in public for the rest of his life. He was strenuously and noisily against the establishment. He worked for *The New Yorker* only because he needed the money, and he hated what he considered the magazine's namby-pamby, artificially well-bred tone. His "Talk of the Town" stories were always full of tough-guy writing, well seasoned with four-letter words. As a result, very little of his stuff got printed by the well-bred magazine, and then only when sanitized. He idolized William Saroyan as a spokesman for the dispossessed, and wrote him long mash notes. He would show them to me, mainly, I think, so that I could see what really good writing was like. One of them (which I still have) read: "No shit, Saroyan, the end of the second act nearly made me puke, my pulse was racing so hard. It was goddam close to holy." Critical writing of this sort was a vein of ore that Seymour mined for years. After he left *The New Yorker,* he wrote for various little avant-garde magazines and took up with people like Jack Kerouac, Allen Ginsberg, and Lawrence Ferlinghetti. He lived for years in a dark and scaly apartment on West Tenth Street, and he wrote a couple of books, one of which, *Memoirs of a Near-Sighted Cannoneer,* caused a transient stir. Behind his manly truculence and theatrical cross-grainedness he was a warmhearted man, endlessly helpful to younger writers in the Village. Occasionally, he would send a particularly promising candidate to see me about a job, and a couple of times we took on a Krim product as a "Talk" reporter. They never stayed—we were too old-fashioned and well-bred for them. Every now and then, I would have lunch with Seymour (always at some god-awful dump of his choosing), and every couple of years I would send him a Christmas card, just to stay in touch. The last card I sent him—"Merry Christmas, you old fart!"—came back stamped "Not known at this address," under which somebody had written "Deceased." Seymour, I found out, had committed suicide rather than face a slow death from cancer.

As for Robey Lyle, my third roommate, she was a mystery. Her only known function at the magazine was as a reporter for the annual Christmas shopping guide, but she was at her desk just as frequently in July as in December—a *New Yorker* groupie. About forty years old, dark and good-looking, she was married to a rich and elderly investment banker, but whenever I saw her, which was every day, she had in tow a young man of my age named Ham—if he had an additional name, I never heard it. Ham, a very laid-back youth, was an almost professional college dropout (Princeton, Brown, Adelphi). He carried packages for Robey, opened doors for her, hung up her coat for her, ran errands for her, and very probably did other things for her, though not in the office. Whenever Ham was not needed, he sat in a hard chair by the standing electric fan not efficient enough to keep Seymour Krim dressed. Then one day, without warning, Ham disappeared—drafted. About three weeks later, he reappeared, on a three-day pass. Robey, an elegant dresser, was so horrified by the fit and quality of his private's uniform that she whisked him over to Brooks Brothers and superhumanly got them to run up a bespoke uniform for him overnight. It certainly fit him better than the old one, but I can't think it did him much good with his sergeant back at camp.

Robey and Sally Benson were friends. They would often have lunch together and come back to the office giggling and knocking things off the desks. Sally was then at the peak of her "Junior Miss" stories and her Kensington Avenue stories (which ended up as *Meet Me in St. Louis*). She would return from lunch tipsy and tittering, roll a sheet of paper into her typewriter, and bat out a title. After one last bit of chaff with Robey, she would start typing at top speed, and do twelve or fifteen pages without stopping. Then she would pull the last page from the machine, tap the sheets into a pile, take them up to Ross or Gus Lobrano, and have the story accepted on the spot. I never once saw her read over a manuscript before turning it in.

In the middle of August, all my indecisions were resolved: my draft notice arrived in the mail. "Greetings," it began warmly, like a host welcoming a guest at a party. "Greetings! Come on in!" It was an invitation I couldn't refuse, and I didn't. I went in.

It turned out to be quite a party, and I thought it would never end. Three years elapsed before the party favors were distributed and I could go home: "Here's a Bronze Star for you, my boy, which you can wear at the American Legion sock hops, and here's a Croix de Guerre and a Purple Heart to go with it, plus five campaign stars and, best of all, a shoe-ration coupon so you can get a pair of civilian shoes."

2

The partygoers who were able to straggle home after the ball looked nothing like the bunch who had been greeted so nicely at the door. For one thing, there were fewer of them, and for another they were completely out of sync with the world they were returning to. Some of the dislocations were unavoidable. In my case, I arrived at my apartment from Fort Dix at the wrong time, around 10:30, long after Susan, now almost three, was asleep. She and I had our first real look at each other the next morning. She knew I was coming, of course—I don't suppose much else had been talked about for weeks—but when she saw this total stranger in her mother's bed she fled, howling, and a lot of days—weeks, months—went by before she began to come around.

There were other domestic thorns. Tass and I had been together for two years and then apart for three, and the disparities were many. During those three vacant years, our daily lives had been completely disconnected, not even within hailing distance of each other. Tass had made many new friends (most of them war-separated women like herself), she had a job she liked, working as a volunteer in the operating room of the Manhattan Eye, Ear and Throat Hospital, and she had Susan to take care of and keep her company. She had, in short, a life of her own, and it was ridiculous of me to think she could change it overnight—or would want to. For my part, I found civilian life plodding and spiritless. Tass's friends bored me, her hospital work was incomprehensible, and Susan disliked me. Bad times all around.

Much of the breakage was my own fault. During my first months back on the streets, I continued, out of habit, to seek a physical solution to every difficulty. I got into endless fights with cabdrivers, and in Central Park one day I flattened a man who told me to shut up when I complained about his spilling Coca-Cola on me. In the office, I told Rogers Whitaker, a senior editor, that I would knock his teeth in if he didn't stop hazing me (he stopped), and when Hamilton Basso, a writer and critic, tried to use my phone to complain to Ross about my editing, I not only literally kicked him out of my office but chased him down the hall to the men's room, where he locked himself in a stall to escape me. I can only say in my own defense that I had been a soldier longer than I had been anything else in my adult life, living in a soldier's un-nuanced physical world. A long time went by before I came to my senses, and the man who brought me there was William Shawn—Shawn and his logical, Shawnian reaction to a battle I had had with an unidentified victim. I was leaving the office very late one night, hoping to get a cab home. Cabs were scarce, and it was ten minutes before one finally appeared. I hailed it and was about to step off the curb and get in when another man darted up from nowhere and jumped in ahead of me. I was right behind him, and before he could slam the door I had him by the leg and hauled him out. At this, the cabdriver yelled that he wasn't going to take either one of us if we were going to fight, so I gave up. I grabbed my rival by his coat collar and pants and rammed him back into the cab, where he lay, half on the seat and half on the floor, as the cab drove off. In all this, he had never said a word. The next day, I was telling Shawn about the perils of working late, and Shawn said, "What if he thought it really was his cab? He gets in, and suddenly this madman, for no reason at all, pulls him out and then throws him back in." Such a thought had never occurred to me. Shawn was perfectly right: I hadn't seen the man, and very possibly he hadn't seen me. For the first time, I began to realize that I had been behaving pretty badly—not only to this poor sod but to a lot of other people—and I returned, permanently and unequivocally, to civilian life. I never hit anybody, or threatened to hit anybody, again.

With the passage of time, as might be expected, the sun began to come out again, and after a long spell of being a pain in the neck to everyone, I started to behave. Tass's new friends (in edited form) became more entertaining, her work at the hospital, now enlarged, seemed interesting and useful, Susan had not only come to accept me but even admitted to liking me, and there was new Margot to make much of. Then the roof fell in.

On Saturday of the Thanksgiving weekend of 1948, Tass and I had two invitations: to Betty Kaufman's to meet a visiting Argentine editor over drinks, and to Hal Scott's, in Tarrytown, for a farewell dinner marking the final chapter of the sale of his old family mansion—a voluminous stone Victorian pile in Washington Irving country. Tass, unfortunately, had a bad cold, aggravating her asthma, which her doctor, Anne Belcher, was treating with a new drug called an antihistamine. At Betty's, she had one drink—a Scotch—but it only made her feel worse, and when we left she said I should go on to Hal Scott's without her, she just wanted to go home and get into bed.

So that's what we did. I saw her into bed with a book and plenty of Kleenex, sent the sitter home, and drove out to Hal's. I got home by one o'clock, and when I went up to our bedroom, on the third floor, at the back of the house, I found all the lights still on, just as I had left them. The room was freezing. The window was open, and the bed quilt had been pulled up, but there was nobody in the room. Or in the bathroom. Or in the guest room. The girls were sound asleep, but alone. I went all through the house. Nobody. My brother Steve and his wife lived directly across the Turtle Bay gardens from our house, and I thought that Tass must have gone over there, for whatever reason. So I went after her. I had just stepped into the backyard garden when I heard an odd little noise off to my left. It was Tass, sprawled out on the ground in her nightgown, filthy dirty, unconscious. How had she got there? Had somebody beaten her up? She was still breathing, so I picked her up and somehow carried her upstairs and laid her on the bed. She was still out cold. The whole thing was not only horrifying but mystifying. I called Dr. Belcher, got her out of bed, and asked her if there was something destructive about those antihistamine pills. When she heard what had happened, she said she would be right over, and was. She took Tass's pulse and blood pressure and told me to call an ambulance. When it came, she and Tass went off to New York Hospital; I stayed behind with the girls. It was now just beginning to get light. The bedroom was still cold. I went over to the window: why had she opened it at all? I leaned out and looked down. I could see that something had rammed a hole through the wisteria arbor that extended into the garden from the back of the house. That something could only have been Tass; she had fallen out the window.

Within the hour, Dr. Belcher called from the hospital: Tass had a broken neck, as well as countless contusions and scratches and layers of dirt. Dr. Bronson Ray, the head of neurosurgery, would be operating immediately. My two sisters-in-law also went into action: Cynthia Botsford took Margot in with her, and a couple of days later Nancy Fleischmann escorted Susan out to Minneapolis to stay with Tass's sister, Betty Lowry.

That was in November; in February, Tass came home from the hospital. In between, I spent a lot of time wondering what had really happened. Tass herself could remember nothing of the events of that night—or of the events of two or three days preceding and following. Dr. Belcher at first thought that the combination of alcohol and antihistamine had caused Tass to black out and fall as she was opening the bedroom window, but when she learned that there had been only one drink, she abandoned that theory. Then she thought that the antihistamine pills themselves had been somehow contaminated, and she had the remaining pills chemically analyzed; they passed. As for me, I didn't see how she could have fallen at all, either conscious or unconscious: the window wasn't open far enough—only about eighteen inches. But if she hadn't fallen, how *had* she gone out? Was she pushed? A burglar? I became so obsessed with this last possibility that late one night, still gnawing on it, I called the local police precinct and said I wanted to report an attempted murder. Apparently, the precinct did not receive many such calls, because the duty sergeant almost choked with incredulity. Not a chance, he said, unless there was a lot more evidence than I could offer. He would send a man around in the morning to look the place over, but there was not a chance I was right. The next day, an officer did come around, but after he had poked about for fifteen or twenty minutes he, too, said I could forget about a burglar. It was not until several years later that Dr. Z. Rita Parker, a psychiatrist whom Tass was seeing, brought up the possibility—in fact, the probability—of suicidal depression. In all the time between the accident and Dr. Parker, nobody, medical or otherwise, ever mentioned depression as a cause. In any event, even if such a diagnosis had been advanced, Tass would have rejected it. She would never have admitted to the cyclical depressions that (we know now) had been afflicting her ever more severely over the years. Someone of her New England upbringing (and of mine, for that matter; it was a generational attitude as well as a regional one) did not admit to being hobbled by any sort of impairment of the mind or of interior balance—to do so was just coddling oneself. So she simply put on a brave mask and faced down the dragon. She did a marvelously good job of it, too; she certainly took me in. But after Dr. Parker brought everything out in the open and Tass could finally talk about her trouble as a trouble and not as a failure of character, I learned that the first faint manifestations of the affliction had started in Jacksonville, and that it had got much worse during the war. (And why not?) In fact, it was not until the discovery of competent pharmacology that the dragon was slain—not slain, I suppose; just put to sleep. And, providentially, it remained asleep until Tass's death, from cancer, on October 21, 1974.

3

If my return to civilian life had been difficult at home, it was not much smoother at *The New Yorker*. I started out where I had left off—as a reporter for the "Talk of the Town" department—but neither I nor the magazine was the same. In the past, I had done "Talk of the Town" stories on things like the history of the golf ball and the culinary applications of the fiddlehead fern without once stopping to think how essentially silly they were. But now I did stop to think. Moreover, I was not the only one who had grown up, or at least shifted gears: everybody in the office was grayer and more serious—especially Shawn. Before the war, he had been, if not quite a rollicking fellow, at least a cheerful partygoer—a timidly rollicking fellow. He and Cecile gave lively, boozy parties (he drank water) in their apartment on Park Avenue South. He would play a lot of piano, and there was a lot of singing—I particularly remember Stella Brooks doing her celebrated cabaret turn ("I'm a little piece of leather from the skin of life . . ."), and Kip Orr singing, or quavering, his one published song ("Lady, play your mandolin; Lady, sing your song of sin . . . I'm a sinner too"). In those days, the whole office was self-consciously bohemian and determinedly unorthodox. Everybody strove to be what Ross was by nature. If Ross took great interest in the trivial, such as golf balls, then golf balls were worthy of serious attention. His endless curiosity and appetite for *facts* led him into all sorts of milieus, and he had dozens of disparate out-of-office friends—people like Raymond Schindler, the head of the Pinkerton detective agency, and Dave Chasen, the owner of a trendy Hollywood restaurant, and, surprisingly, a number of money men from Wall Street. From them, he would pick up a wild assortment of arcana, which would then be translated into ideas for "Talk of the Town" stories. In those prewar days, stories for the "Talk" department were divided into three categories: Fact, Visit, and Personality. The fiddlehead fern and the golf ball were Fact pieces. A typical Visit piece was a story I did on a man and his wife who built a fourteen-foot sailboat in their two-room apartment in Greenwich Village, and a Personality was anybody interesting who happened to be in town. I think Ross divided all of life into these categories. He went to the theater one night and found that his seat did not have the customary hat wire—the wire holder beneath the seat where a man could park his hat during the performance. Was this a trend? Whatever it was, it was a Fact piece, and the next day, I was out on the streets collecting the facts about hat wires. Somebody told Ross that wine flies would find an uncorked bottle of wine no matter how remote and well hidden it was—so an open bottle of Chianti was installed in the porter's hall closet on the nineteenth floor to research the matter. Bets were made on when the first wine fly would show up. Nothing happened, and there was no story, probably because it turned out that there was no such thing as a wine fly. Taking such research seriously (as Ross did) was the mark of a real *New Yorker* staffer. So was the sentimentalizing of saloon life—e.g., Joseph Mitchell's McSorley's Old Ale House, John Lardner's Bleeck's, John McNulty's Third Avenue saloons, John Bainbridge's Toots

Shor. The one piece of fiction I wrote for the magazine was set in a Third Avenue bar. One can hardly credit now how important drink was in social life then—at lunch, before dinner, after dinner (practically nobody drank wine at dinner), during theater intermissions, at football games, while waiting for a train, seeing someone off on a ship, before christenings, after funerals, whenever there was an empty half hour. Accompanying this celebration of drink was a a collateral interest in the workaday world and its inhabitants, fed by Joseph Mitchell's old Mr. Flood, the denizens of A. J. Liebling's Jollity Building, John McCarten's bookmakers, and Robert Rice's Grand Central night workers.

Altogether, life at the magazine before the war was the Hollywood version of journalism—and if you were the right age (as I was), it was an exciting place to be. A lot of the excitement was generated by Ross himself. He was like no editor that I or anybody else had ever seen before. Harold Cohn had been a star in an old tradition; Ross was sui generis. He himself had originated the role he played—relentlessly curious, devoted to detail, endlessly fascinated by the curlicues of grammar and syntax, a Lancelot in pursuit of error. He read every word in the magazine through a jeweler's loupe and wrote long notes about what he found. Here is one:

> Mr. Botsford
> Mr. Lobrano
> Mr. Shawn
> Mr. Vanderbilt
> Mr. Weekes
> Mr. Whitaker
> Mrs. White:
>
> I think the word "fabulous" should be regarded with great suspicion. It seems suddenly to have become a fad word and, worse, a *Vogue* word; it is said

> to appear on every page of *Vogue*'s every issue. Also, it appeared twice in last week's *Collier's,* in blurbs about stories in the issue.—H. W. Ross

Ross had no sense of hierarchy; he called everybody, from the managing editors (Shawn and Gus Lobrano) down to the office messenger (a retired mailman named Gebhardt), by his last name and nothing else. (Shawn, in contrast, never called anybody anything but "Mr." For thirty years, Milton Greenstein was his most intimate confidant, but he remained "Mr. Greenstein" to the end.) Ross would ask advice from the first person he met in the hall, and he wandered the halls a lot. He even asked me, the lowest man on the pole, whether a Thurber piece, then in galley proof, was funny enough to print. Another time, when I was only a couple of heads higher on the pole, he asked me if I thought Shawn had a good-enough sense of humor to be editor of the magazine one day; I gathered that he thought not. On the other hand, Ross's nitpicking and literal-mindedness could be maddening, and even destructive. At some point after the war, I edited a piece by Gerald Brenan, the Bloomsbury figure and an authority on Spanish history. He was a superb writer, much honored for his active role in the Spanish Civil War. His piece for us, called "A Search for the Poet's Tomb," was about Garcia Lorca, who had been shot, presumably by the Franco forces, and buried no one knew where. The finely spun tension started in the first paragraph and never let up. Would Brenan find the tomb? Would he ever come to know exactly what had happened? It was a marvelous piece of writing—eventually a famous piece of writing—and Ross couldn't stand it. He sent me a note:

> I've put through, annotated, the piece entitled "A Search for the Poet's Tomb," but I herewith go on record that I

> think it is a very hot piece, with possible comebacks from the Catholic Church, Generalissimo Franco, the State Department, and God knows who else. Another point, while I think of it: We ought to fix the piece so that the author sounds like an American, and not like an Englishman. I picked up a couple of things in it that sounded as though they were written by an Englishman. There may be more.

This bleat was accompanied by a heavily marked proof and a sheaf of typewritten notes filled with complaints and proposed correctives—the main one being that we ought to state at the very outset whether or not Brenan ever found the tomb. "Just a tease, otherwise," Ross wrote. The whole thing so infuriated me that I went down to Ross's office intending to do combat, or at least turn over his desk. (I was still in my military mode.) Nothing happened. Ross was charm itself and said that he had probably read the piece too fast, and that of course I should do whatever I thought proper. So I did, and a couple of weeks later, when I had another piece going to press—a "Letter from Shanghai"—he wrote me an almost deferential note:

> Mr. Botsford: I put my notes on that Letter from Shanghai through channels. I had quite a number of queries. I hold that this writer [I can't remember who it was—possibly Christopher Rand] isn't precise as to words and expressions, and frequently falters in constructions, too. He has some style, which God forbid I should smother, but he ought to think twice, and he might well look some of his words up. I suggested some fixes, but as usual these are not regarded by me as conclusive or definitive. I don't take the time to think these things through very far, but I claim, in this case, that 80% of the queries are sound.—H.W.R.

It is common opinion today that Ross was a great editor—maybe even *the* great editor. At the time, however, I thought of him not as an editor at all. To me, editors were men like Walter Lister and, pre-eminently, Harold Cohn. They knew what they wanted, they told you what they wanted, and they wouldn't accept anything less. Ross wasn't like that. He never seemed to be a boss. He never ordered or hectored; he just asked endless questions and complained to heaven about the idiocy that surrounded him, present company excepted. He got your best work out of you by getting you interested in the things that interested him. A. J. Liebling had this to say (rather restrainedly) about him upon his death:

> It is hard for a writer to call an editor great, because it is natural for him to think of the editor as a writer *manqué*. . . . I say, despite occupational bias, that Ross, the first editor of *The New Yorker*, was as great as anybody I ever knew, in his way. He couldn't write as well as Thurber or Joseph Mitchell, or draw as well as Steinberg. But he had his own greatness—he put the show together. . . . One thing that made Ross a great editor was his interest in the variety of forms greatness assumes. He wouldn't book a dancer who couldn't dance just because he liked the shape of her *derrière*. This is a higher integrity than either right-wing or left-wing editors possessed in those days. The writing in *New Masses* was as bad, in a different way, as the writing in *Time*. Ross's loyalty was to his readers.

Richard Rovere, who joined *The New Yorker* in 1944, had this to say about Ross: "Ross was all of a piece, and what he was showed in his appearance, his dress, his voice, his idiom. Almost everything about him was on the exterior, visible and audible. Nothing of the sort is true of Shawn."

And here are some recollections of Ross written by Geoffrey Hellman in 1975, twenty-four years after Ross's death, and following the publication of Thurber's terrible book *The Years with Ross* and Brendan Gill's *Here at the New Yorker*. Hellman wrote, in part:

> I joined the staff of *The New Yorker* in March, 1929, when the magazine was barely four years old and I was barely twenty-two. . . . I was given an interview with the managing editor, Ralph McAllister Ingersoll, [who] hired me as a "Talk of the Town" reporter. . . .
>
> I met Ross almost at once. He took a great interest in "Talk of the Town," generating ideas, editing the copy, and sometimes giving out assignments as well. I had an enormous admiration for Ross as an editor. I thought he was one of the funniest and most original men I had ever met. I do not recognize the buffoon of Thurber's book about him, or the foul-mouthed man with dirty fingernails of Brendan Gill's memoir. Ross was profane, in a rather mechanical and old-fashioned way, but his vocabulary was nothing like as cloacal as that of our most revered novelists today. As for some of the outside remarks about Ross, they are equally misleading. John Leonard, in the *Times,* called him an "idiot-savant" and characterized the magazine as "a smarty-pants parish tipsheet that dreamed its way through the thirties." Ross was not a savant, and only an idiot would call him an idiot. I found Ross sensitive and tactful, rather than boorish, but he *was* a character, and he sometimes played the part deliberately. I remember going to his place in Stamford one weekend, driving up in my seasoned Buick, which I parked next to his brand-new Cadillac. He came out to greet me. "Got a better car than you have, Hellman," he said, and then, having in mind my frequent requests for higher pay, he realized that he had

> said the wrong thing. "Couldn't afford it on my salary, of course," he said. "I got a little windfall from an old investment."

To Hellman's assessment, I can add that Ross had no equal in making a great deal out of practically nothing. A single word would release enormous clouds of minutiae, in a performance that second-rate writers found close to deranged and good writers found awe-inspiring. Here is Richard Rovere on an editing session with Ross—in which, incidentally, he perfectly records Ross's way of talking:

> Once, in an article on the New York District Attorney's office, I wrote, rather thoughtlessly, about an express elevator that made its first scheduled stop at the seventh floor. This annoyed Ross very much. "I'm a specialist on elevators," he said. "You probably weren't born when I started studying them, and, by God, this is the first time I ever heard of an elevator 'schedule.' It sounds pretty damned ridiculous. What do you mean, Rovere—that they've got an elevator timetable down there at Centre Street? You catch the, for God's sake, 8:19 elevator, or something like that? I just don't believe it. I'll put one of the checkers on it."
>
> If he had only stopped talking, I would have quickly conceded that I had chosen a misleading word and was glad he had pointed it out. But I couldn't bring myself to interrupt the flow, for I liked it. I liked those times in his office very much.

As for me, I first met Ross in October 1941, when the magazine was sixteen and a half years old, and I, just up from Jacksonville, was barely twenty-four. (I never saw Ross once during my first passage at the magazine.) My prewar impression of him coincided with Hellman's, but everything had changed by 1945, when I got back from the Army. For one thing, Ross was working too hard to give much time to wine flies or hat wires. Not only was he running the whole show but he and Shawn alone had to deal with every line of copy generated by the factual side of the magazine. Factual writing—"Profiles" and "Reporter at Large" pieces, the critical departments, "Goings On About Town," etc.—has always taken up at least three-quarters of every issue, and when I returned from the Army, there were no fact editors around to help carry the load. Sandy Vanderbilt (no relation—or, more likely, a connection so distant as to be invisible), who had been the prewar workhorse of the fact side, was still in Fort Dix, trying to get discharged. Russell Maloney, who had helped Ross with the "Talk of the Town" department, was still off somewhere in a government job. Hobey Weekes had not yet got out of the Air Force, and Rogers Whitaker was deep in the Army's Transportation Corps. McKelway was still in the Air Force, but he never came back as an editor anyway. Katharine White and Gus Lobrano were on hand, but they did only fiction. Ross had experimented with turning writers into fact editors—Brendan Gill, Berton Roueché, Geoffrey Hellman, and Hamilton Basso, among others—but without success: the writers-in-wolfs'-clothing had enraged their fellows by rewriting everything, and imprinting their own style and tone on the copy from beginning to end. To ward off a full-blown insurrection, Ross and Shawn had gone back to doing the editing themselves. So no more parties, no more Stella Brooks.

Just before I was drafted into the Army, I had started writing a Profile, mainly to show Ross that I was ready to graduate from "Talk of the Town," but I was drafted before I could finish it. Now that I was back, I proposed to Shawn that I move on to writing Profiles instead of hat-wire "Talk" stories. He said he had a better idea: Why didn't I take a whirl at editing? So I did, and continued to whirl for forty years.

As a guide to the work, Shawn gave me a piece he had edited, by Helen Mears, a writer now long forgotten. The thing was a revelation. Every page of the manuscript was black with Shawn's crabbed little corrections and transpositions. A paragraph on page three had been moved back to page nine. Requests for more facts or better explanations had been written in the margins. If you studied all the emendations—and I did—you could see the reason for each one: here, to get rid of an amateurish repeated construction; there, to achieve a logical sequence of events; a bit further on, to clarify the thinking. What distinguished Shawn from Gill, Roueché, Hellman, and the other makeshift editors was that, unlike them, he left no trace of his passage; the voice you heard was Helen Mears's. In a heavily edited E. J. Kahn piece he gave me as my second set of training wheels, the voice you heard was Kahn's. I had to sympathize with Gill and the others—who wanted to be a party to ungainly writing?—but you couldn't run a magazine that way.

The first piece I was given to edit was a "Popular Records" department by Douglas Watt (who later became the first-string drama critic of the *Daily News*), and I instantly fell on my face. Watt had written, "Lyrics are now considered to be as important as melody in the construction of a popular song," and he went on to elaborate. But a *New Yorker* typist, copying Watt's original manuscript for editing, had typed "not" for "now," and this, of course, stood all the rest of the paragraph on its head. Nevertheless, without thinking twice, I reworked the paragraph to support the "not." If I had been less green, I would have spotted the trouble right away (anytime you have to reverse the thought in six sentences in a row, you can be sure that either you or the writer has lost his mind), but green I was, and I plowed right on. Watt was such a mild fellow that when he got his proof, his first thoughts were not homicidal, but despairing: he figured he must have run afoul of some unfathomable *New Yorker* policy, and he asked me how he had offended. It was an embarrassing moment.

As the new boy on the block, I also inherited the worst editorial drudgery in the place: editing the annual Christmas shopping guide. It was like being on KP on Christmas Day. The lists were devised by Ross as a cheap and easy way of supplying sufficient editorial text to carry the ever-increasing columns of advertising. The device may have seemed easy to him, but it was mighty hard on the editor who had to put the mess together. The shoppers and writers who produced the text were nonprofessional friends of friends who wanted to pick up a dollar or two for Christmas, plus Marion Miller, who couldn't write, and Robey Lyle, who couldn't either but thought she could. This made Robey's copy the greatest scourge of the season—e.g.:

> Lily Daché, 78 East 56th Street: A mad, mad boutique burgeoning with accessories for worldly folk with a sense of humor . . . Eduard, at 18 West 53rd Street, is the special God of merry creatures from society and the stage (including TV), who have flocked to him for individualistic accessories ever since he pioneered in making handbags and lounging shoes of tough but transparent plastics like vegetables in a de-luxe market. . . .

When Sandy Vanderbilt finally returned to work, he took up some of the load, and life became easier. Sandy soon became my best friend at the magazine. He was eight years older than me and the most undistinguished-looking man I ever saw. His eyes popped slightly, he had next to no chin, he was short and wispy, with a little potbelly, his clothes looked as though they had previously been worn by a much bigger man, and for some reason he always tied his necktie so that one end reached to his groin. He was seriously farsighted, and when he edited copy, he had to pull so far back from it that he looked as though he was afraid his pencil would touch a live wire. For a long time, however, he refused to go to an ophthalmologist, because he knew that the doctor would look straight back into his brain with his little machine and find a cancer growing there. But he was sharp, funny, and perceptive, and an almost flawless editor—as good as Shawn. Before joining *The New Yorker* and after graduating from Amherst, he had worked as a reporter at the *New York Herald Tribune*, where he was all too often scooped by his brasher rivals. Despite his timidity, however, he was always getting into scrapes that, for a man of his temperament, must have been excruciatingly embarrassing, as when he was thrown out of the Hotel Taft one night, wearing only a shirt and pants, and carrying his shoes in his hand as he was marched through the lobby. The Taft's house detective had caught Sandy not only sharing a bed with a woman not his wife (then a crime only a shade lighter than matricide) but, even worse, sharing a bed that had been paid for at the single-occupancy rate.

Sandy and I worked in complete harmony. If he went on vacation or stayed home with a cold, I could pick up the manuscript he was editing, instantly see what he was doing and why, and complete the job, and he could do the same for me. We had adjoining offices, and we practically lived in each other's pockets, trying out editorial fixes on each other, consulting on how to quietly circumvent various Ross queries, comparing idiocies that had turned up in the work of our artists.

Sandy didn't like Shawn much. They had joined the magazine at almost the same time, and Sandy had had the better credentials: Ross had accepted a couple of his "Reporter at Large" pieces, written when he was still working on the *Herald Tribune* (one of them, "Owl Man," made it into E. B. and Katharine White's *Subtreasury of American Humor*), whereas Shawn, a one-time reporter on the Las Vegas, New Mexico, *Optic,* had published nothing in the magazine, and had been taken on simply because he was bright and ardent. I think Sandy was galled by Shawn's rise to managing editor, and he may have said something of the sort to Ross (though never to me). In any event, Shawn and Sandy exchanged jobs for a period of about six months. It was a disaster. Sandy couldn't manage a goldfish bowl, much less the *New Yorker* menagerie. Moreover, in his first week on the job, he ran head-on into a steamroller. Wolcott Gibbs had tarried at the bar too enthusiastically before attending the opening of a Lillian Hellman play, and he had slid out of his theater seat right before the eyes of the playwright herself. Then he gave the play a lukewarm notice in the magazine. Sandy had hardly sat down in Shawn's chair before Lillian Hellman was on the phone, with a few things to say. Shawn was a master at obfuscating the issue when he found himself in an indefensible position ("owing to an unfortunate misunderstanding . . .", "for certain humanitarian reasons that I'm not at liberty to go into . . ."), and a genius at giving a seemingly forthright but actually disconnected answer to a question. Sandy, however, was hopeless at this sort of thing, and Lillian Hellman almost skinned him alive. Over the next months, Sandy, always a big drinker, started drinking more, and one evening, drawing a bath, he forgot to add any cold water, and then stepped or fell into the steaming tub. He came close to being scalded to death, and was in the hospital for weeks. When he got out, he was so rickety that he clearly couldn't continue in his new job. So Shawn returned and started his climb to the editorship.

Sandy, for his part, started a slow decline, and gradually lost his remarkable editorial gift. Like the wartime ersatz editors, he started rewriting every line of every manuscript to root out what he alone saw as syntactical, grammatical, factual, logical, or structural error. With each passing day, with each fortifying drink, he worked ever more feverishly, and more ruinously. Writers who had revered him as an editor and felt lucky to have him were now ready to kill him. Shawn and I took to re-editing everything Sandy did. He never noticed; he was obsessed with eradicating demon error from the next manuscript on his pile. He and his wife, Tinka, were now living across the river in Palisades, and at first I often used to drive over to see him. Then I went less and less, and finally hardly at all; my later visits were very strained. One morning in January 1967, Tinka called: Sandy had died in his sleep that night. I wrote his obituary for the magazine, and the day after it appeared, Tinka called me again. She was crying—a tough-minded, sardonic, witty woman, whom I had thought incapable of tears. We talked for a while, and she seemed to be implying something—something I wasn't getting. Later, piecing together our conversation, it came to me that what she was trying to tell me was that Sandy's death was suicide.

Sandy and I may have been interchangeable as editors, but I was indisputably his junior in point of service, and therefore I was designated the Sunday-night man—as he had been before me. The magazine went to press at two o'clock on Monday afternoon, and the last things to close were the critical and sports departments—"The Current Cinema" (John McCarten), "The Theatre" (Wolcott Gibbs), "Of All Things" (Howard Brubaker), "Musical Events" (Robert A. Simon), "The Race Track" (George Ryall, writing as Audax Minor), and a number of on-again, off-again columns like "Horseshows and Hunts," "Yachting," and "Court Games." On alternate Sundays, Mollie Panter-Downes and Janet Flanner would file Letters from London and Paris. All these creations would be edited and set in type on Sunday night, because Ross felt that the critical departments should pick up the very latest performances, and that the Letters from London and Paris should be as up-to-date as possible—a holdover from the war. Such a load of copy made Sunday night heavy duty, and I can say quite truthfully that I never worked so hard in my life, before or since. I got Friday and Saturday off, and at two o'clock on Sunday afternoon, a checker and a switchboard operator and I would show up at the office. From then until 11:30 that night, when the last messenger left for the printing plant in Greenwich, I could not let up for an instant. It was no use trying to get a jump on the work by starting earlier: often enough, there would be no copy waiting for me at all. Gibbs would have called in to say that he was having a little trouble getting started (bad hangover); McCarten had not even been heard from; Simon had gone to a concert that afternoon and wouldn't be able to start writing until six o'clock at the earliest; and so on. The difficulty with the London and Paris copy was not fecklessness but transmission. The Letters were sent by very erratic cable (nothing better was available so soon after the war), and the frequent passages of garble would have to be traced back to Paris or London for correction—a lengthy business, since it was not possible to telephone. On one occasion, the cable from Paris was delivered to *The New Yorker* as twenty-six pages of the letter O, and nothing else.

The only writers who were always on time were George Ryall and Howard Brubaker. Brubaker was *The New Yorker's* most venerable contributor. His name first appeared as the author of "Of All Things" in the issue of May 9, 1925, but the department, signed only "The New Yorker," had been running since the very first issue, February 21, 1925, when it held the spot that "The Talk of the Town" holds today. Brubaker probably wrote those earlier departments, too. By the time I became Sunday-night man, "Of All Things" had shrunk to a single column, buried in the back of the book. I guess it was kept on out of sentiment; it certainly wasn't very good. As for George Ryall, he was another venerable contributor. He had started covering the metropolitan racetracks on July 10, 1926, and in twenty years, his columns had not changed a particle in style, tone, content, or coverage. The only thing that distinguished one column from another was the names of the horses; you could edit him in your sleep.

As for Gibbs, you didn't edit him at all, asleep or awake. In the first place, he didn't need editing: until he decided to devote himself entirely to writing, he had been (I was told) the best editor the magazine had ever seen—better even than Shawn or Vanderbilt. Bad writing was an affront to him, and he could be cruel, almost vindictive, in his reaction to it. When the literary editor of a Chicago magazine asked him to review a book by Claudia Cassidy, the well-known drama critic of the *Chicago Tribune,* Gibbs wrote back:

February 19, 1954

Dear Miss Ellis:

I have received your request that I submit a review of "Europe on the Aisle," by Claudia Cassidy. The idea, I must say, interested me, but since I have now undertaken a preliminary exploration of the book I feel I must decline your offer. So far, I have read only up to the second page of the Prologue—the paragraph beginning "So we went, and we kept going . . ."—but even this much of the text appealed strongly to my editorial instinct, and I would like to append the following notes for your attention:

1. "Rivers swirled into silver dragons" is, I think, a phrase without felicity, conveying no pleasing or natural image. It is *Saturday Evening Post* imagery—sound divorced from meaning. An illiterate practice.
2. "Craters in some unthinkable landscape" is more of the same, and "unthinkable" is not an adjective employed by the judicious writer. If something is unthinkable, the reader should not be asked to think about it.
3. "Blurred pastel bouquets of a lyric come to life" means precisely nothing, and "blurred" in this context is a fine example of the non-functional modifier, diminishing, if anything, the force of the word "pastel."
4. "For it was apple-blossom time in Normandy" is, I'm afraid, arch at best, and the ragtime beat is not appealing to the ear.

> 5. "Highways and byways" and "capacious maw" are scarcely arrangements of words that would recommend themselves to the fastidious writer.
>
> There are 230 more pages in this book, and they all seem very much the same.
>
> Sincerely yours,
> Wolcott Gibbs

Gibbs did some fact editing, but he worked primarily in fiction, and he once set down a few observations on how fiction should be handled:

> The average contributor to this magazine is semi-literate; that is, he is ornate to no purpose, full of senseless and elegant variations, and can be relied upon to use three sentences where a word would do. It is impossible to lay down any exact and complete formula for bringing order out of this underbrush, but there are a few general rules.
>
> 1. Writers always use too damn many adverbs. On one page recently, I found five modifying the verb "said"—"he said morosely . . . violently . . . eloquently," and so on. Editorial theory should probably be that a writer who can't make his context indicate the way his character is talking ought to be in another line of work.
>
> 2. Collaterally, the word "said" itself is O.K. Efforts to avoid repetition by using "grunted," "snorted," etc., are waste motion and offend the pure in heart.
>
> 3. Our writers are full of clichés, just as old barns are full of bats. There is obviously no rule about this, except

that anything you suspect of being a cliché undoubtedly is one, and had better be removed.

4. Funny names belong to the past. Any character called Mrs. Middlebottom or Joe Zilch should be summarily renamed. This goes for animals, towns, books, and many other things.

5. Our employer, Mr. Ross, has a prejudice against the use of such words and phrases as "little," "vague," "confused," "faintly," "all mixed up," etc. The point is that the average *New Yorker* writer, unfortunately influenced by Mr. Thurber, now believes that the ideal *New Yorker* piece is about a vague little man helplessly confused by a menacing and complicated civilization. Whenever this note is not the whole point of the piece (and it far too often is), it should be regarded with suspicion.

6. The repetition of exposition in quotes went out with the Stanley Steamer: "Marion gave me a pain in the neck. 'You give me a pain in the neck, Marion.' I said."

[It may have gone out with the Stanley Steamer, but it came back with the Ford Thunderbird. Here is a passage from Philip Roth's *Great American Novel*, of 1975: "When he [Hemingway] was having a good day, they didn't make them any more generous or sweet-tempered, but when he was having a bad day, well, he could be the biggest prick in all literature. 'You're the biggest prick in all literature,' I remember telling him one morning . . ."]

7. I suffer very seriously from writers who divide quotes for some kind of ladies-club rhythm: "I am going," he said, "downtown." This is a horror, and unless a quote is pretty long it should all stay on one side of the verb.

8. Editing on a manuscript should be done with a black pencil, decisively.

9. On the whole, we are hostile to puns.
10. Try to reserve the author's style, if he is an author and has a style.

My Sunday-night problem with Gibbs was not what he wrote (even when on a tear, he wrote lucidly and aptly; the review that so outraged Lillian Hellman was well constructed and well turned) but where he could be found in order to write it. Stanley Eichelbaum, the Sunday switchboard operator (he later became Janet Flanner's favorite checker and, even later, the culture editor of the *San Francisco Chronicle*), had put together a chart of Gibbs's favorite hideouts, and if no copy was forthcoming by four o'clock, Stanley would start trying to pick up our critic's tracks.

Fortunately, there was not a theater opening every week. With John McCarten, who *did* have a new movie every week, I had the same problem, but mitigated. He was almost as slippery as Gibbs, but he was such a fast (if rather sloppy) writer that, once cornered, he could produce a column in about an hour, and he didn't care how much it was edited; in fact, he never even read his proofs on Monday morning.

The first long non-Sunday piece I edited was by Christopher Rand—an account of his wartime experiences in China. He was another writer who never read his proofs. I, being so new at the game, wanted to ask him all sorts of questions and get his approval of various changes I had made, but he would have none of it. Whatever I did was all right with him, he said, so count him out—once he had finished a piece, he had no further interest in discussing it, correcting it, or even thinking about it. It was not an ideal arrangement; no editor should be given such latitude to get things wrong.

Chris was an odd, friendly man, who looked like Rudyard Kipling (the rufous hair, the round gold-framed glasses) and who walked entirely on his toes, bouncing along like a terrier. He came from an ancient Waspy family in Salisbury, Connecticut, and was an elegant dresser—for the most part. His suits were made to measure at Dunhill, and they fit like an English banker's, but somewhere along the line, Chris had become a Buddhist (no leather), and his impeccable Dunhill pants were held up by a length of frowsy rope, and instead of narrow, fastidious shoes he wore dirty sneakers. He wrote a lot for *The New Yorker,* all of it good, until a sad day in the late sixties when he jumped to his death from the roof of a Mexican hotel.

Rand and McCarten were almost alone in not caring what happened to their copy, and I soon learned about the difficulties of trying to steer a course between, on the one hand, the Scylla of the demands and suggestions from Shawn, Ross, Eleanor Gould (the staff grammarian), and the fact-checking department, and, on the other, the Charybdis of preserving the beset and badgered writer's prose. The way the system worked was this: A writer would turn in, say, a "Reporter at Large." It would be accepted by Ross and sent to Shawn for assignment to an editor. (In the beginning, that meant Sandy or me.) Once the editor had done his work, the emended copy would be sent off to the printer to be set in type. When the first proof came back, all those other hands would get to work. Ross would examine the piece with his jeweler's loupe, making splotchy corrections in the margins (his proofs were always defaced with erasures and coffee stains) and appending many pages of typewritten notes. ("How could he know this? He hasn't been in Vidalia in twelve years, and it stands to reason that the situation would have changed in his absence. Needs fix for credibility.") Of all the mice nibbling away at the piece, Ross was the only one who complained about dullness. ("This is all stuff a twelve-year-old girl would know. Boring. Suggest cut.") Shawn, on his proof, would tiptoe through the copy, sniffing out questions of taste. ("I don't think the police sergeant's description of the stolen brassières is right for us. Funny, but taste?") Eleanor Gould, the grammarian, would test for sentence structure, word repetitions, and such, and the checker would chase down every windblown fact the writer had used, and endeavor to prove it wrong. The pensées of all these people would be sent on to the editor in charge of the piece (to me, that is, or to Sandy), and it was up to him to accept or reject them. For me, greenest of the green, this was the trickiest part. To accept everything these sharpshooters proposed would be to turn the piece into a translation from the Armenian and the author into a gibbering madman. Yet the impulse to do exactly that was almost overpowering—the sharpshooters were all so particular, so logically unassailable. In my greenness, I recklessly accepted every change they proposed—until I made a couple of really howling errors. Here (to my shame) is what Eleanor Gould did to me and, through me, to Christopher Rand in a piece he wrote on the research-and-development firms on Route 128, outside of Boston.

> Rand: A research-and-development firm must be able to attract and hold scientists. It can't do this by money alone, for in the end most firms will pay about the same for men of equal ability. So it does it by offering nice surroundings.
>
> Gould: A research-and-development firm must be able to attract and hold scientists. It finds that it can't accomplish this with money alone—in fact, most firms have given up any attempt to do so and now pay about the same for men of equal ability—so it accomplishes it by offering superior working conditions.

It was a fortunate thing that Rand never read his proofs, allowing me to reunite him with his writing in a later proof.

Eleanor Gould had me completely mesmerized for a long time. She had begun her career as an organic chemist, not as a grammarian, and you can't beat an organic chemist for logic. Barely a week after falling into the Rand pothole, I did the same thing again. Wolcott Gibbs had included in his theater column a review of a play that had already closed—something he rarely did. He started his review, "While it is not my custom to dissect dead cats, I must say of 'Somewhere Out There,' recently at the Belasco, that . . ." Miss Gould fell on this sentence at once, proposing to delete the word "dead." "A pleonasm," she wrote in the margin. "You can't dissect a *live* cat." The point was not only classy (I had to look up "pleonasm" in the dictionary) but beyond argument: you certainly cannot dissect a *live* cat. So I took out "dead," and the next day when I read in the revised proof "While it is not my custom to dissect cats . . ." I wondered whether Gibbs would just have me fired or would shoot me first. He did neither: he put the "dead" back in without comment. Actually, Gibbs was unfailingly polite to me. Whenever his Sunday-night copy was a bit erratic, he would write me a charming little note of apology the next day, and then fix everything up on his Monday-morning proof. He was polite but distant. His best friends on the magazine were John O'Hara and Charles Addams. In the summer of 1958, Addams was visiting the Gibbses on Fire Island, and he and Elinor Gibbs and some other people were sitting on the porch, having a drink before lunch. Gibbs was upstairs in his bedroom, reading proofs. Periodically, Elinor would call up to him to remind him of lunch, but there was never an answer. Finally, she asked the maid to go up and rout him out. The maid came back and said, "Maybe you'd better go up, Mr. Addams." Charlie went up, and there was Gibbs, dead in his chair. "He had his feet up on the windowsill," Addams told me later, "and the proofs of his book *More in Sorrow* were in his lap. He had a cigarette in his hand, and it had burned right down to his fingers."

It was Jane Grant, Ross's first wife and a newspaperwoman on the *Times* (a rare thing in those days), who, in 1925, recruited Janet Flanner, then newly arrived in Paris, to be *The New Yorker's* voice from abroad. Flanner was thirty-three years old, two years older than an acquaintance of hers in New York—my mother. Both of them came from the Midwest (Indianapolis, in Flanner's case), and both were guided onto the New York scene by Neysa McMein. Janet was dazzled by Neysa; my mother had known her too well and too long for that. Janet practically camped out in Neysa's studio—she even posed for her, as a dairymaid—and could well have been a bit in love with her. Probably she felt a tacit rivalry with my mother; whatever the reason, the two of them never became real friends., although they professed to admire each other greatly. ("And how is dear, beautiful Ruth?" Flanner would ask me whenever I went to Paris.) It was Raoul who was Flanner's great pal. He even stoutly said he liked her "Profile" of Adolf Hitler, which offended practically every other Jew in New York, though she considered it apolitical.

The earliest issues of the magazine had run a couple of anonymous hit-and-miss letters from Paris, but Ross wanted a letter that would be a regular feature. It was to be signed "Genêt" (his invention; Janet proposed "Flâneuse," an idler [*f.*]), and he said he would pay forty dollars for each one (thirty-five, in the event). On October 10, 1925, the first Flanner "Letter from Paris" appeared. By the time I came along as the new Sunday-night man, Flanner had been writing her Letters for twenty years, but we had an instant rapport even so. Maybe because of this, maybe because of dear, beautiful Ruth, Tass and I saw a lot of Flanner when she was in New York. She took a particular fancy to Tass (unsurprisingly, I suppose), who once endured an interminable performance of *The Magic Flute* sitting between Janet and her lover/friend Natalia Murray, being surreptitiously patted and whispered to by Janet on one side and glared at and growled at by Natalia on the other. We even spent a raucous New Year's Eve together at the Stork Club, of all places, along with the Brendan Gills. We drank champagne, and Janet raised her powerful baritone in "Auld Lang Syne" to such effect that the waiters applauded. And whenever Tass and I were in Paris (which was almost every year in those days), we would see still more of her, because she was ravenous for news of New York and *The New Yorker*. One day in the late fifties, Tass and I were having lunch with her in a little restaurant on the Rue des Saints-Pères, when a remarkable-looking raven-haired woman came in—tall, elderly, very gaunt, hawklike of face, and heavily made up, with scores of thick bracelets—jade, gold, Indian, amber, Aztec—reaching from her wrists to her thin elbows. Janet, who was sitting on the banquette, facing the door, recognized her instantly. "Nancy, darling!" she cried, leaping up, and they kissed: Janet Flanner and Nancy Cunard, the *ur*-figures of the Paris twenties—Janet, the survivor, still at work, still of today, and Nancy, now existing only in the past. In the twenties, Nancy had been the larger figure on the Paris canvas—beautiful, independent, rich, a poet, the founder of the Hours Press, Louis Aragon's lover, the Iris March of Michael Arlen's *The Green Hat,* the Lucy Tantamount of Aldous Huxley's *Point Counter Point.* Heartbreakingly beautiful and talented, she could be, and was, careless of her power. ("His voice trembled, his eyes were imploring," Huxley wrote in *Point Counter Point,* surely from personal experience. " 'Please, *please,*' he begged. 'Impossible,' said Lucy, and stepped out of the cab. If he behaved like a whipped dog, he could be treated like one.") Now she and Flanner were two older women, kissing. They had met in 1924 and had instantly fused. "We became a fixed triangle," Solita Solano, the third leg of the tripod and Janet's lifelong companion, wrote after Nancy's death. "We survived all the spring quarrels and the sea changes of forty-two years of modern female fidelity." Now, stared at and whispered over by the other diners in the tiny restaurant, Nancy Cunard was simply a curiosity. Three years later, at sixty-nine, she died—alcoholic, schizophrenic, paranoid. Her ashes are buried in Père Lachaise cemetery, under a plaque installed by Janet and Solita.

As a writer, Flanner was completely unbuttoned and impressionistic. Her words would pour out as from an open faucet, yet every Flanner sentence was instantly identifiable as her own. Its construction may have been loose and undisciplined, and she often used a word because it sounded right even if it didn't mean right, but there was not a line that did not carry a full freight of meaning and feeling. She was a great one for rewriting, or trying to rewrite, a piece after turning it in—not, I always felt, because she had detected a flaw in it but because she didn't know how to turn off the faucet. Whatever the reason, her rewrites seldom improved matters, and often left them in greater disarray. One of her least successful works was a "Profile" of Bernard Buffet, an artist whose popularity rose like a rocket in the fifties and then dropped off just as precipitately. Janet came to him at the highest point in his trajectory, but by the time she had done the writing he was already on his way down. She knew it, and no amount of rewriting could push him back up. She wrote me:

> Gardner, dear boy, it is always later than you think & slower than you could believe when I begin rewriting, especially rewriting Buffet once more. This has been the most tiring, worrying rewriting I have ever done except for the Malraux Profile, when on the second go it felt like the second of a pair of twins, born one year after the first. I've been a clumsy fool about this Profile generally, as puzzled as a beginner in putting it together again & again. I was slow in my mind while writing it—those mud baths (though the mud never went higher than my shoulders) soothed the brain disproportionately. I've added bits here and there as you suggested, such as Buffet's fall-off in sales, this being unpleasant, even damaging, but vital news in reporting on his career. I also included the anti-Buffet criticism which you rightly said had to appear somewhere. . . . My sense of protection for my profilees always seizes me only when the head-severing is done & finished. I probably become attached to them through intimacy, and am prompted always to try to put the head back on over the last pages. Love. Please push the galleys darling.

Janet and I worked together very well. By fortunate chance, I happened to be in almost perfect tune with her thinking and with her style, and she, in turn, came to lean on me for support. I offer a case in point, starting with a telephone call I received from Simon Michael Bessie, than an editor at Harper & Row. The following March, Bessie said, Harper would be publishing a collection of Flanner's *New Yorker* art writings under the title *Men and Monuments.* However, one chapter, which he admired greatly—a "Profile" of Picasso—had not yet appeared in *The New Yorker,* although it had been in the magazine's hands for more than a month. He would greatly appreciate it if I would get off my butt and do the editing so he could keep to his production schedule. I would have to edit it sometime, so why not now? I said I didn't have time right now, and if he needed it so badly, why didn't he edit it himself? We parted not on the best of terms. I now go, shamelessly, to *Genêt,* Brenda Wineapple's biography of Flanner:

> Janet decided that the Picasso article should appear in "Men and Monuments" without the benefit of Gardner Botsford's editing. . . . It appeared in the *New Yorker,* in edited form, in March, 1957, coincident with the publication of "Men and Monuments." The magazine version, decidedly better written, differs little in substance, but Gardner Botsford's fine reorganization clarified the somewhat confusing chronology of events and descriptions.

The fact is that book editors don't know the first thing about editing. It may be that they don't need to. Most of their day is spent on acquisitions, sales, lunches, promotion, and internecine warfare, with very little time left over for work on the manuscript. Editing a book is nothing like editing a magazine article anyway. The pace of a book is lazier, the organization is looser, and the permissible level of blather is higher—generally too high. On the other hand, cutting a book down to manageable proportions for a magazine often loses the book's flavor and the sense of completion. John Bainbridge's *Texas* worked better as a book than as a series of very long *New Yorker* articles. I edited Geoffrey Hellman's "Profile" of the Smithsonian Institution twice—once as a *New Yorker* piece and once as a book—for which he sent me a case of Gruaud Larose. Joseph Mitchell, the nonpareil, never did write a book; some of his *New Yorker* pieces appeared *as* books, but that's different. Similarly A. J. Liebling (except for *The Republic of Silence*). Similarly Janet Flanner (except for *The Cubical City*).

Flanner died on November 7, 1978, and I wrote an obituary. (Over time, writing obits became my secondary career at the magazine: Sandy Vanderbilt, Sam Cobean, Hobey Weekes, Geoffrey Hellman, Hawley Truax, Raoul Fleischmann, Mollie Panter-Downes, Brendan Gill, and, as noted, Janet Flanner. The two most memorable obits—of Ross and of Wolcott Gibbs—were by E. B. White, and he wrote Ross's in the space of one Monday morning, under the pressure of press time—an unbelievable piece of work. White's own obit was done by various hands, chiefly Roger Angell's.) As things turned out, my Flanner obit was never published, owing to internal conflagrations at the magazine; at the time, Shawn would not have published the Gettysburg Address if I had written it. Of Flanner, I said:

> The years after the war were years of great political events and artistic occasions in France. The country had changed enormously, and Flanner had changed, too, spreading her net ever wider to gather material for her fortnightly Letter from Paris. She had to work demonically. She was everywhere—in art galleries, at political meetings, in bookstores, at criminal trials, in theatres, at riots, at state dinners, in concert halls. She always seemed to know

which event had at that moment ripened for the plucking. It was not entirely her own prescience that informed her. She had a system. For some twenty years after the war, Flanner lived in the Hotel Continental, on the Rue de Rivoli, and almost every afternoon, at around five-thirty, she would descend to the bar—a huge, cavernous room, opulent with cupids and goddesses painted on the ceiling and gleaming with gilt everywhere: the hotel's grand ballroom in the days of Louis Napoleon—and take her usual seat on a great horseshoe sofa at the Tuileries end of the room. A perfect dry martini would be brought. (She had early on told the barman, Henri, how.) The firm was now open for business. Within minutes would arrive the first of the afternoon's friends, petitioners, gossips, visitors from New York, political aspirants, bearers of tidings, bearers of manuscripts. Some would have been invited; others would simply have dropped in, knowing that "Mademoiselle Flannère's" salon was the best in Paris. For each of them, in his or her turn, she was critic, arbiter, questioner, reminiscer, or prodder, in English or French or both. (She spoke completely fluent, strongly accented French. She sounded like a Frenchwoman from Indianapolis.) Henri was kept busy. Before long, the places on the horseshoe sofa would be filled, and late arrivals—carrying their first chapters or second acts in their briefcases—would have to wait their turn on little gilt chairs that Henri had forehandedly lined up against one wall; every time a postulant on the horseshoe sofa left, the person at the head of the line would take his place, and all the others, in unison, would move up one notch. It was a scene that unfailingly transfixed the other patrons of the bar. As Flanner dispensed advice and judgment, she also listened, picking up word of an out-of-the-way art exhibition, news of a paradox in a forthcoming statement of policy by a government minister, a bit of literary gossip worthy of the retelling. ("There was difficulty at first in finding a French publisher for General Charles de Gaulle's 'Memoires de Guerre' . . . owing to the astronomical price the General demanded.") Often enough, she would simply have a good time. She liked to tell stories, and she loved to hear them. If the raconteur was particularly gifted, he would be rewarded by the Flanner laugh: she would first widen her eyes and open her mouth in delicious disbelief, and the first chuckling intimations could be heard of the eruption to come. And then it came—a great baritone trombone hoot, followed by little coarse yelps of pure ecstasy.

When the last guest had gone, Flanner would return to her tiny room on the top floor of the hotel—a maid's room in the days when travellers had maids—and shove things around until she had made space for herself to write. It was not easy: every interior surface—the bed, the chair, the desk—was spilling over with manuscripts, periodicals, catalogs, brochures, letters. But she loved the room. Outside were the Tuileries and the great broad sky of Paris; inside and in place (at last) was her ancient Hermès typewriter with the pale-blue ribbon. She would sit down and, drawing on all she had heard downstairs, all she had read, all she had reported, all she had thought during the day and during the week, she would start putting together one of those marvellous, torrential, perceptive Letters with which she brightened this magazine for almost precisely fifty years.

Glenway Westcott, Flanner's friend for more years than either of them could count and now aged, infirm, and dotty, was the principal speaker at the memorial service held for Flanner in Frank Campbell's chapel. When his moment came, he shambled to the dais, clutching to his breast an untidy haystack of notes. Our hearts sank. He balanced his stack on a corner of the lectern, gathered us all in with a benign, mad smile, and started to speak. All our fidgeting stopped. He spoke so well and so gracefully that his sense of loss was almost palpable. Not a movement, not a whisper came from his audience. Then, as he reached for another page of his notes, he knocked the whole pile off its perch. The papers cascaded to the floor, swooping and fluttering everywhere. There was a murmur from the audience. Westcott, undismayed, waved off any help and prepared to go on. But he couldn't remember where he was or what he was going to say, and after a dreadful pause, he began to cry. Monroe Wheeler came forward and collected him from the dais, and they went home. It was the kind of event that Flanner would have perfectly reported in a "Letter."

M*onroe Wheeler*. He was one of Flanner's oldest friends (they had met in the early 1930s in Paris, both under the spell of Gertrude Stein), and an even older friend of Glenway Westcott, whom he met in 1919, and with whom he lived, on and off, for sixty-eight years. A slight, wiry man with black hair, a dark complexion, and brilliant, darting black eyes, he came from an artistically inclined middle-class family in Chicago; Westcott was from a farm family in Wisconsin. Wheeler got a job at the brand-new Museum of Modern Art in 1935, and rose high in its ranks; for years, he was its director of publications. He and Westcott had previously lived abroad for a dozen years, mingling with what was then called "the smart set," ranging from Jean Cocteau to Georges Auric to Somerset Maugham. They knew everybody. Now, in New York, Wheeler met everybody else. There was nobody in the art world he did not come to know, and since art museums are kept going by the titans of the financial world, he became entirely comfortable with the Stephen Clarks, the various Rockefellers, the various Whitneys and Vanderbilts, the Guggenheims. He moved in a section of society where the culture, care, and maintenance of celebrity is almost a profession. "Monroe has an excellent raconteur's mind, memory, vocabulary, tongue," Janet Flanner wrote of him somewhere. "He brings in a story at just the right time, in the right manner, serves his anecdotes perfectly, either piping hot or ice-cold, as tragedies." The difference between Wheeler and the hundreds of ordinary celebrity culturists was that he was never the hero of his stories or reminiscences. He genuinely liked art, he liked the people who made it, he liked the people who paid for it, and they liked him. The names he dropped in prodigal numbers did not so much drop as float gracefully to the ground.

A few days after Flanner's memorial service, I ran into Wheeler at the Coffee House club, where he was having lunch with a discreet young acolyte. I asked after Glenway Westcott.

"Oh, he's all right," Monroe said. "The trouble is, he'll be eighty before long, and he can't remember anything. (Wheeler was well over eighty himself, and could remember everything.) So far, he's left three suitcases behind in taxis—every time he's been in a taxi with a suitcase, in fact. Cartier-Bresson was asking about him today"—and off we went on another of Wheeler's whirlwind magic-lantern tours. As always, when it was over, I went back to my office and wrote it all down.

"Cartier-Bresson was on the phone from Paris," Wheeler said. "He wanted me to get him what he called a 'dingy' hotel room in New York—didn't want to spend a penny more than he had to. He's from Normandy, you know, and the Normans pinch every penny. My friend Philippe de Rothschild wasn't a Norman, but he certainly pinched every penny, too. Jean Cocteau told me once that he and Philippe left a party together late at night and shared a taxi, even though they were going in opposite directions. As it happened, the taxi stopped first at the Rothschild house, and Philippe simply said good night and walked away, leaving Cocteau to pay the fare when he finally got home. So the next day, Cocteau went around to see Philippe and complain that he really didn't think it was fair to make him pay the Rothschild taxi fares. Philippe still didn't offer to pay his half. He simply told Jean that to the Rothschilds the pictures of famous men on the French banknotes were like family portraits—never to be let go of."

"Oh, he *didn't*!" said the acolyte.

"Yes, he did," said Monroe, and moved along to the *Times'* John Russell—or, rather, to Russell's wife, Rosamund Bernier. "Rosamund was born Rosamund Rosenbaum, daughter of a big Philadelphia lawyer," he said. "She went to Sarah Lawrence, where she took an art course under René d'Harnoncourt. Rosamund went on a trip to Mexico, and there fell in love with a young American who was dealing in Acapulco real estate. He was the best-looking of three orphan boys in the town, and Rosamund wanted to marry him. Daddy said no, you're too young, so she eloped with him anyway, and set up housekeeping in Mexico. There, as we all know, Orozco fell in love with her—her second contact with the art world. Possibly because of Orozco or maybe because she and her husband both spoke Spanish—I really don't know—the two of them were recruited by the Museum of Modern Art to shepherd an exhibit of modern art on a tour of South America. Anyway, it wasn't long after that that her husband grew tired of her, and when he met Dolores Del Río, generally considered to be the most beautiful actress in Hollywood, he got a divorce and married Dolores. Oh, how hard Rosamund took it! She came back to New York and wept up and down Fifth Avenue endlessly. But eventually she brushed her tears away and went to France, where she met and married a Frenchman named Bernier. Together, they started *Oeil,* which became an enormous success. But then Bernier, too, got tired of her and went off to become an art dealer on his own. Rosamund returned to the United States and wept up and down Fifth Avenue again. Pretty soon, she went back to France and took to weeping up and down the Faubourg St. Honoré, until John Russell ran into her there and fell in love with her."

Monroe, shifting gears, continued: "I just gave a collection of two hundred letters I received from Marianne Moore to the Public Library's Berg Collection. Now that I'm falling apart, I'm getting rid of a lot of things. I've sold a lot of my books—ten thousand dollars' worth. I'm using the money to eat. Marianne Moore always had a low opinion of the value of her letters. When her friends would say that they were collecting them because they were so wonderfully quirky and illuminating, she would scoff and say that she couldn't understand it at all. 'Sell them, if you can get anything for them,' she would say. She knew the value of a dollar. She, too, was a tremendous penny-pincher. I remember calling on her in Brooklyn one day. It was just about lunchtime, and she was fixing her lunch. I invited her to come out and have a bite with me, but she said no, she had already started cooking. And what cooking it was! She was boiling a potato, and when it was almost done she put some string beans in the same pot—to save gas. That was her lunch: one potato and about six or eight beans. She loved to travel—that is, she loved to think about traveling, because she never went anywhere. She did her traveling at Town Hall, where she would go to hear Burton Holmes lecture. She loved Burton Holmes. People wondered how she managed to live—poetry is not a high-paying profession. The answer is that she had dozens of solicitous, generous friends, who would do anything for her, and who watched over her like nannies. During her last illness, I called her up to see if she needed any sort of financial help, and the woman who was looking after her—her great friend, who moved in to nurse her, and whose name I've forgotten—told me that everything was all right: Marianne had three hundred thousand dollars in the bank. She had squirreled away every prize she had won over a long life, and every grant she had ever been awarded, and had not spent a penny of the money.

"The Berg Collection was founded and named for a famous gallbladder surgeon in New York, and I was one of his patients—the only one still alive, I don't doubt. I was twenty-six at the time. He was already forming his book collection, and he took a liking to me and would sit on my bed in the hospital and talk books. He also removed Mrs. W. K. Vanderbilt's gallbladder—she had hers done a year or so ahead of me. It was his custom—it was the custom of all the really big surgeons in the city in those days—to bill patients for one month of their incomes. Of course, he didn't know what one month of Mrs. Vanderbilt's income was, but he took a healthy guess and, considering who she was, added a couple of digits for good measure. The resulting bill was a whopper. Even she thought it was awfully high, and the next time her lawyers came to call—which must have been the next day, because her lawyers feasted on her—she showed it to them. 'Preposterous,' they said. 'Leave it to us.' But then she thought about how the lawyers were always going to handle things for her, and how they always made everything worse, and she thought about how poorly she had felt for so long because of her wretched gallbladder, and about how much better Dr. Berg had made her feel, and she told the lawyers to all go away. The next day, she took a pouch of her jewels down to Cartier and paid Dr. Berg with the proceeds. Hence the Berg Collection, or a lot of it."

"How did you get to be a patient of Dr. Berg's?" I asked. "At twenty-six, a month of your income could hardly have interested him."

"It's as E. M. Forster said—'only connect,'" Monroe said. "My life has been nothing but connections. In those days, I had a friend named Hope Weil. Her husband was a cotton broker, and she was a bookbinder—a truly gifted, truly artistic bookbinder. Another big doctor in town then was a Dr. Crohn. He was so important that a disease was named after him—Crohn's disease. I forget which organ it attacks, if I ever knew. Well, Dr. Crohn was insanely in love with Hope Weil. He was after her night and day. Couldn't live without her. Never let up. But Hope loved her Mr. Weil. Her Mr. Weil, I must say, was either very tolerant or very thick in the head, because he liked Dr. Crohn and was always saying, 'Let's have him to dinner.' And every time Dr. Crohn came to dinner, I came, too, because Hope felt that I was her ally and would be helpful to have around if things got sticky. Of course, Dr. Crohn was in seventh heaven at these dinners, and he took a liking to me, probably because I was a friend of Hope's and he thought I would be *his* ally. And all the time, Mr. Weil laughed and joked and was delighted with Dr. Crohn's company. So then I had this gallbladder trouble, and Dr. Crohn looked me over and said that it would have to come out and that he would put me in the hands of the finest gallbladder surgeon in New York—Dr. Berg. And that's how I became Dr. Berg's patient. What's more, I think Dr. Crohn made some kind of arrangement with Dr. Berg about the fee—he no doubt felt that I would still be of service to him in his Hope Weil campaign. In any case, Dr. Berg's bill, when it came, was nothing like a month of my income, even at twenty-six."

"But what happened to Dr. Crohn and Hope Weil?" I said.

"Hope held fast. A couple of years later, her husband died, and I would like to say that romance triumphed and she married Dr. Crohn. But she didn't, because Dr. Crohn had given up by that time and married someone else. He lived to be ninety-nine years old. Hope went on with her bookbinding. She died only last year.

"Old age is a terrible nuisance. Everything gives way. The other day, someone was telling me about Iphigene Sulzberger, Punch Sulzberger's mother. Doyenne of the *Times.* I've known her for years. She has a bad heart or circulation problems or something, and her doctor insists that she get proper exercise. So every day she takes a little walk—always the same. She lives on Fifth Avenue, and she walks over to Madison, and along the avenue for a few blocks, and then back to Fifth and home. Her difficulty is that at her age she always has to—how shall I say it?—relieve herself during her walk. At first she would stop in at the Carlyle, but the ladies' room there is down a flight of stairs, and that was too hard for her. So then she asked at the Frank Campbell funeral parlor, where the ladies' room is on the ground floor, and they said of course. She changed her route to take in Frank Campbell's every day, and things went along like that for quite a while. One day as she was coming out of the ladies' room a very smooth young man—a newcomer to the staff—asked her if she would sign their guest book. So she did, and thought no more about it until she got a check in the mail for five thousand dollars. What she had signed was the visitors' register at some rich woman's funeral—the smooth young man thought she was one of the mourners—and the deceased in her will had left five thousand dollars to everybody who had come to her funeral and signed the book."

* * *

In early 1948, the filing of both "Letter from Paris" and "Letter from London" was moved from Sunday to a more civilized day of the week, and I was moved with them. A new man took over the Sunday nights, and I spent most of my time editing long fact pieces—"Profiles," "Reporters at Large," and such. I continued to edit Flanner and Mollie Panter-Downes—in fact, from then on I edited everything that either one of them wrote for the magazine—and I also acquired a number of the other first-class *New Yorker* writers, with many of whom I formed permanent alliances. This meant less time with the lesser writers I had started on—the Helen Mearses and the Joseph Wechsbergs. Helen Mears was a forgettable writer; Joseph Wechsberg, I will remember forever. He was a hair shirt, a Dreadful Example, and a rite of passage for every junior editor. For one thing, he was a Czech who never really learned English. (Here is an undoctored Wechsberg biological insight I have saved over the years: "Without the long snouts of the humble-bees, pansies and red clover can't be fructified.") For another, he had started life as a fiction writer (he is best known today, if he is known at all, for some stories he did for the magazine before the war), and whenever the facts he needed proved elusive he made them up. Since his writing was disconnected from grammar, vocabulary, and sanity (see above), he could write at great speed, and no one was more prolific. Sandy Vanderbilt always claimed that he had edited more Wechsberg than I—that he had edited more Wechsberg than Wechsberg had even written, because of a recurrent bad dream he had about working on a relentless, never-ending Wechsberg manuscript that continued to ooze forth no matter how fast Sandy labored—but when the two of us went to the morgue and got out the Wechsberg file, neither of us could remember who had edited what, or, to be more accurate, who had written what. The thing that galled us both was that Wechsberg was immensely popular with the readers, meaning that *we* were immensely, if anonymously, popular with the readers. With the arrival of some new editors junior even to me—Bill Knapp, Bill Fain, Bob Gerdy, and a couple more transient figures—Wechsberg was passed down the line, and I was free at last.

Not entirely free, of course. Because the magazine published fifty-two issues a year, most of them (then) containing at least two fact pieces, it was too much to expect that the first-string writers could produce enough to fill the demand. This opened the gate to the second-raters, and I (and Sandy and Shawn and everybody else) had to lend a hand. It was the kind of work that led me to several conclusions about editing.

> **Rule of thumb No. 1:** To be any good at all, a piece of writing requires the investment of a specific amount of time, either by the writer or by the editor. Wechsberg was fast; hence, his editors had to be up all night. Joseph Mitchell took forever to write a piece, but when he turned in, the editing could be done during one cup of coffee.
>
> **Rule of thumb No. 2:** The less competent the writer, the louder his protests over the editing. The best editing, he feels, is no editing. He does not stop to reflect that such a program would be welcomed by the editor, too, allowing him to lead a richer, fuller life and see more of his children. But he would not be long on the payroll, and neither would the writer. Good writers lean on editors; they would not think of publishing something that no editor had read. Bad writers talk about the inviolable rhythm of their prose.
>
> **Rule of thumb No. 3:** You can identify a bad writer before you have seen a word of his copy if he uses the expression "we writers."

Rule of thumb No. 4: In editing, the first reading of a manuscript is the all-important one. On the second reading, the swampy passages that you noticed in the first reading will seem firmer and less draggy, and on the fourth or fifth reading, they will seem exactly right. That's because you are now attuned to the writer, not to the reader. But the reader, who will read the thing only once, will find it just as swampy and boring as you did the first time around. In short, if something strikes you as wrong on first reading, it *is* wrong, and a fix is needed, not a second reading.

Rule of thumb No. 6: One must never forget that editing and writing are entirely different arts, or crafts. Good editing has saved bad writing more often than bad editing has harmed good writing. This is because a bad editor will not keep his job for long, but a bad writer can, and will, go on forever. Good editing can turn a gumbo of a piece into a tolerable example of good reporting, not of good writing. Good writing exists beyond the ministrations of any editor. That's why a good editor is a mechanic, or craftsman, while a good writer is an artist.

One of my earliest star acquisitions, who resisted all rules of thumb, was A. J. Liebling—Abbott Joseph Liebling. He was both a wonderful reporter and a stylish writer. Anything his eye fell upon took on life in three dimensions, and in color and sound, as well; he could make a laundry list fascinating. Nobody else writing then (except, of course, Joseph Mitchell) was so shrewd of eye and sharp of ear, so quick and deft at setting a scene, so sensitive to anomaly and humor, so responsive to character. He even made himself an interesting participant in his writing—as an eater, as a sports fan, as a conversationalist, as a reader, as a Francophile. If he had been barred from using the first-person *I* in his reporting, he would have had to find another profession. He could get a story out of anybody. Men and elderly women (there are very few young women in his work) would talk to him in a way they would not talk to their spouses or accountants. They simply could not shut up in his presence. They were victims of the Liebling technique, which was to park himself in a chair across from his prey, his face creased in smiles and good will—and never say a word. Total silence. After three or four minutes of this, the victim would be seized by the universal abhorrence of a conversational vacuum and start singing like a bird. It was easy to imagine an art dealer or a fight manager or a coon-dog fancier—or anyone else in the huge theatrical troupe of characters Liebling knew and quoted—falling into the same trap.

Liebling was helped, too, by having a literally photographic memory—the only such I ever encountered. It was first revealed to me when I was editing a piece of his that started with a long and pertinent quote from Hakluyt's *Voyages*. As always when Liebling plucked a passage from Haroun-al-Raschid or George Borrow or Stendhal or one of his other favorites, I wondered how he had managed to dig up a quote that applied so exactly to his text. (I even irreverently wondered sometimes if he had not started with the quote and cobbled together the text.) In the Hakluyt case, the quote was about twenty-five lines long, and when the checkers got to work on it they made a number of changes—nothing serious, five or six words at most. I showed the changes to Liebling, and he said the checkers were wrong—they had been working from a different edition. "My edition is the one I had at Dartmouth," he said. "It's in my mother's attic, along with my other Dartmouth books. I'm going up to see her this weekend, and I'll get it." He did so, and it proved his point. Except for a couple of commas, he had remembered the text exactly for something like twenty-five years.

Nobody else ever enjoyed his own work so much as Liebling did. Sitting at his little beat-up portable typewriter, drumming away with his short, fat fingers (he had remarkably small hands and feet for a man of his size), he would snort and chuckle and hum to himself as he appreciated his own stuff. Yet he was not a careful workman: he was a newspaper writer, rather than a *New Yorker* writer—slam-bang at top speed. His copy was always one of God's great messes. Walking down the hall to deliver it to Ross or Shawn, still reading it over with the utmost enjoyment, he would stop to prop it against a wall and correct typing errors or write long inserts in the margins—all with a thick black pencil that hadn't been sharpened in weeks. He was a hard man to edit—at first at least. "In the newspaper trade, confirmed reporters think that confirmed editors are mediocrities who took the easy way out," he wrote in his memoir of Harold Ross, and it was an attitude he publicly maintained all his life. However, I had one advantage: I had been with the First Infantry Division on D day and in Normandy, and Liebling had seen me there. His admiration for the First Division—it was almost an infatuation—went back to its earliest days of combat in North Africa, which he attended as the magazine's first war correspondent. He wrote a "Profile" of Terry Allen, the division commander at the time, and a number of "Reporter at Large" pieces about ordinary infantrymen caught up in the fighting. Altogether, there was no better reporting done during the war.

When Liebling learned that the First Division was going to lead the Normandy invasion, he pulled every wire and lever at his command to be allowed to accompany it. This was the big one, he knew, and he was determined to be ready for it. When I first met him, in London (the catalyst, obviously, was *The New Yorker*, even though our paths had never crossed in New York), he was in training, working out in a gym and doing a daily five-mile run in Hyde Park. I could see that he had a long way to go: he was still a remarkably fat man—or, to be more exact, he was a standard-size man with a remarkable paunch. It was all out front: from fore to aft he was enormous, but from side to side he was unexceptional.

Liebling and I left for Omaha Beach at the same time and

from the same port, Weymouth, but on different vessels, and I didn't see him in France until he showed up one afternoon when the First Division was parked at Caumont. One's first view of Liebling dressed for combat was a memorable one. The only Army pants big enough to button around the magisterial paunch left him with a vast, drooping seat behind, a flapping void big enough to hold a beach umbrella. The legs of the pants were tucked into knee-high gaiters left over from the Spanish-American War, leading to a pair of thin-soled lounge-lizard civilian shoes. Other correspondents generally tried to look more military and more warlike than any soldier—parachutists' boots, aviators' scarves, tankers' jackets—but Liebling was not one to pretend. He was a correspondent, not a soldier, and he looked it. Unfortunately, we didn't get a chance to talk much, but he noted that he would be in New York before I was, and promised to bring word of my well-being as of June 22, 1944, to the office and my wife. He did so.

When I saw Liebling next, it was back in the *New Yorker* offices, and I had just been given my editor's baton. Although it was an article of faith with him that all editors were incompetent losers, he must have decided to be nice to me as a gesture to the First Division. In any case, whatever the reason, he accepted me, in a way he never accepted the editors of *Collier's* when, in 1949, he left *The New Yorker* and went there to work. *Collier's* had been sliding downhill for several years, and a new editor—a noisy, assertive tough guy named Louis Ruppel—had been installed and given a lot of money to bring it back up with a powerful staff of new writers. He did his first shopping at *The New Yorker,* but the only writer lured by his siren song was Liebling, who was, as always, strapped for money. He signed a contract to do a big caustic piece on Henry Luce and Time, Inc., and another on Col. Robert R. McCormick and the *Chicago Tribune*—no holds barred. The contract also contained a clause saying that not so much as a comma could be changed in his copy without his consent. He was to do the *Time* project in New York and then move to Chicago for the *Tribune* piece. In November, Liebling turned in an enormous manuscript on Luce, and moved to Chicago for the winter. At that point, everything broke down. *Collier's* thought the *Time* piece too nose-thumbing to print, and Liebling refused to accept their changes. (Nobody knows what happened to the manuscript, which is too bad.) As for the McCormick project, it never got off the ground at all, leaving Liebling stuck with a winter's lease on a Chicago apartment and no assignment. He used the time to write his celebrated "Profile" of Chicago, the "Second City." In the spring, he returned, perhaps sheepishly, to New York and *The New Yorker*.

Liebling's attitude toward editors was, I am sure, more ritualistic than heartfelt, but I didn't know that when I got my first Liebling manuscript to edit, and I didn't dare make a change: I simply put the piece into type and went to Liebling the next day with a couple of suggestions. "No!" he said. "Leave everything alone." But when Ross complained about the same things on his proof, he paid attention and fixed them. That was no way to work, so when I was given a second Liebling manuscript, I simply did the editing I thought was unavoidable, put the piece in type, and waited for the earthquake. No earthquake—not even a rattle. He accepted my changes, or perhaps never noticed them, and said not a word. As time went on, I did more and more editing, to the point of reorganizing sections of a piece, and sometimes even cutting it. Still not a word, or very few. Every now and then, he would take issue with something I had done, but he always came to see the difficulty, and his corrective rewrite was often better than his original. He turned in a long "Comment" one week when I was editing the department in Shawn's absence, and when I reduced the three pages of copy to half a page, he even wrote me a note: "Thank you for making me look like a writer."

Liebling was also, it must be said, capable of jolting bad taste, as in a long passage about the smell of a certain French girl's feet. This appeared in an ill-advised memoir of his youthful ventures into amour in Paris. It was a sort of sequel to his highly successful recollections of his youthful ventures into French cooking. He wrote many reverent pieces about French cooking, but the fact is that he loved any kind of cooking, if there was enough of it. Bob MacMillan, Jack Ruge, and I used to lunch regularly at the Villanova, a very good Italian restaurant on West Forty-sixth Street, and one day we arrived, to find Liebling alone at a table there. He was drinking an espresso, and on the busboy's stand behind him were the tombstones of a formidable meal: an empty soup tureen, a fish skeleton on a poaching rack, a denuded bread basket, an empty ice-cream-sundae glass. We invited him to bring his coffee over and sit with us, and he did so while we studied the menu. When we ordered, he ordered, too—an entire second lunch, from antipasto to another ice-cream sundae.

When I first knew Liebling, he was married to Lucille Spectorsky, former wife of Augie Spectorsky, fiction editor of *Playboy* and one-time checker on *The New Yorker*. She was Liebling's second wife; his first wife was Ann McGinn, a beautiful but schizophrenic waif from Providence, whom I never met—she had been institutionalized long before I met Liebling himself. Joe was devoted to her—he kept in touch and paid all her expenses until the day he died—but in 1949, he went to Reno and got a divorce so he could marry Lucille. Lucille was out of a different box altogether—a big blonde from rural Kentucky, amiable if dumb. She had an acquisitive streak that kept Liebling broke: when they bought a house and land in Springs, near East Hampton, he put up the money, but she held the title, and when they divorced, he had to buy the house a second time, from her.

The next chatelaine of the house in Springs was Jean Stafford, and that was not a marriage made in heaven, either. It started out well enough, but by the time Liebling died, it was seriously eroded. She stayed on in Springs after his death, and Tass and I saw her now and then; somehow, Tass got stuck with putting her up for membership in the Cosmopolitan Club and shepherding her through the formalities. Jean was drinking a lot and slowly turning into a harridan. When she died, in 1979, she left the Springs house and its contents—including all Liebling's books, papers, manuscripts, notes, first drafts, and project outlines—to her maid.

When Liebling dismissed the writing in *New Masses* so sniffily ("as bad, in a different way, as the writing in *Time*"), he may not have known that a lot of the writing had been done by his *New Yorker* colleague Richard Rovere. During his *New Masses* days, Rovere—a writer just as competent as Liebling, with less panache, perhaps, but with a higher critical faculty—was a rather flighty Communist. In his book *Final Reports,* he says he was not sure whether he was actually a registered member of the Party or not—an unlikely assertion, but plausible under the circumstances: in 1936, he applied for membership while on a vacation job at a summer theater in Connecticut, but his application had not been accepted by the time the job was over, and he never heard anything more about it. But he tried. In his journal for June 15, 1936, he writes, a bit prematurely, "Joined Communist Party under assumed name of Dick Halworth," and the entry for the next day reads "Went to my first unit meeting and—quick like an arrow—gone was the sham and the four-flushing, the hypocritical histrionics." He was twenty years old. He devotedly supported the Party's positions, but he found the meetings so boring that he quit attending, and he had a hard time with the Party's authoritarianism and discipline. Even this tenuous adherence was severed, however, on August 24, 1939, when the Stalin-Hitler nonaggression pact was made known. The news knocked him flat. He quit *New Masses* and eventually got work on *The Nation* and on *Common Sense,* until the spring of 1944, when he joined *The New Yorker*. (He was exempted from the draft because of his eyes.)

I became Rovere's editor in 1949, almost as soon as he started writing his "Letter from Washington." Until then, "Letter" articles were supposed to be from abroad—London, Paris, Minsk. Ross was convinced that no *New Yorker* reader would be interested in a "Letter from Pittsburgh," say, because if anything important happened in Pittsburgh, the New York newspapers would have it. But abroad was different. Everything that happened over there was rather weird—Ross was not an internationalist. Shawn and Katharine White, who were, persuaded him that Washington *was* abroad, in a sense. Foreigners practically ran the city—particularly its social and artistic side—from their embassies and trade missions. This argument may have led Ross to expect the "Letter from Washington" to be a sort of indirect report from abroad, but what Rovere delivered was a quintessentially American report on American politics, and nobody has ever done it better.

Rovere never lived in Washington, or stayed there for more than a day or two at a time. He and his wife, Eleanor, lived in Rhinebeck, on the Hudson, and kept an apartment in New York in the Iroquois Hotel, on Forty-fourth Street, across from *The New Yorker*. The Iroquois was then a run-down derelict, the seedy remains of a solid, respectable hotel of seventy-five years earlier. The Roveres took a long and very cheap lease on a suite of rooms, redecorated them from top to bottom, and moved in their own furniture. Rovere did most of his reporting by telephone, and for this he had one unbeatable asset: a marvelous speaking voice, rich and comforting. Listening to him on the phone, one pictured a calm, assured, and trustworthy family doctor. The physical reality, however, was quite different. His hair, a sort of neglected crew cut, stood up in spikes, his one necktie had seen years of service, his glasses were always askew, and his suit had apparently first belonged to somebody else—somebody a good bit bigger. Most disconcerting of all, however, was his divided gaze. One eye would fix you benignly while the other roved about wildly; Wolcott Gibbs once wickedly said that he would never travel by air because he was sure that the pilot, when he emerged from the cockpit to talk to the passengers, would look like Richard Rovere.

At his death, in 1979, Dick was working on *Final Reports,* an autobiography, of which about a quarter was printable and the rest in first-draft form or in notes. It was in the hands of his agent, and she, at the behest of his publishers, Doubleday, had cobbled together a hybrid manuscript of over six hundred pages. It was a publisher's nightmare, and Doubleday was moaning. Eleanor Rovere asked me if I could help out, which I did. *Final Reports* (230 pages, plus index) was published in 1984. It's unlikely that it attracted more than a couple of hundred readers, which is a shame, since it contained some rewarding stuff. There was one passage I found particularly fascinating because it concerned my old affliction Joe McWilliams, whose thugs chased Steve and me from the Lindbergh rally. Dick is writing of the year 1938, when he was working for *New Masses:*

> There was a particularly inflammatory Fascist rabble-rouser named Joe McWilliams, whose meetings had a way of turning into riots, during which blood, generally Jewish, was spilled. Joe North [managing editor of *New Masses*] asked me to learn what I could about this hoodlum and his supporters. In the course of doing this, I met another reporter with a similar assignment. "Funny thing about McWilliams," this man said. "He used to be a Communist. Somewhere in Texas, I think." I reported my findings to Joe North, who instructed me to go down to Party headquarters, on 13th Street, and tell my story to a man named Durba. Though I thought I knew the roster of Party functionaries fairly well, this was a new name to me. Durba was a huge, menacing man—a Latvian, I was later told—without a hair on his enormous head, and he spoke with an almost impenetrable accent. I told him what I had learned about McWilliams. Durba heard me out impassively, then went to a safe, pulled out an unwieldy ledger of the kind that Bob Cratchit must have toiled over, locked the safe, and began to thumb through the ledger's large pages. In time, he came upon the name I had given him: a Joe McWilliams had indeed joined the Communist Party in Austin, Texas, just two or three years earlier. It was a

common enough name, I pointed out—perhaps it was another man. Durba said nothing, He went back to the safe, replaced the ledger, and pulled out another, of similar bulk. He had not explained what the first volume was, but I had assumed it to be a roster of Party members. In the second, he seemed to find McWilliams listed again, and I assumed from this that it contained the names of defectors, of the Party's enemies, or perhaps of Party agents who had infiltrated other organizations. Whatever it was, he told me that he thought I should drop the project until I got further word either from him or from North. I dropped it, and heard nothing more from either of them.

It was an odd business, and significant in a way I did not appreciate at the time. In later years, when the Party was being investigated by the F.B.I. and a number of Congressional committees, there was always some mystification as to whether or not a master list of Party members had ever existed . . . but none of the investigators—who were saying with great assurance that they knew who was and who was not a member—ever claimed hard documentary evidence. . . . As for the mysterious Durba, I learned from several sources that he was one of the top Soviet agents in the United States, one of those from whom William Z. Foster, Earl Browder, A. B. Magil, and Joe North took their orders. That is more than I ever learned about Joe McWilliams.

By the time Rovere joined *The New Yorker* in 1944, the staff had been undergoing a change. The old-school reporters of Ross's style and cut had been infiltrated by a new breed of journalists—Gibbs, White, and Thurber, primarily—who, like Rovere, thought of themselves as writers rather than as reporters. Many of them had not started as journalists at all—White, for instance, had been an advertising copywriter, and Gibbs had worked on the Long Island

Rail Road. Among this lot was my Sunday-night "London Letter" acquaintance, Mollie Panter-Downes. Her background was in fiction. She published her first novel at the age of sixteen, and it sold so well that she was able to support her widowed mother on the royalties. (Her father, a major in the Royal Irish Regiment, had been killed in the First World War, at which time he was in his forties.) She also wrote short stories, and a number of them appeared in *The New Yorker*. In 1939, with war appearing to be inevitable, Ross decided that the magazine needed a a steady voice in England to match Flanner's in Paris, and Katharine White, Mollie's editor, proposed her for the job. Her first "Letter from London" was written the week war was declared, and appeared in the issue of September 9,1939.

As writers, Panter-Downes and Flanner were almost antithetical: where Janet was torrential, Mollie was a miniaturist. Both, in their separate ways, were exactly right for the "Letter" format. Producing a Letter from Wherever is quite different from reporting an event. The writer has to deal not only with the actuality of what is happening in local politics, art, theater, sports, and a dozen other arenas but also with what people *think* about what is happening—the sort of reporting that requires a lot of telephoning and listening to gossip and reading of newspapers. Panter-Downes and Flanner were nonpareils at this sort of work, and when they quit their desks and telephones and moved to the window—when they reported on what they had actually seen, rather than read or heard about—they were even better. Mollie was at her best working on a small scale—a visit to an air-raid warden's house, for instance—while Flanner excelled at big events, such as a criminal trial or a Bastille Day parade. Their sharpness of eye was extraordinary; they didn't so much report as absorb.

One reason for the difference of style between the women may have been in the way they lived. Flanner was unrepentantly what she was: an upper-class bohemian, a lesbian intellectual, a left-wing internationalist. Mollie was a middle-of-the-road conservative and an unflagging defender of the Royal Family. Where Flanner ate in restaurants and lived in hotels, Mollie was a superb cook and lived with an amiable husband (Clare Robinson, a high-level civil servant, Oxford, bookish, quirky, very intelligent) and two delightful daughters in an ancient timbered house surrounded by fifty acres of Surrey countryside. Where Janet knew all about filing copy at press offices and how to get one's story on the wires ahead of a rival's, Mollie dispatched her Letters in a homemade, maddeningly English manner. "When the piece was finished," I wrote of her later, "and every comma in place, something close to farce took over. A local boy on a rattle-trap bicycle would wheel the copy over to the railroad station, if he didn't have a flat tire, and deliver it to a train conductor on the 6:43 to London; this man, in turn, if he didn't forget, would trot it over to the cable office, and the people there, if they hadn't mislaid the address, would dispatch it to New York. Over the years, every one of these possible disasters took place, but, true to form, muddling through eventually prevailed."

When I was in England during the war, running around Dorset with my rifle platoon, I tried a couple of times, at Shawn's urging, to call on the Robinsons in neighboring Surrey, but the travel requirements were too complicated and I didn't have enough leave. When I finally did meet Mollie—in 1950, on her first visit to the magazine that had made her name a byword in this country—it was at a dinner given by Raoul in the Plaza Hotel. We hit it off right away, and Tass and I saw a great deal of Mollie and Clare from then on. They stayed with us when they were in New York, and we spent much time with them in England and, later, in France, ambling down to Provence, where they had a tiny house near Claviers, among the obligatory olive trees. The British have been flocking to Provence for ages, some of them humdrum vacationers like Mollie and Clare, and others an exotic breed of expatriates, on the run from debt and taxes at home, as their forebears started doing in the eighteenth century. In the twenties and thirties, they were memorably anatomized by Evelyn Waugh, Scott Fitzgerald, Cyril Connolly, and P. G. Wodehouse, and it seemed to me when I was in Claviers that they had not changed a particle since—all of them upper-class, rich, and garrulous at the top of their lungs. Provence for them was a sort of private, sun-dappled Forest of Arden, created expressly for their unfettered gratification and staffed by a resident population of ingratiating, invariably little, rustics. ("I have a wonderful little man in Clochemerle who is an absolute genius with curtains. . . ." "The *notaire* was a darling little old man who . . .") There were perhaps a dozen of this breed living permanently around Claviers, flitting among their various houses like water bugs. Mollie and Clare were in a different social loop, but once in awhile they would cross over, and the local fauna always performed on cue. On one occasion when Tass and I were visiting the Robinsons, a neighbor, Lady something or other, had us all over for a drinks party and talked to us entirely through a marmoset perched on her shoulder. ("Nikki says you were sweet to come, and he'll be very cross if you don't try his favorite champagne daiquiri.") This was pretty good, but even better was a flourishing young woman guest from London who, as she said more than once, was dressed solely in a thirty-foot silk scarf. "The way it's wrapped around me, I can't wear a stitch under it," she added, interestingly.

With the Robinsons in Surrey, life was calmer but just as unreal. It was all so unremittingly *English* that to a visitor from a lesser country it seemed as never-never as a television ad for Beefeater gin. The lawns were thick and smooth, the brook was musical, the ancient gardener would clomp up in his Wellingtons to report that a fox had carried off two hens, the cows in the pasture nearby would low as required. But the charming casement windows of the main house leaked quantities of good English air, generally freezing; the dining room was fitted out with electric plate warmers and griddles to keep food hot after its chilling passage from the kitchen; and the downstairs bathroom, though obviously the reading nook of somebody with a taste for the *TLS*, farm journals, and publications of the Royal Archaeological Society, was paralyzingly unheated. The great fireplace in the living room was stocked with mighty logs of British oak, but even in winter the fire was kept at the level of a candle flame—to save wood and remind one that life is real, life is earnest, and this was not a New York apartment.

Mollie and Clare fit perfectly into this cardboard cutout of Olde England—Clare, with his patched tweeds, his amiable bull-terrier, his high-minded intellectual curiosity; Mollie, with her faultless manners, her patrician nose, her clear blue eyes, her elegance of posture, diction, and dress. She lost nothing with age (she died at ninety), and at the end you could hardly tell her from the Queen Mother herself.

Mollie's funeral was held in the ancient church at Chiddingfold, close by the Robinson home. The pews were hard, the January air was frigid, and the mourners, who seemed almost as venerable as the church, stayed wrapped in their woolly overcoats and heavy scarves, and surreptitiously stamped their feet for warmth. The service was formal and severe, and when the congregation joined in singing "A Mighty Fortress Is Our God," little puffs of congealed breath emerged from every open mouth. Mollie was right at home.

4

With the advent of writers like Mollie Panter-Downes and Richard Rovere, and of a new-style editor in the person of William Shawn, the day of the Old Prophets—the irreverent, Ross-style reporters who would have been right at home in the cast of *The Front Page*—began to wane. A. J. Liebling and Joseph Mitchell, who came to work at the magazine from the *World-Telegram* in 1934, were both thoroughgoing newspapermen, it is true, but they were a bit too literary for Prophethood. The Old Prophets were a self-contained bunch, and I have a feeling that they rather terrified Shawn with their complete self-assurance and their easy familiarity with Ross, whom they curtly called "Ross," or sometimes "Harold." (Shawn never in his life called him anything but "Mr. Ross.") I was having one of my rare lunches with Mr. Ross—he was "Mr." to me, too—at the Algonquin when Joel Sayre came by and sat down, uninvited. "God, you look terrible, Ross," he said. "Getting too much hump these days?"

Trying to picture Shawn confronted by such a question is—

well, let us move on to Maeve Brennan, who bowled over the Old Prophets' successors, one by one, in the early fifties, when she came to the magazine from *Harper's Bazaar.* She was tiny—no more than five feet tall—but hugely spirited and enormously attractive. Her father was an important figure in the Irish struggle against the British—he was in jail when Maeve was born—and later he became the Irish consul in Washington. Maeve, who was born in Dublin the same year I was born in New York, had an entrancing Irish brogue. She graduated from Catholic University, in Washington, with a degree in library science, moved to New York, and got a job at *Harper's Bazaar* writing fashion copy. She was a writer through and through: she simply could not *not* write, filling endless notebooks with observed incidents, trial phrases and sentences, and overheard conversations. After a couple of her short stories appeared in *The New Yorker,* she quit the *Bazaar* and moved to West Forty-third Street. Brendan Gill was the first to topple. He was followed by Joseph Mitchell, and Mitchell by Charles Addams, and Addams by McKelway, whom she even married. Wolcott Gibbs also checked in somewhere along the line.

Despite the length of this roster, I always thought of Maeve as a loner. I believe she accepted the constant buzz of men around her as not of her doing and beyond her control. What she liked best was to be alone—the only passenger on a month-long freighter trip to Ireland to see her family; locked up in her cabin for a summer of writing at Yaddo or the MacDowell Colony (when she could manage it); a winter tenant of various East Hampton summer houses otherwise closed for the season. Several of these East Hampton houses belonged to friends of Gerald Murphy, one of Maeve's staunchest allies, and they were big. Maeve would establish a little zone of warmth in them, and there she would write and write, taking time off only for long walks on the deserted beach with Bluebell, her black Labrador. She wrote stories and book reviews and "Talk of the Town" pieces about her fictional character the Long-Winded Lady. I had got to know her in these post-McKelway days, when I was her ("much-feared") editor on the "Briefly Noted" fiction reviews she wrote every week for the magazine, and we became good friends. She wrote me many long, wonderful letters from East Hampton about her life and thoughts there—about writers and writing, for instance:

> I forgot to tell you—Howard [Howard Moss, poetry editor of *The New Yorker*] gave me the new English edition of his book on Proust. It is a much smaller and more handsome book than the American one, and I have read it all now, and, Gardner, it is magnificent. I have it beside me, and I keep looking at it. It is a book to look at when you wake up in the middle of the night. It is such a pleasure to hear your brain stretch a little bit. Now I have gone to Colette again—the part where she describes the lady who clipped caves for wild birds in her garden hedge, and the birds settled in with their bassinets and humidors. . . . Most of the magazine's fact writing, which used to be sensationally good, has become selfish writing. The writers don't think about the reader but about themselves. They are all trying to express themselves, and they are envious of "fiction" writers, because they seem to believe that this is what fiction writers do—show their wonderful minds and their unique unhappinesses and their fascinating adjustments and so on. I have been screaming for years that there is no difference—writing is writing, and it is for the reader. *For the reader* always comes first. We are writing to make a living, and if we don't give value, we don't get any money.

About her troubles with her cleaning lady:

> I hope you are well and cheerful and happy. I am not. But the sea has been so loud that I cannot remain angry. The

Lady Who Helps Me turned her ankle in her garden a week ago last Saturday, which meant moans and groans all last week. She would *not* go to the doctor, and then when I got here from town yesterday it was only to hear, with moans and groans, that the pain had Got So Bad that she had finally called the doctor at *5:30 a.m.*, and went a-barrelling over there, to hear that Inflammation Had Set In, and "I'll be on crutches at least a week, Miss Brennan." God damn. That's me—she is a rigid Catholic and never even says "Darn." Instead she says "AOUEW CHEEZE."

About office doings:

Dear Much-Feared:

Howard called yesterday to say that he had had lunch last week with a Somebody from Scribners who talked only of Me. Only of Me, Much-feared, not a word, not a syllable, about Vous, or as you and I would say, Toi. This personage is fascinated by me. Now he wants to buy me from Lippincott. I am going to be the Dizzy Dean of the New Yorker Magazine, and if Capt. Billy Shawn doesn't change his attitude and get as friendly as he used to be, I may become an Independent. I am full of ideas—they are twirling around in my head. I had to turn off the record-player, because as long as I can listen to Mozart I see no point at all in doing anything else. But about Howard: He told me he had the most fearful day Friday at the office. Apparently, somebody *in the office* has turned in a long, long, long piece partly in verse, which is why Howard was in on it. He was prostrate with shock after reading it, it is so bad, but recovered himself and stormed down to

Shawn, who agreed that it was a bad piece, but said hopefully that it could be fixed. Well, on and on. Finally, at the door, Howard turned and squeaked that if they print the piece they have to have a subtitle: "Over the Dead Body of Howard Moss." He wouldn't tell me who wrote it, but I gather the person is Poor. I quoted Gibbs quoting from "The Boy Friend": "He only does it because he's poor."

O I nearly forgot. Do you remember I told you I thought there was Trouble Brewing at the Lieblings'? Well, I am telling you. [The Liebling house was only a few miles away, in Springs.] I knew Jean Stafford would wear Joe Liebling out, but it still is not altogether her fault—he despises *women writers,* and she has more talent than he has, and more intelligence. I may be making a mountain out of a—well, really, Much-Feared, what do people usually make mountains out of?

And, most memorably, an account of Christmas with Jean Stafford, Howard Moss, and Mark, Howard's particular friend, a big-time New York hairdresser, who fancied himself as a cook and was forever oiling his frying pans and such:

Dear Gardner:

The Portuguese bed is now all furnished with a wooden floor and two mattresses, and is said by both Mark and Howard to be very comfortable. However, it will be a long day before I have "house guests" again. Mark peels potatoes directly onto the floor, and just when the kitchen has been cleaned and scrubbed, by me. He likes to go in there and make himself a cup of tea and an English muffin from the toaster, and for some reason the entire floor and the kitchen counters are covered with crumbs and wet tea bags. I threw that toaster with all my might, what a crash, and what a thundering of hooves when I ran after it to start throwing it again. And why put one of my cups, a favourite one, on the latch part of a window that somebody is just about to open. The cup filled with olive oil, of course. No more home-cooked meals in this house, ever.

Jean Stafford had to be invited to Christmas dinner. Howard called her on the morning of Christmas Eve, and she asked to speak to me, and told me she had stomach flu and didn't think she could make it, but maybe, if Mark would go over there and get her. She also said that she had sciatica and palpitations, and her biopsy on her bosom hadn't healed, and that she had thrown up in the Woolworth Building last Monday afternoon.

Then on Christmas Eve night I was determined to be taken to Herb McCarthy's in Southampton for fish, but the fog was too strong, so we went to the Hedges here instead, and as we walked through the posh empty lounge to the cocktail room, Howard and Mark, who were behind me, suddenly disappeared, and reappeared several minutes later to say that Jean was in the restaurant, dining on chicken à la king with two friends. She then appeared herself, in a fine-looking red dress with a stand-up collar, and apparently quite fit, and said she was feeling much better thank you.

But on Christmas Day, a sepulchral voice on the phone commanded Mark and Howard over there, and she showed up here quite drunk, wearing sawed-off fisherman's fleece-lined boots that reached half way up her calves, man-cut trousers tucked into them, gray trews, a loose, long-sleeved sweater with a high neck, made of old bits of gravel, and thin uncombed hair, a dirty face, and the bleary eyes of those old men who ask you for money early Sunday mornings. She couldn't drink champagne but must have bourbon, but settled for Scotch, and brought with her one of those eternal bottles of wine that A.J.L. was always carting about and insisting that people drink.

The din. was turkey and stuffing that Howard and I had laboured over, and bread sauce, and turnips for Howard, and mashed pots, and some other specials, including a revolting gravy that Mark had spent hours over. Then there was plum pudding in blue flames, with a sprig of holly, which Mark and I had to light several times before it would stay flaming long enough for us to charge into the "festive" room with it, holding it with all our hands, and hard sauce and cranberry jello that Mark made in "pretty little dishes" that he forgot to wipe the bottoms of, so that my large white-linen table cloth was all over red jello, not that it mattered, because Jean had spilled a very large glass of beastly red Chat. Haut Brion, first one way, over the cloth, and then the other way. And then insisted on the big box of salt, so she could strew salt over it, and most of the salt went on the newly waxed floor, so that the cats and Bluebell almost went insane with thirst from their paws and with rage at all the disorder. She talked about the wine all during dinner, and insisted that everybody drink it and admire it. Really, Gardner, she is a horror. It was my dinner. And the house was all done up and decorated. When she wasn't discoursing on the fucking wine and crying because it was the late Fatso's wine, she told stories we had all heard fifty times, and the table looked as though something anemic had bled to death on it. Christ it was awful. And most of the time we couldn't hear her, but we did hear her say that Edmund Wilson, who is up at the college she is at, *hates* me and Howard and thinks we are stupid. I was flattered, but Howard, sensing a *crise littéraire* (letters in the *Times Book Review*), got all white and tense and dramatic, and Mark got very angry, because he was drinking his wine like a Greek god and nobody was looking at him.

Immediately after eating her plum pudding with expensive home-made hard sauce (which Mark made with too little rum and too damn much butter), she announced that she was going to vomit. Mark and Howard took her tenderly by the elbows of her queer sweater and led her off. Bluebell and Rupert [a cat] cavorted after the trio, hoping for some *real* fun, but Jean spotted a comfy chair in the living room and sank into it and got another glass of whiskey. I went in with coffee and sat smiling, even though Mark had made the coffee with some special Italian flavouring, arsenic I think, but after a while Jean tottered up and said she'd better go home, and they put her muskrat coat on her and she embraced me, which I hated, and they wouldn't let Bluebell go along for the ride, which enraged me, and Bluebell was fed up with them from then on.

When the coast was clear, I raced into the kitchen with all the cats and Bluebell after me, and I gave them all large slices of turkey and other nice things. That was about 11:30. At about 1:30 I was still cleaning up when the two Dreamers arrived back, having pacified Miss Stafford and put her to bed. She sleeps in a high hospital bed with three photos of the Departed around her. Howard confided to me the the reason Bluebell wasn't allowed along for the ride was because Jean had *promised* to vomit in the car, and Howard thought it might be easier if Bluebell wasn't along. Easier for who. Howard and Mark were having a row because Jean wanted to ride into town with them Monday morning, and Howard said "Well, Mark, I don't want Jean to drive in with us, because it means stopping so she can have a drink and stopping so she can throw up, and all." I said, "Why do you have to stop for her to throw up?" Mark thought that this was funny, but Howard said, "Well, after all, Jean is one of my Oldest and Dearest Friends." They then offered to "help" with the rest of the dishes. Helping meant putting full pans of grease in the bottom of a little basin and putting glasses and the Waring Blender on top and filling it all with lukewarm water and Lux and leaving it to jell. I said no thanks, and they went to bed, and I laboured until 2:30 and then tottered up to my bed.

But we did have champagne at noon, and Edward Albee came with his friend Bill, who lives with him. I adore Albee, and his friend is very mysterious and only 21. They stayed three hours. The last time they came, they stayed three hours and then Albee invited me back with them for dinner, and I must say I enjoyed myself, and sat around beaming. Albee's house is on the edge of a cliff overlooking the sea in Montauk.

The next night, Saturday, we went for a drink at Albee's and to see his Christmas tree, which was enormous and all furnished with ornaments from Geo. Jensen. Then we went to the Rouechés, and really Berton Roueché is too dreary for words. He was very flirtatious and kept trying to maneuver me into a corner to kiss me. I am nearly fifty, and too old for Berton. Jeffrey Potter was home with the flu, but his new wife was led up to me by Kay Roueché, who then vanished, and that poor girl, Jeffrey's wife, trembled with fear while she tried to explain to me that she had asked Kay to introduce her, and would I please come and see Jeffrey, who talks about no one else, and would I come and see the baby, and would I please come and see them. She was trembling and trying to smile. It was really awful. She asked me how I did my hair and told me about all my "stories" and said that every day last summer she drove to the Maidstone beach and that she always walked along the beach looking for me. I didn't tell her that I am to be found on the beach only in the middle of winter. Oh dear somebody has done a very good job of pulling that girl down. She is 30 and it is her second marriage, but she seems 17. And she must have been so happy when they were married. I would like to break his neck, but he is only a child himself.

Howard and Mark drove off this morning, leaving me to call Miss S. and tell her they were gone without her. But I don't mind being a villain.

Written in solitude by the winter sea, they are cheerful letters, full of good sense and a warming humor; it was when Maeve returned to town that the voltage started to climb. Her enthusiasms became obsessions, unpredictable but overpowering. At one point, for instance, she discovered Billie Holiday, and bought every one of her hundreds of records, which she played over and over again, for hours at a time, even in the office, on a portable phonograph. In New York, Maeve lived in hotels or in short-lease apartments. Sometimes she lived in two apartments at once: she would sign a lease on one, happen upon another she liked better, and sign a lease on it, too. Sometimes she lived in hotels near the office—the Royalton, the Iroquois, the Prince Edward—and at other times in hotels farther afield: the Westbury, the Lombardy. When she moved, as she did so often, she could transport her entire household—all her possessions and her cats—in a taxi, like the big blonde in Dorothy Parker's story. Maeve had more cats than possessions. They were all strays, each with a name—Juno, Basil, Rupert, and Daisy ("that black daughter of Satan") were the core ménage—and each with a distinctive (to Maeve) personality. The doyenne of the establishment was Bluebell, the amiable black Labrador. ("I am sitting in my *bar,* which has two ice buckets," she wrote from her latest winter retreat, "and I just this minute heard a crafty rush of fur in the living room, and a few tiny squeaks, and I ran in there, to find nothing but drowsy Bluebell, but saw Rupert's tail twitching outside and ran out there, and there he was, hiding behind a bush with a whole bird in his mouth. A very small bird, upside down, with Rupert's teeth clamped gently on its tiny gray stomach. I said, 'Rupert, give me that little bird.' And so he did, and I took it upstairs and opened a window and off it flew, to the *Daily News,* I suppose, to make a complaint against me for having such a cat.")

As for Maeve's possessions, they were strays, too, each with a history and almost a personality: the set of teaspoons left to her by her aunt Nan, the one who had run away with the chartered accountant when she was not yet twenty, only to have him die in her arms in Genoa a week later; the riding crop she had been given on her twelfth birthday because she loved horses so much, even though her family could never in the world have afforded to keep one; and so on.

And slowly, slowly, as this kaleidoscopic life went on, she became demented. Her living arrangements became ever more chaotic. Paranoia set in. She called me one day from Yaddo and said, in a whisper, that I was to meet her in a certain West Side coffee shop at eleven sharp the next day; she was leaving Yaddo secretly and had to talk to me before "they" could trace her. We met, and she told me in a perfectly controlled and reasonable voice that "they" were getting perilously close to her: "they" had even put cyanide in her toothpaste, but she had detected the almond odor just in time. Now she was going to hide out for a bit in Howard Moss's apartment, because he was in Greece, and "they" didn't know she had a key. She was confiding in me because she wanted somebody to know the facts. Who were "they"? I asked. She said that was a silly question, because I knew perfectly well who "they" were, and she was certainly not going to mention their names in public, where anyone might overhear. All this was related in such a calm and plausible way that I began to doubt my own reason.

From that day on, things got worse. Eventually, Bill Maxwell, Howard (back from Greece), and I managed, with the greatest effort, to get her to sign herself into University Hospital, where the doctors brought her around with drugs and started her on a psychiatric program. It worked, and for a while, out of the hospital, she prospered and began writing once more. But then everything went to pieces again, mainly because she refused to take her medication. Once again, the three of us got her attended to, and once again she relapsed. In the end, she turned on Bill and Howard, and then on me, too, saying we had been corrupted by her enemies. She refused help of any sort (though I did ascertain that she had enough to live on in the form of benefits of some kind from *The New Yorker*), and then she disappeared—right out of sight. I next saw her, at least a year later, for a moment on Forty-fourth Street. She had cut her hair and dyed it orange, but otherwise she looked to be in control. She still would not speak to me, however, and I never saw her again. She died in a nursing home in 1993, and a memorial service, thinly attended, was held for her in a temporary chapel of St. Agnes Catholic Church, on East Forty-fifth Street.

I walked back from Maeve Brennan's memorial service with Daphne Hellman, Geoffrey Hellman's former wife, who had known Maeve since her *Harper's Bazaar* days, and had had a heated affair with St. Clair McKelway, the man Maeve later married. It was not a cheerful walk. Daphne's mind was on McKelway, who, like Maeve, had gone over the edge of sanity and died in a nursing home. Talking about him made me think of the high number of untoward *New Yorker* deaths there had been: not only Maeve and McKelway but Chris Rand on his Mexican hotel roof; and Richard Harris, who, full of dope, had gone through a high window in a Riverside Drive apartment; and Dave Lardner, of course; and Mark Murphy and John McCarten, dead of booze; and Berton Roueché, Seymour Krim, and Sandy Vanderbilt, three more suicides—and probably others I couldn't remember just then. It was a depressing thought, but it matched my other thoughts as I listened to Daphne talk on about McKelway. "He was such a good writer," she said. "Do you think we could find a publisher to bring out a selection of his work?" I thought, but did not say, it would be hard enough to find a publisher who had even heard of McKelway. The fact was, *The New Yorker*'s great days, when its writers were revered and sought after, were over—the days when I, for instance, and every other right-thinking undergraduate at Yale read every word of every issue and could hardly wait a week for more. As I say, the walk was a melancholy one.

Daphne left me at Lexington Avenue to take a taxi to the Village Gate, where she would be playing her harp that night, and I went on across town, still thinking about what had happened to the magazine. I had left it eleven years earlier—in 1982, when I reached sixty-five—and even then it had been sliding for quite a while. The trouble, I felt then and still felt, was that the editors at the top—including me—had grown too old. Back in the days when these editors had first come to work, they were of the same generation as the readers they hoped to address. On February 21, 1925, the date of *The New Yorker*'s first issue, Harold Ross was thirty-two. Shawn, when he signed on, was twenty-six, and Sandy Vanderbilt about the same. Rogers Whitaker and Hobey Weekes were just out of college when they showed up. In the fiction department, Katharine White (then Angell) was in her thirties, and so was Gus Lobrano. Forty years later, the same editors were still there (or dead), and now the readers of their own generation—the readers they understood by instinct rather than by calculation—were getting senior-citizen discounts at movie theaters and poring over brochures for round-the-world cruises. There were, of course, younger editors of talent—Bill Whitworth, John Bennet, Chip McGrath—but they were kept on a short leash, and reverence was expected of them. The man who held the leash was Shawn, now a senior citizen himself, and he held it, as always, in a grip that never relaxed. In the beginning, it was the tightness of his grip that brought about *The New Yorker*'s greatness. But in the end it also brought about the magazine's decline.

William Shawn and I both went to work at *The New Yorker*

as reporters for the "Talk of the Town" department—he in 1933, I in 1939. He, as noted, was twenty-six; I was twenty-two. There was another difference between us: I got fired after two weeks; he got fired after forty-seven years. In the six years that preceded my arrival at the magazine, he had moved from "Talk of the Town" reporter to idea man, and then, just weeks before my arrival, to managing editor, a post he shared with Gus Lobrano. (Gus managed fiction, Shawn managed fact, and Ross, then in full cry, managed them both.) An idea man was an integral part of the magazine's structure in those days. He thought up assignments for the "Talk" reporters and the long-fact writers—the writers of "Profiles," "A Reporter at Large," and other full-blown fact pieces. He initiated new departments, like "Horseshows and Hunts" and "Yachting" and "Oar and Oarsmen," and found the people to write them. ("Yachting" was written by Bunny Riggs, who later reappeared as commander of the landing craft that carried A. J. Liebling to Omaha Beach.) Another of the idea man's functions was to keep files of possible subjects. Writers stuck for a topic would go through the entries and reserve candidates. A grazer in the files would invariably reserve with abandon, not so much to jump-start his typewriter as to prevent anybody else from moving in; E. J Kahn, for instance, was able to reserve to himself the entire continent of Africa. Reserving an idea did not, of course, mean writing about it; in fact, most of the ideas in the files never got written about at all. Geoffrey Hellman at his death was still reserving an interview with Grover Whalen, who had preceded him to the grave by sixteen years.

As an idea man—he remained one in spirit all his life—Shawn was a demon, as good as Ross himself, but with a difference. Ross's torrent of ideas came from simple curiosity: how did something work, or not work? Why had something happened, or not happened? Shawn had plenty of curiosity, but it was analytical rather than simple. He would take a fact or an object—any fact, any object—and think about it. A golf ball, for instance. It was hard as a brick but it bounced prodigiously. Bricks don't bounce, so there must be a resilient inner composition. Rubber, no doubt, but there was no rubber in the early days of golf, so what was used instead? Did early golf balls bounce? An interesting question. A history of the golf ball might make a good piece for "Talk."

Ik Shuman, the executive editor who came across my column in the *Yale Daily News,* was an old newspaper pal of Ross's and a very courtly man. He was courtly when he hired me, and two weeks later, he was just as courtly when he fired me. He said he would be glad to see me apply again someday, but right now, to his great regret, I was fired. I stayed fired for two years, and during my forced sabbatical, Shawn had begun to settle in as managing editor, but there was little job security in the post; in the fifteen years since the magazine's founding, managing editors had come and gone like bluebottle flies. (One of the first, back in the twenties, when the magazine was new and flat broke, was a man named Art Samuels. Because of the cash shortage, he was paid, week after week, in company stock, and in the 1980s, when the magazine was sold to Newhouse, his widow, Vivian, had squirreled away so many shares that she was listed as one of the magazine's principal owners.)

Shawn's predecessor as managing editor was St. Clair McKelway, probably the worst of the lot. He was a good editor but in no way a manager. He was Mr. Congeniality, giving out assignments apologetically, like a man forced to bring up business affairs at a cocktail party. Shawn, on the other hand, delivered every assignment as if it were a judge's charge to a jury. This was serious business, he intimated, and no particular of the assignment was left unexamined. If you were new to Shawn and his ways, the process was apt to make you doubt your sanity. Was it possible that the two of you, both sober and of voting age, were sitting here discussing the interior construction of a *golf ball,* for God's sake? Yes, it was possible, and Shawn was so persuasive and low-key about it that very soon you were ashamed of your coarse and frivolous nature. "So, Mr. Botsford, perhaps you could find time to look into this for a 'Talk' piece?" Mr. Botsford could and did. A golf ball's innards suddenly *mattered*.

At the time of my golfing treatise, I did not know Shawn at

all. Over the golf ball, he and I were still "Mr. Botsford" and "Mr. Shawn," and we stayed that way until I went into the Army. I wrote him from training camp, and he answered, and now we were "Gardner" and "Bill." By the time I got back, three years later, in the fall of 1945, it was as though we had been intimate friends for years.

Shortly after my return, I switched from writing to editing—there was an imperative need for editors, since all the old ones were still in the service—and in my new job I naturally saw more of Shawn. In the office, Shawn was still the Pope and I the postulant, but outside we were *en famille*, at our house, at the Shawns' house, in Central Park, wheeling our respective baby carriages. Still, we were not friends in the way that, say, Sandy Vanderbilt and I became friends. Shawn and I were just too disparate. Fundamentally, he was a hermetically sealed intellectual, and I was anything but. He was alert to every nuance of contemporary thought and opinion, while I studied at the feet of Ethel Merman, Carl Hubbell, Eddie Condon, Red Smith, and their like. He tiptoed through life as though through a minefield, on guard against ambush by germs, heights, insolent civil servants, elevators, and cold weather. I was nothing like that. I was forever catching cold, arguing with cab drivers, forgetting my gloves. He thought things out; I was wildly irrational. In short, he was in control, and I was all over the place. On the other hand, his response to a situation often seemed to come from a book or a seminar—certainly not from experience. In the physical world—the world of how things work and get done—I was way ahead of him. In that world, he seemed to just not get it. When he started taking driving lessons, his astonishment at what a driver can make a car do was genuine. He had been riding in cars all his life, of course, but he had never *noticed*. He would know that the new editor of *Poseidon* was an unreconstructed New Critic, but he didn't know how to change a tire. When he was summoned to jury duty, he managed to get his doctor to attest to his physical inability to serve, but when it came to laying this excuse before the jury clerk, he was helpless, and asked me to go with him and do it.

As an editor, rather than a writer, I was on a subtly different footing with Shawn. Previously, he had been my editor, my boss, and to some degree my adversary, representing the magazine, its policy, and its taste against any heretical cavorting on my part. Now I was an editor myself, on his side of the fence, a colleague. He was still my boss, but now I, too, could speak, in a small way, for the magazine's policy and taste. This was an expansion of authority that in many situations could have grown into a rivalry—in many situations, but not in this one. It takes two to make a rivalry, and as a rival I was sound asleep. I liked and admired Shawn, and, in an indefinable, upside-down way, I naïvely thought of myself as his protector, his front man in the outside world he found so alien. It never occurred to me that I was responding to an old, old force—the power of weakness. I was as unschooled in such matters as he was in the ways of jury clerks.

A larger question is what Shawn felt about me, and here, of course, we ride off into speculation. I think he liked me—I know he liked me—but always with an almost subliminal reservation: the shadow of my connection to Raoul Fleischmann. "Botsford, unfortunately, is a Fleischmann ex-stepson," he wrote Ross in the 1941 memo recommending that I be taken on the staff. For years, that "unfortunately" remained a tiny grain of sand in his relationship with me. I didn't know it was there, and even he must have sometimes forgotten it, but it *was* there.

Shawn's animus toward Fleischmann could have come only from Ross. (It's quite possible that at the time of the "unfortunately" he had never met Fleischmann.) Ross by then had reached a sort of Punch-and-Judy relationship with the publisher. He loudly asserted that, as a publisher, Fleischmann was nothing but a money-grubbing businessman, while Fleischmann asserted, only a trifle less loudly, that Ross, as an editor, was a suicidally profligate spendthrift. The fact, of course, was that neither of them cared a straw for anything but the integrity and success of the magazine. Shawn's "unfortunately" echoed Ross's sentiments, but the difference between the two men was that Ross forgot his suspicions of me as soon as the two of us began working together on "Talk" stories (he found other things to complain about, but they all concerned my work), whereas Shawn, far more internally complicated than Ross, never entirely let down his guard. "Behold, there ariseth a little cloud out of the sea like a man's hand." I was the cloud, almost invisible at the moment, but, as Shawn must have thought, you never can tell about clouds.

This all seems like reasonable analysis to me today, but at the time, for whatever reason—insouciance, thickheadedness, other distractions—I made no analysis at all. Edith Oliver, who had known Shawn far longer than I had, was more perceptive. "Control—that's what drives Bill," she told me once. "Control, control, control—he's got to have it. He doesn't know what to make of you—he can't understand why you don't seem to give a damn." Maybe that was it—I *didn't* give a damn about control. To Shawn, however, control meant power, and the prospect of getting it and exercising it was so enticing that he couldn't believe that anyone, anywhere, might be of a different mind.

It was, I am sure, Shawn's loss of control over events that lay behind his corroding anguish over the article that Tom Wolfe wrote about *The New Yorker* in the fall of 1963. This was a pivotal moment for Shawn. Until Tom Wolfe, Shawn's fanatical pursuit of public invisibility had been pretty much a success. He had been left alone to manage his private world without criticism, or even much comment, from the outside. He did everything possible to avoid being interviewed, and the interviews he consented to were almost reverential. In short, he was in control. Then along came Tom Wolfe with his cheeky unveiling of Holy Mother *New Yorker*. He said the unsayable, spoke the unspeakable, and couldn't be controlled, though Shawn tried mightily to do so.

Tom Wolfe's article was unkind and unfair but it did cast light on a paradox that everybody except Shawn was aware of: the more Shawn struggled to remain invisible, the more he was becoming a full-blown celeb, and celebs were what kept all too many journalists in business.

The article appeared in two parts—"Tiny Mummies: The True Story of the Ruler of West 43rd Street's Land of the Walking Dead" and "Lost in the Whichy Thickets"—in the Sunday-magazine section of the *New York Herald Tribune*. I read the first part while I was having breakfast in a Lakeville, Connecticut, coffee shop (I forget why I was in Lakeville), and it was a lulu. During the Ross years, a lot had been written about him and his magazine, but invariably the tone was admiring and/or gee-whiz—"Look at what this unpredictable *New Yorker* and its zany boss have done *now*!" The writers seemed to feel that they might someday be asking Ross for a job. It was clear that Wolfe had no hope for a job. He made fun—sometimes pretty funny fun—of the magazine in an exclamatory, shotgun style that would never have been permitted in the chaste, elegant drawing room of *New Yorker* prose:

> If there was no ashtray on his desk, he would go out himself!—Mr. Shawn of *The New Yorker*!—and bring back a Coca-Cola bottle for use as an ashtray. Easygoing!
>
> "Why—hello—Mr.—Cage—um—yes—how—are—you—here—let—me—how—is—Mrs.—Cage—um—take—your—coat—oh—oh—didn't—mean—to—um—there—if—I—can—just—slip—it—off—here—have—a—"
>
> "Well, thank you, very much, Mr. Shawn—"
>
> "a—seat—right—over—here—well—uh—it—always—does—that—ha—ha—well—now—oh—I—see—you're—smoking—let—me—"
>
> "Oh, I'm sorry, Mr. Shawn, I didn't—"
>
> "No, no, no, no, please—perfectly—all right—it's—please—keep—your—seat—I'll—be—right—back—"
>
> Whereupon he goes out of the office, smiling, and

comes back in a moment with an empty Coca-Cola bottle in his hand. He puts the Coca-Cola bottle on the desk for Cage to use as an ashtray.

So one can imagine Cage saying something like he has a great many *viable* ideas about this story, but it is funny, he can hear his own voice as he talks. The words are coming out all right—"several really very *viable* approaches, I think, Mr. Shawn"—but they sound *hollow*, as if in an echo chamber, because inside his brain all he can focus on is the cigarette and the Coca-Cola bottle. The thick glass in those bottles, and, Jeezus, that little hole in the top there—it *looks* big enough, but if you try to knock the ash off a cigarette here into the Coca-Cola bottle you see that the glass is *thick* and the hole *isn't* big enough. Cage is practically down to the end of the cigarette—"Well, I'm not absolutely sure the ethnocentric *works* in a case like this, Mr. Shawn but"—and then what is he going to do? There's nothing to put the cigarette out *on*. He's just going to have to drop the cigarette down the hole in the Coca-Cola bottle, and then it is going to hit the bottom of the bottle, and then just keep on *burning*, you know? And there is going to be this little smelly curl of smoke coming up out of the Coca-Cola bottle, like a spirit lamp, and this filthy cigarette lying in the bottom right there on Shawn's desk, and obviously Shawn is not crazy about cigarettes in the first place, and old Cage hasn't even sold him on the idea of the story—

This was one of the more congenial pictures of Shawn, and long before I got to the final "Zoom! Grace!" of Part One, I knew that Shawn would be having a fit, and I also knew he would do something dumb in response. Ross would have dismissed the Wolfe conniptions with profanity and a lot of stamping around, but Shawn would—well, what *would* Shawn do? Here was Part

Two coming up in a week, and he couldn't bluster Wolfe into silence (Shawn bluster?), he couldn't buy Wolfe's silence, he couldn't count on Wolfe's spiritual rebirth in next week's installment. In fact, he couldn't do anything at all. To cross swords with his tormentor in public would be disastrous—Wolfe would delight in being challenged; in addition, he would always have the last word. But, sitting there at my Lakeville lunch counter, I was sure that Shawn—being convinced, as always, that logic and high principles were omnipotent—would manage to ignore reality and do something dumb. He would do or say or write something that might win laurels at a debating society but would allow Tom Wolfe to eat him up in a bite. It seemed to me that the best thing I could do for him would be to persuade him to take comfort from his army of supporters, both in and out of the office, and silently, if painfully, allow the Wolfe thing to run its undoubtedly short course. As his self-appointed big brother and know-it-all counselor in the ways of the world, I resolved to tell him so on Monday, when I went back to work.

I could not have been dumber myself. I ran into Shawn in the hall, on my way to my office. "That was a lousy thing Tom Wolfe did to you, but you shouldn't let it bother you," I said. "I know it's tough to take, but everybody is behind you, and in ten days the whole thing will blow away."

I might just as well have said that I thought Jack the Ripper was a playful scamp. Shawn gave me a cold and scornful look, went into his office, and shut the door. But I did have one thing right. He had indeed made a dumb move. He had written a letter to Jock Whitney, the *Herald Tribune*'s owner, urging him, as a gentleman, to pull the second part of Wolfe's article, and Whitney had made the letter public. The daily press and the news magazines picked up the story and gave it wings. Moreover, the letter to Whitney was only the first maneuver in an elaborate and useless defense—useless and counterproductive. Loyal letters by loyal staffers were encouraged, and specimens were sent to any publication that might print them. Wolfe's piece was combed for factual errors, and several were found. (Thurber's old office was not next to the men's room but across the hall from it.) Renata Adler and Gerald Jonas went to Chicago to search out further error. The factory hummed day and night, and a journalistic spat that might have lasted ten days went on and on. In all this time, Shawn and I never spoke of the mess. He clearly felt I had let down the side. I had taken an insensitive view of a Deep Personal Tragedy.

I think Shawn never got over the Wolfe article. Within weeks of its appearance, he went into a fury of editing—he would show them *The New Yorker* was no land of the walking dead—and, indeed, he produced a series of brilliant issues, each one outshining the last. One could say that Tom Wolfe made the magazine better than it had ever been before. But I remained the truant who didn't go to Chicago.

Shawn's heart attack in December 1971 was his nightmare come true. For one thing, he was a world-class valetudinarian; he saw every cold in the head as terminal, and one can imagine how he felt about a twinge in the heart. For another, his doctor ordered complete isolation, and for six weeks Shawn received no visitors, no phone calls, no manuscripts. All his control over events evaporated, and I was left in charge. I, unfailingly insensitive, saw nothing amiss in any of this. For six weeks, I sat at his desk doing the things he had to do. I finished editing pieces he was working on, I assigned ideas to writers, I rejected failed manuscripts. I worked as hard as he did—harder, because I had my own work to do, too. When we heard that he was on the mend and would soon return to the office, I prepared an account of my stewardship to bring him up to date on everything that had happened during his absence, and I gave it to him on his first day back. He didn't want to see it. In fact, he didn't want to talk about his absence at all, and he made it clear that I and the rest of the world were to act as though he had never been away—that he had been in command the whole time. Therefore, no reports on stewardship were needed, and no thanks were due for work done in his behalf.

For the first time, I thought that Shawn was behaving rather shabbily. But I soon got over it. Once he was back in his chair and the machine was clicking along at its normal pace, it was hard to go on being miffed. I was a big part of the normal pace, and a triviality like Shawn's refusal to say thanks was not going to make me regret my job; *The New Yorker* was the only place I had ever wanted to work. At one time, I had been asked to become the editor of *Harper's Bazaar*, and at another I was taken to lunch by Fairchild Publications and offered the editorship of a new magazine that *Women's Wear Daily* was about to spin off. Nothing doing: *The New Yorker* was the place to be, and the reason this was so was that Shawn had made it so. He might put out a tepid issue or two, but then along would come a skyrocket of a piece that was as much his creation as it was his author's—Truman Capote's "In Cold Blood," for instance, or James Baldwin's "The Fire Next Time." You couldn't stay miffed at a man like that. Or, rather, you could stay miffed at his ingratitude, and irritated by his shortcomings in dealing with the here and now, and upset by his prevarications, and exasperated by his inability to delegate anything to anybody, and derisive about the way he played favorites, but you couldn't deny that he was the *fons et origo* of the whole works. The man was a goddam genius, and geniuses are famously hard to get along with.

But time takes its toll on geniuses, too. The luster wears off, and it doesn't take all that long. When the sun was shining and all cylinders running smoothly, Shawn could look about him and feel—quite rightly—that he was the beloved daddy of all his children on the staff. Such filial homage is demonstrably fickle, however, and only a couple of years later the staff was bringing in the Newspaper Guild to talk tough on its behalf. This was another watershed moment. Shawn felt not only betrayed and insulted but threatened. You could say that this was the point when the magazine's downhill slide started—the point when Shawn's obsession was no longer the quality of the product but his own survival as editor. He could not accept the fact that time moves, that the seasons change and the tide goes out, and he wore himself to a cinder trying to keep everything as it once was, unchanged. His tactic was as old as the Bible: he would make time stand still by perpetuating himself. He would install an alter ego in his place—a younger alter ego, a portrait of himself as a young man—and to this cloning project he brought a dedication and a ruthlessness I had never seen in him before.

THE PRIEST-KING OF NEMI

It all began in September 1975, on a day when Shawn took me to lunch in the Rose Room of the Algonquin. We talked of nothing for a while, and then, with dessert, he got down to business: What would I think about giving Jonathan Schell a trial as an editor? The question was not only unexpected but mystifying—other potential editors had been given tryouts without fanfare, so why was this such a big deal, worthy of a lunch in the Rose Room? I was not a great admirer of Jonathan's writing—he was certainly on the side of the angels, but as a writer he struck me as wooden and preachy—and I hardly knew Jonathan himself at all. Shawn, though, was obviously very high on him. Schell's prospects as an editor, he said, were so good that he could be considered a likely candidate for the post of editor in chief someday.

Here was the big deal, worthy of the Rose Room. Jonathan Schell, editor in chief! The prospect, I must say, hardly warmed my heart, but there was no denying that Shawn had a superlative nose for talent, and he had known Jonathan for many years. (Jonathan was Wallace Shawn's roommate at the Putney School and at Harvard.) I might not like Jonathan's writing, but writing and editing are two different birds, as I well knew, and it was possible that Shawn was right. Anyway, the whole thing was a long way off, and this was only a trial. So I said okay.

Shawn looked pleased, and we went back to the office so he could get the trial started. At least, I assume he got it started; as the weeks came and went, there were no outward signs of its inception or progress. A couple of "Talk of the Town" writers said that Jonathan was assigning stories, but the groans and sighs coming from Hobey Weekes's office every Monday morning as he put the department to press made it clear that he was still its editor.

A year and a half went by, so quietly that I forgot all about Schell's trial. Then, in February 1977, Shawn again took me to lunch at the Algonquin to bring me up to date. I would be glad to hear, he said, that Jonathan's trial had been a success—such a great success, in fact, that he proposed to make him his deputy in dealing with several low-wattage editorial chores. I began to wish I had paid more attention to the trial. As it was, I had nothing to say about its success or failure. So I said nothing.

It turned out, a few days later, when Shawn went public with his deputy plan, that I was the only one in the place who had nothing to say. The salaried editorial staff—the editors, checkers, secretaries, makeup people, department writers, proofreaders—began to seethe, and so did a number of the contributing writers. Most of the seething was done in my office, probably because I had been on the scene so long. The complaints were so insistent that I ended up writing Shawn a letter. It was pretty sententious and overblown, but I was nervous, and it shows:

February 23, 1977

Dear Bill:

It is with much distress that I write you this letter, because it can only cause you pain, dealing, as it does, with a subject that I know lies close to your heart.

Word of Jonathan's training program and its ultimate objective—his grooming as most-favored candidate to succeed you as editor of the magazine—has now spread, and the reactions have been coming in. Very often, they are voiced to me. I haven't sought them out; they have come unbidden, possibly because I am the Oldest Living Inhabitant. In every case, I am urged to *do* something; if Jonathan is made editor, I am told, we are all in the soup.

Altogether, I cannot impress upon you too forcefully the fact that the atmosphere around here is getting very bad. And it's indeed an atmosphere—not just a couple of cranky voices being raised.

In the twenty-six years since Ross's death, you have made this magazine into something unique, without parallel anywhere. You haven't done it alone, of course; as you yourself have said, the editor of this magazine must have the trust and support of a competent staff if he is to succeed. Trust and support—you have them, you have earned them, you deserve them. But they are qualities that the present candidate can lay no claim to.

There was silence for ten days. Then, on March 4, Shawn came to see me in my office. "I've read your letter," he said, "and I'm also told by Milton Greenstein [the editorial department's legal adviser and its liaison with the business department] that there is some unrest over Jonathan. It's hard for me to understand any of this. Here we are conducting an experiment to see whether Jonathan can do various editorial jobs, and before the experiment is really under way people are protesting. They are judging him before there is anything to judge. Somebody opened the dam by saying this experiment was aimed at preparing a replacement for me, whereas what should have been understood was that Schell was just taking on some editorial chores."

I said, "When you use the word 'deputy,' as you did, everybody is convinced that there's more going on than meets the eye. They feel that any trial in which you are the judge, the jury, and the court reporter is really no trial at all."

"I'll think about it over the weekend," Shawn said.

In all the conversations I had with Shawn on the Schell matter—I quote them from summaries I made later in the day, which may be why they sound so flat—he never once accepted the fact that I was simply speaking for an unhappy staff, and had no agenda of my own. It is true that I couldn't see Jonathan as editor in chief either, but hardly because I wanted the job for myself. I was sixty years old, and there was nothing I wanted less. Tass had died, of cancer, three years earlier, and now I was remarried, to Janet Malcolm, and once more having a very pleasant life outside *The New Yorker.* In Shawn's view, however, the attraction of being the editor in chief of the most influential journal of its time was so overpowering that he couldn't believe that I was immune to it.

One theme kept recurring in our conversations: Why did people distrust Schell when he hadn't yet had a chance to show what he could do? It was a good question, and there is probably no single answer. Certainly Jonathan was no ambitious Iago; he was personable and pleasant-spoken, and he had more than a few friends among the other writers. But there was always something of the holy man—something of Shawn—about him; one would hesitate to say "shit" in his presence. He was serious, and seriously concerned, just like Shawn (though without Shawn's esprit and sense of humor). People saw in him an extension of Shawn, and Shawn was by no means popular with the editorial staff just then—its negotiations with the American Newspaper Guild attested to that.

As for the writers, they were, with exceptions, more tolerant of Jonathan. "It used to be said within the offices that Shawn loved his writers and resented his editors," John Bennet, an editor himself, wrote in a memorial appraisal of Shawn. "This was true. Writers are pathetically easy marks for editors. In creating a piece of writing—Shawn's term for a magazine article—an author risks everything, and is more vulnerable during the editing process than a hospital patient in the hands of a surgeon. Little wonder that the writers idolized a man who took their proposals and ideas—who took their very psyches—and validated them."

There were weak spots in the idolatry, however. Writers vying for a place in the sun of Shawn's attention would sulk and speak harshly of Father if he spent too much time with a rival. Even writers whose work had been accepted and excessively praised by Shawn (a weakness of his) would be plagued by the difficulty of getting their stuff published. The competition for space in the magazine was strenuous, and some pieces got left in limbo for months, or even years. Jonathan's pieces, however, got published still warm from the typewriter, and all of them were edited by Shawn himself. For Jonathan, the sun of Shawn's attention never set. Envy of teacher's pet may not have been a worthy reason for resenting Schell, but it was a human one.

The level of uproar that was rocketing around the office halls by this time is indicated by the following notice, which was posted five days later:

TO THE STAFF

March 9, 1977

It is not my intention to make frequent appearances on the bulletin board in order to deny rumors. However, all the talk of the past couple of weeks suggests that I should provide some information. Contrary to

> rumor, no one has decided when I will retire, and no one has made any decision on who will succeed me.
>
> William Shawn

I've decided—for the moment anyway—to call off the Schell experiment," Shawn said to me. "All I was doing was conducting a test to see whether Jonathan could carry out certain editorial duties, but the heat, and even the hysteria, of the reaction were such that it became clear that he would not have enough support."

Thus did Shawn begin his defense of his title—for this was a beginning, not an end, as every Shawnologist realized on hearing the words "for the moment." In this case, the moment lasted two months. Then I got an enormously long letter from Shawn minutely detailing the manifold merits of Jonathan. It was practically an announcement of the Second Coming, and it ended with nothing less than a proposal to make him managing editor. I hastened in to see Shawn, fire buckets in hand. Worst possible move, I said. Gasoline on the fire—particularly since the staff thinks the Schell matter has been permanently laid to rest. I was just in time. Shawn listened, and conceded. Then he showed me a notice he had prepared for posting on the bulletin board that afternoon:

TO THE STAFF

> Some weeks ago, I had in mind conducting an experiment involving Jonathan Schell. It was my feeling that he might be the person who should succeed me in my job. Before the experiment had got started, a rumor ran through the office to the effect that I was soon to retire and that *a decision had been made* for

> Jonathan Schell to succeed me. This rumor created a troubled atmosphere in the office, and the experiment did not take place. It is against this background that I write what follows.
>
> When the time comes for me to retire, a successor will be appointed by *The New Yorker's* publisher, Peter Fleischmann. I have told him that I will recommend someone when I reach a conclusion about who I think it should be. Mr. Fleischmann may or may not accept my recommendation, but he has assured me that he, too, understands the crucial importance of the editor's having the staff's support.
>
> As we think of who the next editor should be, we have to gauge his talent, appraise his editorial judgment, examine his taste, measure the range of his interests, and look searchingly at his qualities of character. Jonathan Schell may be the right person. I have now asked him to take the job of Managing Editor, so that all of you will have a chance to work with him and get to know him. I ask merely that you do what you can to make this try-out as Managing Editor—unavoidably, under a stronger spotlight than is usual in these situations—as pleasant as possible.

The notice was never posted, and a few days later Shawn said, "I would like to put this whole matter off for a while. There still seems to be some turmoil in the office."

Once again, a Shawnologist would take note of that "for a while." This time, the time-out lasted a year, until the spring of 1978. During that time, the office remained quiet, but not the outside world. The public interest in the doings at *The New Yorker* has always seemed to me to be out of all proportion to the doings themselves. If a change of editor had been proposed at *The New Republic* or *Esquire* or *Cosmopolitan,* it would have been worth two days' coverage, but when it was *The New Yorker* the journalistic gossips and sibyls never let up. Who would succeed Shawn, and when? *Time, Newsweek,* and the *Village Voice* all dipped in, and even English and French journals had a go. At the end of 1978, two days after Christmas, I put together the following chronicle in an attempt to chart the twists and turns of events:

The place to start [I wrote] is May 1977, when William Shawn abandoned his plan to install Jonathan Schell as managing editor of *The New Yorker,* with a view of someday making him editor in chief. Until the Schell project came along, nobody had given much thought to Shawn's retirement—though seventy years old, he was healthy and in full command, and the magazine was perking along very well. However, the Schell project, coupled with the magazine's newly adopted policy of mandatory retirement at sixty-five, put the word "successor" into play. Shawn had been exempted from retirement, but everybody else on salary was now aware that life at *The New Yorker* was finite. Shawn may or may not have had a twinge of guilt over his favored position—probably not—but he could not have failed to note that retirement was a hot topic both in and out of the office.

Though the buzz kept growing, however, nothing actually happened for a year—until May 1978, when Peter Fleischmann, the chairman of the board and principal owner, had three conversations with Shawn. (I heard this later from Shawn himself.) In the first, Shawn said, Peter, who had not been deaf to the buzzing, asked what Shawn's plans were for the future. In another, he spoke of the passage of time and of the fact that Shawn was seventy. In the third, he spoke of his dislike of loose ends (he was in very poor health himself) and of his desire to have a plan in place for the future of the editorship.

Shawn saw these conversations as pressure on him to quit. In this, he was partly right. There was indeed pressure on him, but it was pressure to lay a plan for the future, not to quit. His quitting would have scuttled the magazine then and there, and Peter Fleischmann, like everybody else, knew it. The pressure Shawn felt was less draconian, but being asked to think about a successor did not afford him much joy either. He had already thought about a successor, but when he unveiled his candidate the staff had gone into fits. It was an intractable situation for him, leaving no room to move. What could he do? What he could do was to throw up smoke screens and attack.

That, in any case, is the only explanation I can think of for a call I got in early June of 1978 from Jane Kramer. Did I know, she asked, that Shawn was being pushed out of his job by Peter Fleischmann? Not only that, he was being told to clear out his desk in the next couple of days. Couldn't we do something to let him know that his staff was behind him, and at least arrange for a more dignified exit?

At the time, I knew nothing of Shawn's conversations with Peter Fleischmann, and I couldn't imagine what she was talking about. This is all news to me, I said, and I don't believe a word of it. Peter Fleischmann may be ailing, but he is not suicidal. If Shawn leaves, the magazine goes with him.

Needless to say, Shawn did not clear out his desk in the next couple of days. Instead, at the end of July, just before I went on vacation, he came to me and said that the question of his retirement and the succession was again in the air (it had never been out of the air), and that we must discuss it in September, on my return.

During the afternoon of Monday, September 11, on my first day back at work, Shawn came to my office and asked if I had had any new ideas on the succession. I said no—that I thought the last thing he wanted was for me to put my oar in. In that case, he said, we are left with two options. Option A is for me to stay on as editor until I can find a replacement outside the office, since nobody in the office is competent. (I let that pass.) Option B is for you to take over right now.

I was totally flummoxed. I told him this was an enormous and unexpected decision for me to make, and I wanted to think about it overnight.

The next day, following a night of unprecedented self-examination, I wrote Shawn a note (I don't have a copy), saying that after much thought and long consultations at home I had decided to offer myself as a temporary successor to Shawn—temporary, since I was only four years from mandatory retirement myself. I listed three reasons for my decision. The first was that an open-ended search outside the office could go on until we were both too sere and withered to function—and with no guarantee of success even then; potential editors in chief weren't all that thick on the ground out there. The second reason was that Shawn had more than once told me in the past year or so that he had come to hate his job: the contest with the Newspaper Guild, the commotion over Schell, the monthly meetings with the contentious Employees' Advisory Committee (a byproduct of the Guild struggle) had all taken the flavor out of his work. At this stage of his career, I wrote, he shouldn't be expected to go on flogging himself. And if he were free of all that misery, he could think harder about a permanent successor. (This line of thought, I now realize, was pretty naïve, but there it is.) The third reason was that the best sort of succession would be one where the new man slid in almost unnoticed, and I had been around long enough to do that.

Shawn read my note and came to my office. He said okay, so be it, and the only thing left to do was for him to notify Peter Fleischmann of our decision. There existed (as I had learned from Milton Greenstein) a contract between the editor and the publisher which stipulated that if either party contemplated doing something drastic—if the editor should consider quitting or retiring, if the publisher should consider selling the magazine—the other party would be given six months' notice. Shawn's informing Peter of our decision would start the six-month meter ticking.

It was a big moment, but there was no exultation in the air. I was more than a little apprehensive about what I had got myself into. Did I really want to dedicate my every waking hour to the tumultuous doings on West Forty-third Street? Give up all thought of an outside life? At my age? Later that evening, I called up Shawn just to hear what was going through *his* mind. I asked him if he was content with the decision. He said no—he would have preferred Option A—but that the choice had been made. We agreed not to say anything to the staff until Peter had been heard from.

A couple of days later, I faced up to reality: I had made a big mistake. I went to see Shawn in his office to tell him so—to tell him that I didn't want the job. However, he spoke first. He said he could not be entirely satisfied with the prospect of me as his successor, since our personalities were too disparate. Under me, the magazine would change—not necessarily for the worse, perhaps even for the better—and he hated change. Therefore, he was being put in a difficult position. He was flatly incapable of telling a lie, he said, so if someone asked him if he had confidence in me as his successor, he could not say yes. And if someone asked him if he was being pushed out of his job, he could not say no. Also, he was very inept at turning aside direct questions from a reporter or anybody else, and this resulted in damaging answers, since, as I knew, he could not tell a lie.

I must say I found this lecture more than a little irritating. If he felt this way, why had he offered me the option in the first place? I hadn't asked him for it; I didn't even want it. In fact, one of the reasons that had prompted me to accept it was to give him a break. It was understandable that he should hate the idea of change—after all, the magazine was his child, his creation—but why this high moral tone, this lofty insistence on his inability to lie, when all of us who worked with him knew that he was an incomparable liar—as he had to be. Lying is an art no editor faced with a daily budget of tricky decisions, necessary side steps, and unavoidable reversals can afford to be without. Rather truculently,

I said that if my withdrawal would make him happy, he should come right out and say so. No, he said; we will try to work things out.

In the light of future events, I am sorry that I didn't speak up and tell him I had changed my mind. I would have lost nothing, and much bad feeling and acrimony would have been averted. But I was sore at being jerked around, and I was damned if I was going to help him out of a hole he had dug himself. Resentment, as it always does, had left a residue of stubbornness.

Calming down, I said that I didn't see that he was in such a hard bind. A plain recital of the truth would answer all questions. It was reasonable for a man of his age to be looking about for a successor, I said, and it was reasonable for him to come to me, the second in line. The fact that he had addressed me, and not somebody else, cleared up the question of his confidence in me. And the fact that it was he who had offered the option, and not I who had asked for it, cleared up the question of his being pushed out of his job.

"That approach is very interesting," Shawn said. "It might work. I'll try it out on Milton Greenstein".

He would try it out on Milton Greenstein. He couldn't face the evil moment; he had to put off the impossible decision. He and I had become like that pair of performance artists who spent eight months tied together by a six-foot length of rope. He wanted me to go away, but he couldn't fire me for any reason that he could admit to publicly—and, anyway, he was by nature incapable of firing anybody for anything. Nor could he accept me without conceding that he was over the hill, no longer in charge. And I, at my end of the rope, wanted to be out of there, but I couldn't quit without creating a worse quagmire than already existed, or without leaving a hole that would be extremely troublesome to fill at short notice.

Late in October, he had a try at cutting the rope, but pulled back at the last minute.

"Peter Fleischmann is firing me," he said yet again. He was fully aware that Peter Fleischmann was not firing him, but he had repeated this mantra so many times that he may have come to believe it. "He is firing me because he is your brother and does everything you tell him." This was a new line, and a nasty one. It didn't sound like Shawn at all.

"What you are saying is that *I* am the one who is firing you," I said. "If I take over from you, it will only be because I myself—Gardner Botsford, nobody else—fired you."

"Yes, in effect, that is so."

This was my first hint of Shawn's true, or at least recent (i.e., post-Schell), feelings about me. He knew as well as I did—he had known for thirty years—that I was neither the agent nor the creature of the Fleischmann family or *The New Yorker*'s business department, that I had got my job at the magazine *despite* my fatal family connection. Before coming to *The New Yorker,* I had been on two newspapers where the business department felt free to dictate to the editorial department: the advertiser came first. It was a degrading way to work, and I hated it. But at *The New Yorker,* a brick wall had been built between the two departments with the very first issue. Harold Ross was its architect and Raoul Fleischmann the compliant landowner, and in all the years I worked there it was never, to my knowledge, breached. (When the Newhouse people took over, the wall was not only breached but leveled.) Peter Fleischmann would no more have asked me about an editorial decision than I would have asked him how much money Shawn made; to do so would have been a betrayal of everything his father had held to be honorable.

Shawn's new line of attack put me in an impossible position. If I withdrew my candidacy and stayed on as a standard-brand editor, Shawn would consider me a latent time bomb, able to countermand any of his decisions by an appeal to Peter Fleischmann. If I pursued my candidacy, I was a murderer intent on seizing his victim's rights and powers. The only way out, it seemed to me, was to ignore the deterrents and quit on the spot, and I told him so.

"If you quit, I will quit two minutes later," he said. "Nobody will be left to run the magazine." The rope held.

The next day, I canceled my decision to quit and he acknowledged that he had misjudged my relationship with the publishing office. We agreed that I would go back to regular editing, and he would continue to instruct me in the role of editor in chief. We shook hands on it.

During the second week of December, there was another hack at the rope. Shawn told me, in the strictest confidence, that he was writing Peter Fleischmann a long, private letter setting forth every detail of his position, including a broad and final summary of his hopes and recommendations for the future of the magazine. The letter was so secret, he said, so full of personal and staff disclosures, that he had typed it himself, rather than entrust it to a secretary, who might talk. Two days later, on December 13, Bill Whitworth, in a state of anxiety, came to see me. He had just heard from two sources, Renata Adler and Jane Kramer, that unless Shawn won over Peter Fleischmann with an enormously long letter he had written him, he would be out of a job in a matter of days. (A letter so secret that no secretary could see it?) I asked Whitworth where Adler and Kramer had heard all this. He didn't know about Kramer, he said, but Adler, on her first visit to the office in months, had been accosted in the hall by Lillian Ross, who told her that Shawn was being fired and asked her to join a protest group. So Renata had come to Whitworth to find out what was going on.

On Saturday morning, December 16, Peter Fleischmann called me at home. He had been in the hospital, undergoing medical tests and feeling very poorly, so he had not really read Shawn's long letter until that moment. He said I should read it, too, and that I wasn't going to like what I read. So I went to his house and read the letter, making notes on it as I went along. I here append my notes:

"I [W.S.] felt a distinct chill in the air beginning about a year and a half ago." There followed a long history of the

Schell affair, through page 7. "Some editors, not including Gardner Botsford, spread the word among the writers. The story told by the editors was calculated to inflame the writers, and it did." In May 1977, the Schell chapter was closed.

"It has recently been pointed out to me that your confidence in me has been shaken. You believe [I here paraphrase] that the staff is demoralized, that I have become a lunatic who thinks that he alone can edit the magazine, that I still want to install Jonathan Schell as editor, that I want to stay on as editor forever, and that the magazine is drifting." There followed (through page 17) a long account of the magazine's successes on all editorial fronts.

Then: "It is agonizing to talk about my uncertainties concerning Gardner. My aim is nothing less than to avert a tragedy in which he has the most to lose. . . . I have had twenty-seven years' experience as editor and thirteen as managing editor, and Gardner has not, and yet you turned to him for advice. [Peter Fleischmann never in his life turned to me for advice about anything.] In effect, what he advised was to replace me with himself. . . . Gardner is too inexperienced to be editor-in-chief, and he is not equipped to choose his successor, because he does not understand the magazine—we see things with different eyes."

Then: "Maybe you have acted as you have because you think I am too old. I feel fine. Verdi wrote 'Falstaff' at 89. . . . Picasso . . . Titian . . . Casals . . . If I were to become feeble-minded, I would have to be eased out. Instead, I am being brutally thrown out. I am horrified. I cannot believe that you and Gardner understand what you are doing."

And finally: "I ask to remain for two years, so that I can try to find an editor who can carry on."

It was a marvelously well-written letter. When I finished reading it, Peter said to me, "Shawn thinks that the real villain in the story is your wife—that Janet is ambitious for you to become editor, and ambitious for herself to succeed you when you retire."

When I got home, I told Janet about the letter and what Peter had said about her, and she, like me, was knocked flat—and also incensed. She was a writer, she said, and she wouldn't dream of changing roles; the whole thing was not only preposterous but offensive, and she sat down and wrote Shawn a letter telling him so. (Some months later, I mentioned this theory about Janet to Whitworth, and he said that he had heard it long ago from Lillian Ross. It went like this: Point one: For twenty-five years, Botsford has had this power over Peter Fleischmann, but he has never used it. Then suddenly, when Schell is put forward as a candidate, he does use it. Why? Point two: For twenty-five years, Botsford has said, over and over again, that he doesn't want the editorship. Then, suddenly, he pushes Shawn out of the job so he can take it himself. Why? There must have been a change in his life. And there has been: a new wife. She's responsible for it all.)

By this time, I was perfectly aware that whoever Shawn's replacement might be, it was not going to be me. I had no complaint about that—relief was more like it—but I did seriously resent the way I had been treated. Why couldn't Shawn have played it straight with me? Said what he meant, said what he thought, without all this double-talk and swamp gas of the past months? We had known each other for thirty years—worked together, talked together, taken our children to Central Park together—and he still couldn't level with me. Plainly, I was no longer a candidate, but I was damned if I was going to walk away with jovial handshakes all around. And there were other difficulties, still unresolved: the grass fires that Shawn and/or his acolytes had ignited among the writers. Peter had told me that J. D. Salinger called him up and protested Shawn's being fired—took it as a fact that he *was* being fired—and many other writers were no doubt being told the same thing. By now, the truth was irrelevant. As always, it was complicated, diffuse, and needful of explanation, whereas the falsehood was direct, slashing, and effective. Undeniably, Shawn's departure, even under the most commonplace circumstances, would be mourned by a great many writers: their mentor and guide, their economic lifeline—their editor—would be gone. The notion that he had been fired would turn normal regret into outrage, and it was hard to imagine that *any* successor to Shawn could function in that climate. What to do? Salinger was miserable; the staff was miserable. Shawn was miserable; I was miserable. The six-foot rope had become truly galling.

Late on Christmas Eve, Shawn put through my front-door letter slot (Janet and I were not home) the following copy of a letter to Peter:

> Dear Peter:
>
> You and Gardner and I seem to agree that we are in some kind of serious trouble. We also seem to agree that in the present circumstances it would be a good idea for me to stay on for a while, one way or another. I have a simple suggestion to make: Let's set aside the question of my retirement and the succession for the moment. What I suggest is that you restore the situation to what it was before our trouble began; and it began when you asked me to resign. Let us go back to the status quo. As the publisher, just tell me that you want me to continue as editor, and that I'm the editor with no strings attached, with full editorial authority, with no one telling me which of my duties I should retain and which I should give up, with no one telling me which editors I should put in what jobs, with no one telling me how to run the editorial office, and with no one except you telling me when to leave. In other words you would be saying, 'Bill, you are the editor, and just as long as you are editor whatever you say goes.'

> All you'd have to do is initial this letter and send me a Xerox. I could then make a truthful statement to the staff. One month later, when everybody has cooled down, you and I could discuss the important question of my retirement and the succession. Let's clear the air and begin the new year in a new atmosphere of understanding.
>
> Affectionately,
> Bill

Early in the morning of December 26, Peter accepted Shawn's proposal. He did not consult me. I couldn't argue with his decision to restore what stability he could to the magazine by giving Shawn carte blanche, but in my opinion it was a carte blanche reprehensibly obtained. On the other hand, I was now free again, and a little tranquillty would not be unwelcome.

The next afternoon, a notice was posted on the bulletin board:

TO THE STAFF

> Peter Fleischmann has asked me to stay on in my job, and I have agreed to do that. In an atmosphere of friendship and understanding, Mr. Fleischmann and I will continue to discuss plans for the magazine's future—a subject of concern to all of us here.
>
> William Shawn

There my chronicle ended, and thus did we all manage to arrive at nowhere.

We stayed at dead center for five months, motionless. Then

came the wretched Penelope Gilliatt mess, which put the magazine in a serious pickle, and Shawn himself in an even worse one. The former wife of John Osborne, the playwright, and a short-story writer of note, Gilliatt had once been the best film critic in Britain. Now she was alternating with Pauline Kael as *The New Yorker*'s critic, and was also writing Profiles and short stories. Her latest Profile, of Graham Greene, edited by Shawn himself, had just appeared, and its publication was quickly followed by a letter from Michael Mewshaw who demonstrated that she had lifted, untouched, whole paragraphs from an article on Greene he had written for *The New Republic*. This was bad enough, but then it developed that Peter Canby, *The New Yorker*'s checker, had detected the plagiarism and had sent Shawn a proof identifying the purloined passages. (He also found that Gilliatt had lifted from a piece by Victoria Glendinning, but Ms. Glendinning was not heard from.) Shawn's personal pickle was that he could deny nothing: he had seen the Canby proof—he had written notes and queries on it in his own tiny handwriting—and had put the Profile to press anyway, without fixing the disaster. Mewshaw's letter and Canby's proof had been seen by a number of staff members in the course of their ordinary duties, and thus, inevitably, by the staff at large, which meant, in due course, that the outside world heard all about it, too. Newspaper reporters from the *New York Times* and the *Washington Post* called me for comment, and so did Pauline Kael, from the West Coast, where she was being badgered by the press. I fended them off for the moment and went in to see Shawn and find out what line we should take. He was in a state. He had never been in a bind like this before, and when I mentioned the *Times* and the *Post* he blew up all over the place. Somehow or other, the train wreck was now my fault, and he accused me of using it in an effort to take his job.

Things were no better the next day, and it came to me that I didn't have to go on like this. Everything I did (and, in this case, didn't do) drove Shawn to distraction (and vice versa). Anything I edited or wrote became a political assault on him—even my Flanner obituary was too much for him. ("You think that just because of your special position here you can dictate what appears in the magazine.") It was time for me to go—really go this time—leaving him to try to pull things together on his own.

The next morning, before going to work, I called Peter Fleischmann and told him I was quitting.

"For God's sake, not now!" Peter said. The magazine was having enough trouble explaining to its advertisers that it was not falling apart, despite the articles in *Newsweek, Time,* the *New York Times,* and the rest, he said, and my resignation right then would just make things harder. "Give us a chance to prepare for it," he said. "Take a vacation." I finally agreed to do nothing and say nothing until Monday, June 25, when I returned from a week's vacation.

On my return, a letter from Shawn awaited me:

Dear Gardner:

Before I go on with my search for a successor, I wish to say that I need and want your support. I also need and want your practical help, and I will ask you to relieve me of some day-to-day work, so that I can put in more time on the succession. Our working more closely together would, of course, be beneficial to the magazine editorially, and I think it would have a healing effect on the office. For the past two years, you and I have been living and working under nightmare conditions. But I now hope that the nightmare is ended. Our friendship may be tattered, but in a new atmosphere I think we can restore it to what it once was. Certainly our friendship is important to me. Sometimes I think it is as important as the magazine itself. And the two are not easily separated.

With love,
Bill

An irresistible letter—disarming, touching, encouraging. I, of course, abandoned any idea of resigning—new deal, new hopes, new enthusiasm: we were moving forward at last. Shawn and I shook hands (again), and he told me he was working out the details of the reorganization.

So there was a flurry of activity. To start with, I would read final proofs in Shawn's stead, the first being a "Letter from Mexico," then in galley proof. Next, I would take over the "Talk of the Town" department and try to put some vigor back into it. And there was more. Altogether, a great day in the morning.

As things turned out, the "Letter from Mexico" was the first and last proof I read for Shawn, and it never appeared in the magazine anyway. The "Talk of the Town" project and the other duties never materialized at all. And there we were: full circle. Nothing had happened, and nothing was going to happen, and by now, I didn't give a damn. I, at least, had an out: on June 1, 1982, I could retire, honorably, plausibly, and without rocking the boat. As for the politely paranoid priest-king of Nemi, he could go right on endlessly circling his tree at 25 West Forty-third Street: "In his hand he carried a drawn sword, and he kept peering warily about him, as if at every instant he expected to be set upon by an enemy," Frazer wrote in *The Golden Bough*. "And the man for whom he looked was sooner or later to murder him and hold the priesthood in his stead. The post which he held by this precarious tenure carried with it the title of king; but surely no crowned head ever lay uneasier, or was visited by more evil dreams, than his. For, year in, year out, in summer and winter, in fair weather and foul, he had to keep his lonely watch, and whenever he snatched a troubled slumber it was at the peril of his life. The least relaxation of his vigilance, the smallest abatement of his strength of limb or skill of fence, put him in jeopardy."

It was now (belatedly, God knows) clear to me that Shawn didn't want—couldn't even contemplate—any successor at all who was not a clone. The loss of power would be intolerable; he had to be the priest-king, the father, the source of life-giving money and success and celebrity. It had been ludicrous to think that he would ever put forward the name of a candidate successor; he would more likely have driven a stake through the poor fellow's heart.

And, indeed, for three years no candidate was even mentioned. Then, in the fall of 1982, three months after I had thoroughly retired from the magazine, Shawn did put a name forward: Jonathan Schell.

Once again, almost wearily, the staff erupted. Once again, the name was withdrawn, and once again Shawn went back to circling his tree. Then, out of nowhere, there appeared an adversary who would not put up with temporizing or circuitous delays, and who cut off his head with a stroke: Si Newhouse.

So Shawn was out and Robert Gottlieb, the editor in chief of Newhouse's Knopf publishing house, was in. Yet again did the staff erupt, this time in outrage over the arbitrariness of the announcement and the anointed's lack of experience in journalism. On January 17, 1987, more than a hundred and fifty staff members, artists, and writers signed a letter to Gottlieb urging him to decline the appointment—in vain. The protesters were behaving like spoiled children, Gottlieb said. He would stay the course.

And so he did. On Shawn's last day in office, I wrote him a farewell note that said a lot of the things I had long wanted to say. He had given me a hard time during my final days on the magazine, and I resented his mendacity and his two-facedness. But even at the peak of my resentment I had felt that there was another hand doing the knife work against me. Shawn was indeed a liar (but he had to be, in his job) and an artist at the fast shuffle (again, as he had to be), with a thirst for power (this he had on his own), but there was no venom in him, and the campaign against me had been venomous. Jonathan Schell had not a drop of poison in him; Ved Mehta, a foot soldier in the campaign, had enough venom, but he was ineffectual. Lillian Ross had been busy in the ranks, but she was more or less a joke—her and Shawn's assumption that nobody noticed that they were an item was a comic staple in the office. Then I read *Here but Not Here,* Ross's self-aggrandizing effort to establish herself as the real Mrs. Shawn and as privy council to Shawn in running the magazine, and I realized she was no joke. I now knew not only the who but the why.

On February 12, 1987, Shawn sat in his office for the last time, saying good-bye to his colleagues one by one. When I went in, I didn't say good-bye but handed him my note:

Dear Bill:

I know that all too often in recent years you had occasion to think of me as a mindless obstructionist who never got the point (and I know that I got as mad at you as I have ever got at anybody), but things between us go back a lot farther and deeper than that. Forty years, in fact. Good times in abundance: lively parties on Park Avenue South (I hadn't thought of Stella Brooks from then until now), walks in the Park while Wallace and Susan got themselves messy with mud pies, summer evenings in Bronxville, listening to Jess Stacy, wonderful dinners with Mollie P. and Janet F. And forty years of working together.

Without knowing it, you are a gifted teacher. I still remember the revelation of seeing what good editing could do for a piece of writing when, for my instruction, you gave me a manuscript by Helen Mears you had edited. Then, when I was doing my own work, I learned even more from your tutorial proofs. In short, everything I know about editing (and by now I know a lot) I learned from you.

It's hard to face the fact that we've come to the end of the line. I suppose the magazine will go on—I'm sure it will—but it will not be your *New Yorker* or my *New Yorker*. The magazine to which you gave identity and that I worked for unreservedly is gone.

. . . But this is too funereal. We do not say good-bye, dear old friend. I will be here, you will be there; we can meet. All I will say for now, in the words of Our Founder, is

Thanks, and God bless.